CLEARING THE WAY

Combat Engineers in Kandahar

23 Field Squadron

edited by

Major Mark Gasparotto

Library and Archives Canada Cataloguing in Publication

CIP data on file with the National Library and Archives

ISBN 978-1-926582-54-2 (Trade paperback colour)
ISBN 978-1-926582-59-7 (Trade paperback black and white)
ISBN 978-1-926582-55-9 (Hardcover colour)
ISBN 978-1-926582-60-3 (Hardcover black and white)

CREDITS
Imagery / Maps

Afghanistan and Region (MCE 2021): Authorized for publication by the Directorate of Geospatial Intelligence. Produced by the Mapping and Charting Establishment, Department of National Defence, Canada, © 2002. Her Majesty the Queen in Right of Canada.

Kandahar Province: Authorized for publication by the Directorate of Geospatial Intelligence. Produced by HQ RC(S) Geospatial Support Section, Department of National Defence, Canada, © 2008. Her Majesty the Queen in Right of Canada.

Zhari-Panjawi: Op RAMPANT LION 1 Imagery. Produced by the United States Naval Research Laboratory, US Government.

Photographs

All photographs provided by members of the Squadron or Battle Group unless specifically identified in the caption.
DND Combat Camera photographs are reproduced with the permission of the Minister of Public Works and Government Services, 2010.

Individuals' Proper Names

All reasonable attempts have been made to obtain authorization to use a person's proper name in the book. In the case of the deceased, the Fallen's family have been contacted to provide that authorization.

www.23fieldsquadron.ca

By the Squadron, for the Squadron

-

For Shane

*"If, in the future, another unit is raised
to bear the name of this Company,
which was born of this war,
then it shall have a proud tradition to uphold."*

— *The Twenty-Third Story*
(War Diary - 23 Field Company, RCE, World War 2)

CONTENTS

FOREWORD

It is indeed humbling to have been asked to write the forward to a work that explores the actions of combat engineers during the early days of Canada's combat experience in Kandahar Province. This book is decidedly tactical, weaving a multitude of personal stories into a compelling narrative through the eyes of a field commander - Major Mark Gasparotto. If one were searching for the whys and wherefores of Canada's commitment in the South of Afghanistan, they will not find it here. Instead, we are exposed to the raw bedlam, ironic moments and absurdities of war at the soldier-level. The story is replete with little nuggets of wisdom and soldier-philosophy that will bring a wry, knowing grin to those who have 'seen the elephant.' I believe it a compelling read that will only serve to increase one's admiration for the ingenuity of our soldiers, in particular our sappers, regardless of the seemingly impossible demands made of them. Fortunately, many of the characters in this book have moved on to educate subsequent rotations of soldiers in the grim matters of warfare.

As the Commander of 2 Canadian Mechanized Brigade Group in 2006, the brigade from whence 23 Field Squadron emerged, I had the enviable opportunity to see the members of the squadron in Zhari District. I recall meeting a characteristically dishevelled Major Gasparotto (in dress, not wit) along the slowly evolving Route Summit in a leaguer for lunch on October 3rd, 2006. I spoke to a number of soldiers, remembering best my conversation with WO Perrault and his much beaten up sappers. They had already weathered several tight scrapes and bore the look of cagey veterans. That day would prove to be yet another test for 23 Field Squadron as they were hit hard by the Taliban later in the afternoon (an event thoroughly described in the book's text). Sadly, we learned of the death of two Dragoons that evening - Sergeant Gillam and Corporal Mitchell. While we discussed the day's events from the top of FOB Spervan Ghar, the news was broken to the Commanding Officer, Lieutenant-Colonel Omer Lavoie, (a man who figures very large in this work) by the Regimental Sergeant-Major, Bobbie Girouard. The vicious circle is completed for me on reading the multiple accounts of Bobbie's death by suicide bomber, an event labelled aptly by Major Gasparotto as "the day the music died."

This book lets one relive the early days of the war in Kandahar, when each day seemed to bring new challenges. It is the coming of age of a sub-unit that is recorded in graphic detail. It sounds cliché to say that 23 Field Squadron covered itself in glory and runs counter to the professional humility that this book exudes. However, as an outsider looking in, albeit with a reasonable knowledge of things engineer, I can say that they answered the call exceedingly well. I challenge the reader to immerse themselves in these pages and arrive at any other conclusion.

Pro Patria,

Denis Thompson
Brigadier-General
Chief of Staff Land Operations

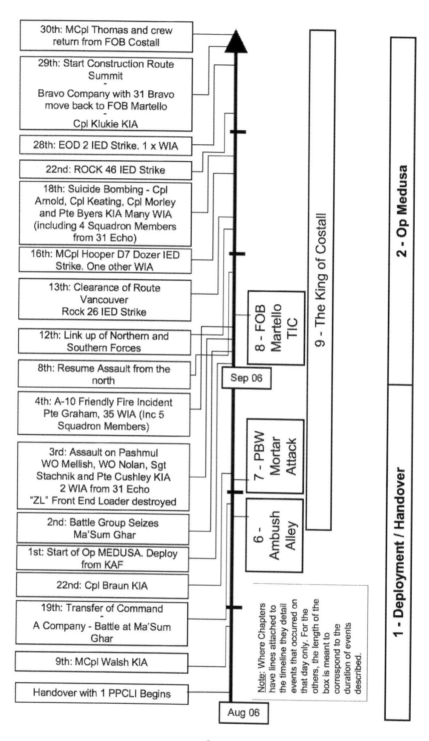

30th: MCpl Thomas and crew return from FOB Costall

29th: Start Construction Route Summit
-
Bravo Company with 31 Bravo move back to FOB Martello
-
Cpl Klukie KIA

28th: EOD 2 IED Strike. 1 x WIA

22nd: ROCK 46 IED Strike

18th: Suicide Bombing - Cpl Arnold, Cpl Keating, Cpl Morley and Pte Byers KIA Many WIA (including 4 Squadron Members from 31 Echo)

16th: MCpl Hooper D7 Dozer IED Strike. One other WIA

13th: Clearance of Route Vancouver
Rock 26 IED Strike

12th: Link up of Northern and Southern Forces

8th: Resume Assault from the north

4th: A-10 Friendly Fire Incident Pte Graham, 35 WIA (Inc 5 Squadron Members)

3rd: Assault on Pashmul WO Mellish, WO Nolan, Sgt Stachnik and Pte Cushley KIA 2 WIA from 31 Echo "ZL" Front End Loader destroyed

2nd: Battle Group Seizes Ma'Sum Ghar

1st: Start of Op MEDUSA. Deploy from KAF

22nd: Cpl Braun KIA

19th: Transfer of Command
-
A Company - Battle at Ma'Sum Ghar

9th: MCpl Walsh KIA

Handover with 1 PPCLI Begins

Sep 06

Aug 06

8 - FOB Martello TIC

7 - PBW Mortar Attack

6 - Ambush Alley

9 - The King of Costall

Note: Where Chapters have lines attached to the timeline they detail events that occurred on that day only. For the others, the length of the box is meant to correspond to the duration of events described.

2 - Op Medusa

1 - Deployment / Handover

— 9 —

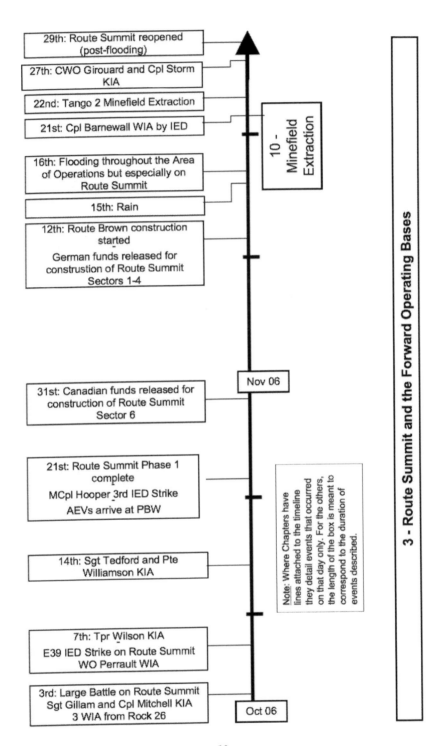

29th: Route Summit reopened (post-flooding)

27th: CWO Girouard and Cpl Storm KIA

22nd: Tango 2 Minefield Extraction

21st: Cpl Barnewall WIA by IED

16th: Flooding throughout the Area of Operations but especially on Route Summit

15th: Rain

12th: Route Brown construction started

German funds released for construstion of Route Summit Sectors 1-4

31st: Canadian funds released for construction of Route Summit Sector 6

21st: Route Summit Phase 1 complete

MCpl Hooper 3rd IED Strike

AEVs arrive at PBW

14th: Sgt Tedford and Pte Williamson KIA

7th: Tpr Wilson KIA

E39 IED Strike on Route Summit WO Perrault WIA

3rd: Large Battle on Route Summit Sgt Gillam and Cpl Mitchell KIA 3 WIA from Rock 26

10 - Minefield Extraction

Nov 06

Oct 06

Note: Where Chapters have lines attached to the timeline they detail events that occurred on that day only. For the others, the length of the box is meant to correspond to the duration of events described.

3 - Route Summit and the Forward Operating Bases

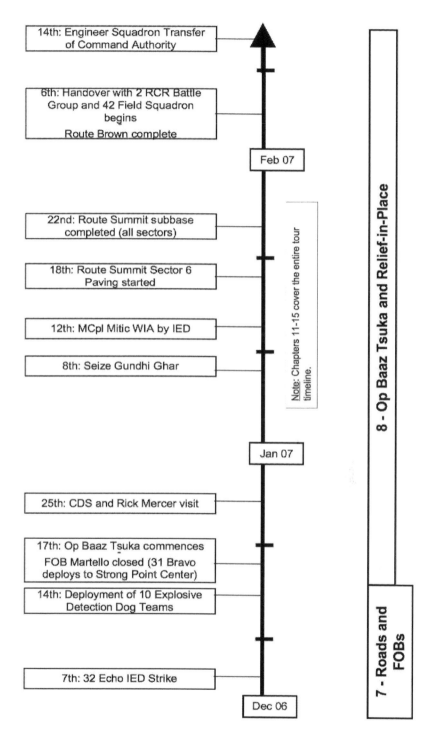

14th: Engineer Squadron Transfer of Command Authority

6th: Handover with 2 RCR Battle Group and 42 Field Squadron begins
Route Brown complete

Feb 07

22nd: Route Summit subbase completed (all sectors)

18th: Route Summit Sector 6 Paving started

12th: MCpl Mitic WIA by IED

8th: Seize Gundhi Ghar

Note: Chapters 11-15 cover the entire tour timeline.

Jan 07

25th: CDS and Rick Mercer visit

17th: Op Baaz Tsuka commences
FOB Martello closed (31 Bravo deploys to Strong Point Center)

14th: Deployment of 10 Explosive Detection Dog Teams

7th: 32 Echo IED Strike

Dec 06

8 - Op Baaz Tsuka and Relief-in-Place

7 - Roads and FOBs

ORDER OF BATTLE

Op Archer Rotation 2:
Canadian Task Force

Higher Headquarters
Regional Command South
Joint Task Force – Afghanistan
             1 RCR Battle Group
             Kandahar Provincial Reconstruction Team
             Operational Mentoring and Liaison Team
             National Support Element

Battle Group

Headquarters		**Call Sign**
- CO	LCol Omer Lavoie	9 (Niner)
- RSM	CWO Robert Girouard /	9 Charlie
	CWO Mark Miller	
- DCO	Maj Marty Lipcsey	
- Ops O	Maj Jay Harvey	
- Adjutant	Capt Kyle Keffer	

A Company, 1 PPCLI

- OC	Maj Mike Wright	19
- CSM	MWO John Hooyer	19 Charlie

Bravo Company, 1 RCR

- OC	Ma.j Geoff Abthorpe	29
- CSM	MWO Ian Boyd	29 Charlie

Charles Company, 1 RCR

- OC	Maj Matt Sprague	39
- CSM	MWO John Barnes	39 Charlie

B Squadron, LdSH(RC)

- OC	Maj Trevor Cadieu	Tango 29
- SSM	MWO Walter Laughlin	T29 Charlie

ISTAR Squadron, RCD / 1 RCR

- OC	Maj Andy Lussier	69
- SSM	MWO Steve Lehman	69 Charlie

E Battery, 2 RCHA

- BC	Maj Greg Ivey	Golf 29
- BSM	MWO Bob Montague	Golf 29 Charlie

Health Services Company

- OC	Maj Erin Savage	
- CSM	MWO Tim Ralf	

Tactical Unmanned Aerial Vehicle Flight

23 Field Squadron, 2 CER
Squadron Headquarters — Echo

- OC	Maj Mark Gasparotto	39
- SSM	MWO Brad Montgomery	39 Charlie
- 2IC	Capt Richard Busbridge	39 Alpha
- Ops O	Capt John Hayward	39 Bravo
- Ops WO	WO Derek Marcoux	
- Int NCO	Sgt Mike Mazerolle	
- Geo NCO	Sgt Isabelle Couture	
- SQ	WO Ted Gombert	39 Golf
- TQ	Sgt Bernie French	

1 Troop

- TC	Lt Anthony Robb	31 Alpha
- WO	WO Earl Rouzes	31
- Recce Sgt	Steve Houde	31 Bravo
- 1 Section	Sgt Louis Proulx	31 Charlie
- 2 Section	Sgt Rene Grignon	31 Delta
- 3 Section	Sgt Jon White	31 Echo

2 Troop

- TC	Lt Justin Behiels /	
	Capt Dan Clarke	32 Alpha
- WO	WO Roger Perrault /	32
	WO Scott Clucas (WSE)	
- Recce	Sgt Scott Clucas	32 Bravo
- 1 Section	Sgt Olie Carruba	32 Charlie
- 2 Section	Sgt Shane Stachnik	32 Delta
- 3 Section	Sgt Neil Coates	32 Echo
- 4 Section	Sgt Sam Ross	32 Foxtrot

7 Troop (Armoured)

- TC	Lt Matt Arndt	37 Alpha
- WO	WO Luc Aubuchon	37
- Recce	Sgt Ted Peacock	37 Bravo
- Badger 1	MCpl Kris Schroder	
- Badger 2	MCpl James McDonald	
- Badger 3	MCpl Marc Barrette	

Heavy Equipment Section

- Commander	Sgt Ron Dix	35 Alpha
- 2IC	MCpl Lance Hooper	35 Bravo

Explosive Ordnance Disposal

- EOD 1 (Chief)	PO1. Paul Walsh
- EOD 2 Team Leader	PO2. Jim Leith
- EOD 3 Team Leader	MCpl Brendan Hynes
- EOD 4 Team Leader	MCpl John Valois

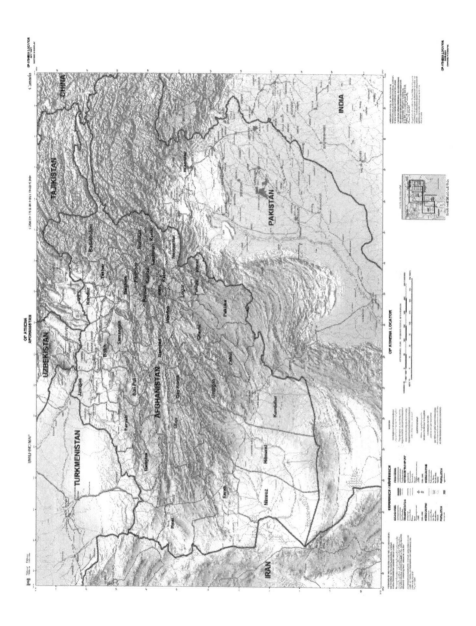

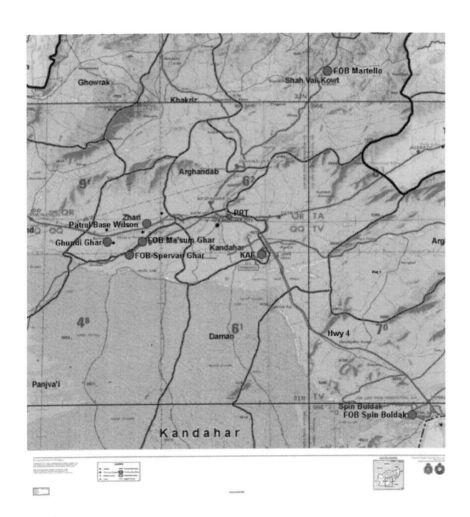

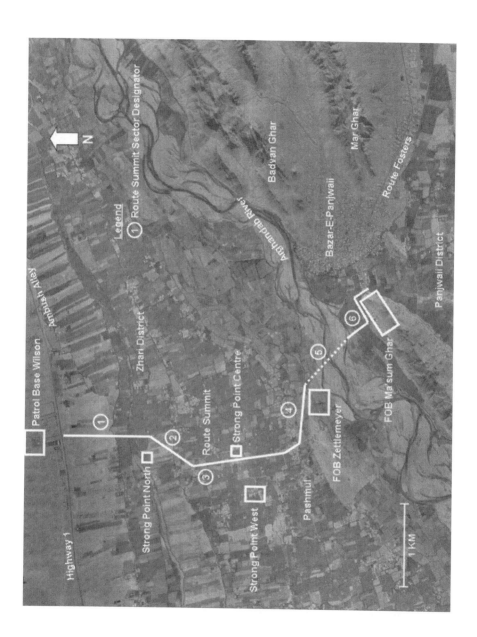

LIST OF ABREVIATIONS
MILITARY WEAPONS AND EQUIPMENT

Miltary Rank Structure

Other Ranks

Private	Pte
/ Sapper	Spr
/ Trooper	Tpr
Corporal	Cpl
/ Leading Seaman	LS

Non-Commissioned Officer

Master Corporal	MCpl
/ Master Seaman	MS
Sergeant	Sgt
/ Petty Officer 2nd Second Class	PO2

Warrant Officer

Warrant Officer	WO
/ Petty Officer 1st First Class	PO1
Master Warrant Officer	MWO
Chief Warrant Officer	CWO

Officer

Lieutenant	Lt
Captain	Capt
Major	Maj
Lieutenant-Colonel	LCol
Colonel	Col
Brigadier-General	BGen
Major-General	MGen

Lieutenant-General	LGen
General	Gen

Appointments

Chief of the Defence Staff	CDS
Commanding Officer	CO
Officer Commanding	OC
Regimental Sergeant-Major	RSM
Squadron Sergeant-Major	SSM
Company Sergeant-Major	CSM
Battery Sergeant-Major	BSM
Squadron Quartermaster	SQ
Technical Quartermaster	TQ
Second-in-Command	2IC

Call Sign Prefix

Engineers	Echo
Artillery	Golf
Infantry	India
Tanks	Tango
Medical Evacuation Helicopter	Dustoff

Units / Organizations

1 Combat Engineer Regiment	1 CER
2 Combat Engineer Regiment	2 CER
Royal Canadian Dragoons	RCD
1st Battalion – Royal Canadian Regiment	1 RCR
2nd Battalion – Royal Canadian Regiment	2 RCR
1st Battalion – Princess Patricia's Canadian Light Infantry	1PPCLI
Provincial Reconstruction Team	PRT
International Security Assistance Force	ISAF
North Atlantic Treaty	

| Organization | NATO |
| United States Agency for International Development | USAID |

Vehicles and Weapons

Light Armoured Vehicle	LAV
G-Wagon	'Jeep'
RG-31 'Mine Resistant Vehicle'	
Bison	'Armoured Personnel Carrier'
Armoured Engineer Vehicle	"Badger"
All Terrain Vehicle	ATV
Rifle (5.56mm)	C7
Machine Gun (7.62mm)	C6
Rifle – short barreled (5.56mm)	C8
Machine Gun (5.56mm)	C9
Plastic Explosives	C4

Miscellaneous

Forward Operating Base	FOB
Reconnaissance	"Recce"
Situation Report	"Sitrep"
Killed in Action	KIA
Wounded in Action	WIA
Explosive Ordnance Disposal	EOD
Improvised Explosive Device	IED

INTRODUCTION

"There is no trap like illusion,...
no greater friend than knowledge,
no greater enemy than pride."
— Gheranda Sumhi

This is the story of the men and women of 23 Field Squadron – Op ARCHER Roto 2, comprising soldiers, sailors and airmen drawn from across the Canadian Forces and beyond. The intent of this book is to mesh their very personal stories with the Squadron War Diary, all within the framework of the overall 1 RCR Battle Group mission.

The Squadron was billed as a multi-national, tri-service, dual-component and combined-arms outfit* that included naval clearance divers, electronic warfare operators (Canadian and Australian), Royal Canadian Dragoons, signallers, geomatics** technicians, and administrative / logistics staff, all attached to a core of combat engineers. Its role was to create the conditions allowing friendly forces to live, move and fight on an asymmetric battlefield and to deny the same to the enemy. More specifically, it entailed the provision of mobility, counter-mobility, survivability, reconstruction and geomatics support to the 1 RCR Battle Group in particular, but also to the Canadian Task Force as a whole. This mission was accomplished by the Explosive Ordnance Disposal (EOD) operators, heavy equipment operators, armoured engineers, geomatic technicians, combat

---

* *Tri-service* denotes personnel originating from the Army, Navy and Air Force. *Dual component* indicates both Regular and Reserve Force members. *Combined Arms* indicates two or more combat arms trades grouped together; in this case Dragoons and combat engineers.
** *Geomatics* is the collection, analysis, reproduction and dissemination of all geospatial data and intelligence. More that just map making, it is used to assist commanders and staff with complete battlefield terrain visualization.

engineers and various support and headquarters staff that were 23 Field Squadron.

It has been said that history is written by the victor. The undeclared caveat, however, is that this chronicling only happens if he or she actually sits down to write it. It is perhaps a reflection of our self-effacing and self–deprecating nature as Canadians that we, as members of the Canadian Army, have not done a good job of telling our story – not only within the organization, but to the Canadian public at large. Part Squadron War Diary, part collection of personal accounts of battle, and part insight on leadership in combat and the human condition, it is this underlying theme that has inspired the writing of this story.

I have written all the chapters contained in Part 1 – they are meant to serve as the foundation of the Squadron War Diary and provide the thread for the specific incidents that others have captured in Part 2. These accounts are taken from my recollections and interpretations of the events. Every attempt has been made to avoid revisionist accounts of the battles fought and decisions made, however prone most of us are to viewing the past through rose-tinted glasses. Compiling these stories 6-24 months post-tour has allowed us some time to reflect upon the events with the benefit of witnessing, in some cases, the delayed apparition of second- and third-order effects as a result of our actions. We have not dwelled on these aspects, as our goal was to provide, to both those interested and to ourselves, a written account of those snapshots in time. Where opinions are stated, they are mine alone.

Chapters in Part 2 are courtesy of my second-in-command, Maj Rich Busbridge, some of my former troop commanders, Capt Dan Clarke and Capt Anthony Robb, my sergeant major, CWO Brad Montgomery, the Squadron Operations NCO, WO Derek Marcoux, the 2 Troop Warrant Officer, WO Scott Clucas and an EOD Section Commander, Sgt John Valois. Sgt Neil Coates, Sgt Justin O'Neill, Sgt Sammy Ross, MCpl Mike Maidment and LS Keith Bruce also contributed greatly. Cpl Matt Austin interviewed many members of the Squadron and wrote four chapters on their behalf. I am deeply grateful to all those who took the time to contribute, especially those who accepted the unglamorous task of editing the initial manuscripts (my wife Shannon, my parents Renato and Stephanie, Capt Ed Stewart, the Battle Group Public Affairs Officer and LCol Frank Egan). I also want to thank every member of the Squadron who took the time to delve into and share potentially painful memories.

I have read many books and accounts of the Canadian Forces in Kandahar. From what I can tell, based on my first- and second-hand knowledge of the events, these various accounts are largely factual, which is to say that there are no gross errors or fabrications. However, they are not entirely representative or complete and this book will inevitably share that same predicament. This is 23 Field Squadron's story as told by its various authors. It is based on the recollections, written documentation and oral submissions at the time. It does not capture every event that occurred to every member of the Squadron, even if those members did agree to be interviewed by Cpl Austin. Therefore, this collection of stories cannot be read through the lens of *Objectivism*, as truth is very much dependent on the individual perceptions of the particular witness.

Lastly, there are many revelations of errors made by the Squadron during the mission. These admissions of error are not an attempt at self-flagellation, an act of humility or a *cri-de-coeur*. While cathartic, they are meant primarily to highlight where we can improve should we ever need to do this again – as we learn in equal measure, if not more, from our mistakes than from our successes. Many have found it difficult to admit fault, as there may be blood on our hands as a result of those decisions made. Guilt and pride are incredibly powerful and potentially consuming emotions. Inevitably they lead to denial. Denial is insidious and is ultimately destructive to both the individual and to the wider organization. Individually, it can be soul-destroying. Collectively, it creates a cognitive dissonance whereby the soldiers who were there and know their truth have to reconcile their personal experiences with the often sanitized, mythicized and impenitent official version. Therefore, to present this story without the inclusion of these faults would be disingenuous, historically myopic and ultimately a disservice to those who will follow in our footsteps.

Major Mark Gasparotto MSM, CD
April 2010
Ottawa, Ontario

PART 1
SQUADRON WAR DIARY
THE ROAD TO HIGH READINESS
AND DEPLOYMENT

The road is long
With many a winding turn
That leads us to who knows where
Who knows when
But I'm strong
Strong enough to carry him
He ain't heavy, he's my brother

It's a long, long road
From which there is no return
While we're on the way to there
Why not share
And the load
Doesn't weigh me down at all
He ain't heavy, he's my brother

— *"He Ain't Heavy, He's my Brother"*
Lyrics by Bobby Scott and Bob Russell. Recorded by the Hollies.

Our pre-deployment training termed "The Road to High Readiness," was a long one, and in our case it led us to war. The result of all this preparation was a highly trained and cohesive fighting force ready to deploy and prosecute combat operations. The downside of the length of training, however, was that the 1 RCR Battle Group was both mentally and physically tired before even deploying to theatre.

In the historical context, deployments during the Balkan peacekeeping era had become a proxy for normal collective training due in large part to funding constraints in the 1990s that severely curtailed our ability to train. For this deployment, extensive vehicle-crew and mission-specific requirements inevitably prolonged the pre-deployment preparations to almost a year for the 1 RCR Battle Group rotation, and to closer to a year-and-a-half for subsequent rotations. Predictably, one of the most common soldier complaints noted by those who do post-tour polling for the military, was the length of pre-deployment training. The Army Commander has recently decreed that this training must be conducted in a maximum of six months.

My own preparations began in early 2005. I was serving as the Regimental Operations Officer for 2 Combat Engineer Regiment when I was informed by LCol Brian Irwin, the Commanding Officer (CO) that I would be taking over as Officer Commanding (OC) 23 Field Squadron that August. For the core of combat engineers that would make up the Squadron, the training started that September, while the majority of the attachments (Reservists, Dragoons, Naval Clearance Divers and other specialists) joined us in early 2006. At the same time the Squadron was detached from the engineers and placed under command of LCol Omer Lavoie's 1 RCR Battle Group.

Battle Group, a term taken from the Second World War, refers to a largely *ad hoc* collection of supporting arms centred on either an infantry battalion or armoured regiment. Modern battle groups are more planned in their nature and for the Kandahar rotations would be built on an infantry battalion. An engineer squadron, a mixed armoured and light reconnaissance (recce) squadron, an artillery battery, an unmanned aerial vehicle flight, a medical company and eventually a tank squadron would join together with three infantry rifle companies to form this combined arms team.

The major challenge at this point was to forge a cohesive team from the eclectic grouping of soldiers, sailors and airmen, not only within 23

Field Squadron but within the Battle Group as a whole. While some of the initial friction could be attributed to personalities, it was in part also due to a clash of Corps and Regimental cultures. Nonetheless, whatever differences were not sorted out by the end of Exercise Maple Guardian – conducted at the Canadian Manoeuvre Training Centre (CMTC) – were certainly put to rest the first time these soldiers came under enemy fire in theatre. The creation of a singular *esprit de corps* was demonstrated to me most vividly when MCpl Greg Murray, one of my field section LAV crew commanders and a Royal Canadian Dragoon, carried the Engineer flag in the guard of honour during Sgt Shane Stachnik's ramp ceremony at Kandahar Airfield in September of 2006.

In April, I was fortunate to participate in the Battle Group's tactical reconnaissance of our eventual area of operations in Kandahar. The heat was already a considerable factor, especially for the members of the Tactical Reconnaissance Group who had not yet acclimatized to the desert conditions. What we saw and heard confirmed the reports of heavy fighting that we had been receiving back in Canada. Furthermore, it steeled our resolve to provide the best war-fighting training available to our soldiers in the time remaining to us.

The many professional development sessions, ranges and training exercises were too numerous to list. However, our time spent on Ex Maple Guardian in Wainright, Alberta during April and May of 2006 deserves special mention. It was a long, somewhat painful and anticlimactic experience - but a necessary evil to ready 23 Field Squadron and the 1 RCR Battle Group for deployment. There was a readily apparent yet usually mild undercurrent of 'us-versus-them' attitude between the Battle Group and the Canadian Manoeuvre Training Centre staff who supervised the exercise. The engineers got over this fairly quickly but the Squadron wanted to express its gratitude for our hosts' 'hospitality' by spelling out the "CMTC" acronym with wrecked cars on a hillside. The derelict cars had been used during the exercise as targets or to simulate Vehicle-Borne Improvised Explosive Devices (IEDs) and we had been tasked to recover the cars to a central location. No direction was given as to how they were to be arranged and even if it had, it would have been ignored. It was an open invitation for the Squadron to employ its artistic talents. It also made for a great photo op. I am told that most saw the humour in it.

The Squadron posing in front of 12 wrecked cars spelling 'CMTC' at the end of Exercise Maple Guardian.

With training completed, all that remained for the months of June and July was last-minute administration and pre-deployment leave. After the long haul of training through the winter, pre-deployment leave was absolutely required. Such leave can be a double-edged sword, however, as the soldiers and their families count down to the inevitable day of departure. As the departure day approaches, the soldier's mind is pre-occupied with the upcoming mission and there tends to be an emotional distancing from his or her family. This is a very common phenomenon, however many soldiers do not accept these emotions for what they are or are in denial about them. As a result, they fail to fully prepare themselves and their families for the possibility of being injured or killed – and given the stream of news coming in from theatre over the month of July, it seemed the odds of getting injured or killed were far greater than originally anticipated.

Consciously coming to terms with and then discussing one's own mortality in real terms is very difficult, but immensely important. Doing so, I believe, takes some of the pressure off the spouse and family in the event of death. For example it would simplify and ease the burden of the funeral decision-making process from, "What would he have wanted me to do?" to "That is what he wanted."

Certainly writing my own 'Death Letter' was one of the most surreal and emotional things that I have ever done. It was a highly personal and uncomfortable experience to expose your soul - even to yourself.

Soon enough our time arrived and we began our journey overseas. We were leaving for the hostile and unforgiving environment of Kandahar

Province, a place the troops called "The Suck," a borrowed expression from the book and movie, *Jarhead* about United States Marines' experiences during the First Gulf War. So off we went, embarked on another long road, a road from which there was to be no return to the innocence of the life we had known before.

DEPLOYMENT

I arrived in theatre on August 3rd, 2006 and was met by my Squadron Quartermaster, WO Ted Gombert. He and his assistant, Cpl Randy Duggan, were part of the Battle Group Advance Party and had been in theatre for almost a week prior to my arrival. The remainder of 23 Field Squadron would arrive over the next two weeks. We were soon moved into our permanent accommodations at Kandahar Airfield, which consisted of two-to-a-room, two-storey, air-conditioned containers. Apart from the 40 degree Celsius heat and the ever-pervasive smell of fecal matter, it was all very comfortable for a war.

After a trip to the Kandahar Airfield range to group-and-zero our personal weapons, a process that ensures that your rifle and the rifle's sight are pointing at the same thing, I met up with Maj Trevor Webb, the OC of 11 Field Squadron. His squadron was attached to the 1st Battalion, Princess Patricia's Canadian Light Infantry (1 PPCLI), the Battle Group that we would be replacing. Trevor is an old friend of mine as we had been students together on our Troop Commander's Course back in 1998. He had been in theatre since early 2006. Trevor was eager to start the handover process, however that day elements of the 1 PPCLI Battle Group, including some engineer attachments, had been engaged in an intense firefight with enemy insurgents in a village called Pashmul. Pashmul is located in the Zhari district, 20 kilometres west of Kandahar City on the north bank of the Arghandab River. After a protracted battle, centred on a soon-to-be notorious building known as the "White School," they broke contact having suffered four killed-in-action (KIA) and several wounded-in-action (WIA). The engagement was notable for two reasons. First, it resulted in the largest number of Canadian soldiers killed in a single combat engagement in many years. Second, it was one of the first times that we had seen the enemy willing to eschew standard guerrilla tactics and dig in to engage Coalition Forces in a conventional battle, using static defensive positions, complete with obstacles on the approach routes (in this case IEDs) covered by direct fire weapons. The enemy contact on August 3rd was an ominous precursor, signalling further engagements that month in both the Zhari and Panjwaii Districts and would ultimately lead to Operation Medusa.

We took over from a very tired 1 PPCLI Battle Group. Their mental and physical disposition after six months in theatre presaged our own at the end of our tour six months later. The surprisingly unrelenting tempo of operations did not offer much of an opportunity for comprehensive maintenance, and thus their (and soon to be our) vehicles and equipment were in very rough shape. Unfortunately for us, included in this inventory was the heavy equipment fleet. In fact, the serviceability rate for the eclectic fleet was hovering at only 20% and had been there for most of 1 PPCLI Battle Group's tour. Since the arrival, or even the notion, of sending tanks and engineer armour into theatre was weeks away, I would have to rely on this heavy equipment to provide the mobility support, such as breaching obstacles and crossing wadis (dry riverbeds), required for upcoming operations. There was much work to be done that would require the Squadron to beg, borrow and reconfigure heavy equipment from a variety of sources. Throughout the handover and acclimatization process we began to take ownership of the issues and applied our fresh-to-theatre enthusiasm and energy to solving them. Without any doctrinal breaching or gap-crossing assets in the in-theatre Canadian inventory, and the majority of the heavy equipment broken and awaiting parts, the Squadron, and 2 Troop specifically, used its imagination and initiative to fabricate LAV transportable / supportable and soldier-portable ramps. These ramps allowed a combat-loaded LAV, weighing roughly 18 tonnes, to cross a 2.4 metre gap, the basic width of a small wadi. They were constructed out of steel I-beam and two-foot metal pickets. Eight ramps in total were built, which was enough for each of the LAVs in 1 and 2 Troop.

Top: The OC and 2 Troop Headquarters demonstrate the portability of a LAV Ramp.
Bottom: Ramps mounted on the side of an Engineer LAV at Strong Point West.

Helicopter and land-based recces were planned and executed as part of the handover. Along with the CO, my first recce took me via a US Army UH-60 Black Hawk helicopter to Forward Operating Base (FOB) Spin Boldak on the Pakistan border to the southeast, and to FOB Martello to the north. These FOBs were in opposite directions roughly 100 and 150 kilometres away from Kandahar Airfield respectively, and delineated the outer edge of the Battle Group's vast area of operations. The only way to see every Canadian FOB in one day was by air.

We landed at FOB Spin Boldak first. The FOB was shared by the Afghan National Army and a US Other Governmental Agency / Security Contractor. Previously, it had been a French Army outpost, occupied by their Army Units and Foreign Legion troops. Consequently, one of the buildings had a bar and beautifully painted naked women adorning the walls. Initially, Charles Company (for reasons that only they can explain, 1 RCR calls its third rifle company 'Charles' instead of 'Charlie') was given the responsibility of occupying FOB Spin Boldak and conducting patrols along the Pakistani border. Op Medusa, and the various follow-on activities that flowed from it would ultimately change that task.

Our second destination was FOB Martello. FOB Martello was built along the Tarin Khowt Road, on the way north to the Dutch area of operations in the Province of Uruzgan. It had been constructed by the previous rotation as a means of securing the northern part of Kandahar Province and NATO's expansion into Uruzgan. While the construction was a feat of engineering, the location of the FOB was both tactically and technically very poor. It was located in a bowl, surrounded by unsecured high features on all sides and sat at the confluence of several wadis. Touring the FOB, I was immediately reminded of descriptions of the French firebase at Dien Bien Phu[1] in Vietnam. Neither the Taliban nor the wet season would be kind to the soldiers who would occupy this barren and forsaken piece of ground. For the rest of tour, I would not set foot back in either of the two FOBs we visited that day.

The recce to the Zhari and Panjwaii districts, immediately to the west of Kandahar City, was done by road, in LAVs. To the north of the Arghandab River lies the District of Zhari, to the south, the Panjwaii. It was a two-day trip, led by the CO of the 1 PPCLI Battle Group, that took us through the bustling streets of Kandahar City as well as the very dangerous Taliban-controlled regions to the west along the Arghandab River.

The Arghandab River flows southwest and borders the western and north-western edge of the city. In stark contrast to the desert that surrounds it, the river irrigates a lush green belt, full of grape, pomegranate, poppy and marijuana fields. It was this insurgent-controlled green belt, north of the river and south of Highway 1, that the Taliban used as a sanctuary and transit route. Highway 1 is the country's ring road. It's generally east-west orientation in that part of the country passes right through the heart of Kandahar City. It links Kandahar City to Kabul to the northeast and Helmand Province to the west. In most areas, it is a two-lane concrete road. By occupying the green belt in the Zhari-Panjwaii area the Taliban were well-placed to strangle the western part of Kandahar City.

Situated in the heart of this green belt lies the village of Sangsar. This collection of mud compounds is the alleged birthplace of Mullah Omar, supreme leader of the Taliban movement. In previous conflicts, Kandahar City had always been taken after the green belts on its periphery were controlled, and the city isolated. In the summer of 2006, the Taliban were trying to repeat history by retaking Kandahar City in this time-honoured manner.

After a day of driving, we arrived at Patrol Base Wilson. Canadian Forces shared this 100-metre-square compound, which housed the Zhari District Centre, the seat of local government and an Afghan National Police station. It was an overcrowded and fetid place which, as I would soon find out, was targeted daily by Taliban mortars. In fact, you could practically set your watch by it. At approximately 6:00 pm the first mortar round that day hit, crashing through the roof of a G-Wagon 10 metres to my left. Luckily for me it did not detonate, although I did count it as the first of my nine lives lost. For some Darwinian reason I did not realize that more rounds would follow until the second round hit. I immediately ran to my parked LAV and jumped into the turret. Trevor was in the gunner's seat and I was in the crew commander's. The other LAVs around us began to open fire, likely at a spotter who was adjusting the mortar base plate's fire. We could not identify any targets, however we decided to test fire our cannon and coaxial machine gun just in case. As would have it, Murphy's Law prevailed and both jammed. The lesson: Never have two majors in the same turret because quoting lines from the movie *Tombstone* to each other will not correct weapon stoppages – "Isn't that a daisy." At the end of my first mortar attack, my crew and I were no worse for wear, but the misadventures continued.

Top: Afghan National Army soldiers assembled at Patrol Base Wilson.
Bottom: Observation Post atop the Battle Group's compound within Patrol Base Wilson.

It was decided that the convoy would depart Patrol Base Wilson in darkness for the move to the town of Bazar-E-Panjwaii, some 25 kilometres away. The town was on the south side of the Arghandab River and was nestled in between three prominent high features – Badvan Ghar, Mar Ghar and Ma'sum Ghar[2]. Naturally, during my first night move, through 'Ambush Alley', the LAV's thermal sights and intercom crashed. The rest of the trip would prove to be no better. Since no harm ensued they now seem comical. At the time, however, I was suffering from a serious sense of humour failure. We drove through the town at daybreak and stopped at the foot of Badvan Ghar, which overlooked the river but more importantly, over Pashmul and the White School to the north. It was with this landscape as a backdrop that I officially took over from Trevor.

Handover from Trevor with the White School in the background.

After our 20-minute stop, the convoy mounted up and prepared to leave. The hydraulics that operated the LAV's rear ramp failed and it was too heavy to close manually. I attempted to tell the convoy over the net, but the radios had crashed and the convoy left without us. Other than screaming at the departing convoy without effect, all I could think of was the movie *The Beast*, based on a lone Soviet tank, lost in Mujahideen country. As we would find out later, electronic warfare intercepts indicated that the Taliban were planning to ambush the convoy during our sojourn at Badvan Ghar. Our only option was to lift the ramp up, so that it was horizontal, and chain it off manually, thereby making the LAV moveable but keeping the entire back exposed. We then guessed at the convoy's location and drove with the rear ramp down through the town linking up with the convoy about a kilometre away. We then thanked certain members for abandoning us and with the help of several other soldiers, we managed to lift the ramp and lock it into position. Upon our return to Kandahar Airfield, Murphy struck again, resulting in a 25mm round being fired into the berm at the weapons clearance area – nicknamed thenceforward, by my friend and the OC of ISTAR Squadron, Major Andy Lussier, as the "G Spot." It was determined that the discharge was due to mechanical failure of the cannon's safety switch. Ultimately I should have known better but a burr on the butterfly switch was caught at 3/4 of a turn. It did not fully activate the safety, and when I proceeded to clear the cannon, a round was fired. As my gunner would tell you, I was the weakest link in the turret. Finally the trip was over. It was the last ride for Trevor Webb and his immortals. For myself, however, it proved to be an inauspicious start to my tour.

After seeing the ground throughout the area of operations, the assessment was made to keep the greatest part of the Squadron's combat power centralized and close to Kandahar Airfield while sending small engineer detachments to both FOB Martello and Spin Boldak. The exploits of Sgt Neil Coates and MCpl Anderson Thomas and their men who were dispatched to these distant FOBs can be found in the Chapters named "Attack on FOB Martello" and "The King of Costall." Knowing that my soldiers would soon be scattered all over the province in support of the various and far-flung elements of the Battle Group, I gathered them all together and told them this:

> *This is likely the last chance that I will get to address the Squadron as a whole. As such, I wanted to pass on some insights into this place and the mission but also to articulate what I see as our keys to success.*
>
> *From the beginning of our training, I've tried to put you in the mindset that we would be fighting a war. I've been here just under two weeks now; with four ramp ceremonies, incoming mortar fire and three rocket attacks later, make no mistake, we are very much in harm's way. A fight is shaping up west of the city in the near future. So we can't waste any time preparing for that eventuality – equipment and vehicle preparations and becoming familiar with the area of operations. In the chaos and fog of war, it will be a section commander's fight. So get yourself ready.*
>
> *Keys to our success defined:*
>
> *This will be a marathon. We may have to sprint now and again but it will be a six-month grind. Therefore, sustainability is paramount. So prepare yourself mentally for the long haul.*
>
> *Flexibility of mind, body and spirit will be essential. Take your job seriously, never yourself. Sense of humour is a must.*
>
> *Do not rush unless ordered to. Most things can wait until tomorrow. So if you have to abort a combat patrol*

because of external or internal circumstances then do so. A vehicle recovery, IED strike or casualty will become the mission at the expense of the original one. So plan accordingly. Remember the enemy has a vote and wants to kill you.

Foster a bullet-proof mind – never talk yourself out of the fight. In LCol Dave Grossman's[3] words, "no pity party, no macho man and avoid a state of denial." Do not feel sorry for yourself and seek help if required. Soldiers experience fear and I've seen many weep for their fallen comrades. It is not to be ashamed of. Some of us will undoubtedly see and/or experience terrible things. We will get through it together. As such, anyone involved in a critical incident will talk to the mental health folks as soon as practicable.

I'll sum up with the orders that General Hillier had passed on to us in Trenton. "Take care of yourself and take care of each other." I have every confidence in each and every one of you to be professional and honourable soldiers. Chimo[4].

By mid-August, the planning for Op Medusa was gathering momentum. Unfortunately, the Squadron was still incapable of offering any meaningful mobility support to the Battle Group as large quantities of our heavy equipment remained unserviceable. We continued to scrounge for equipment and hound the chain of command and the mechanics to get our vehicles repaired. I do not blame the mechanics, as they could and would work around the clock to repair our vehicles, provided they had the parts to do so. The issue was more about commanders prioritizing which fleet of vehicles to fix. LCol Lavoie understood the value of what we could offer with respect to mobility support. He accepted our concerns and threw his weight behind our efforts to get those assets back in the fight. As for the troops, the ones that had not been 'outside the wire' were becoming very anxious to see some action. All I could tell them was to be careful what they wished for. Their time would soon come.

August 19th marked the official Transfer of Command Authority; the 1 RCR Battle Group was formally in charge. Three hours after the ceremony, elements of A Company under the command of Major Mike Wright were involved in a vicious and protracted nine-hour battle with hundreds of insurgents in the vicinity of Ma'sum Ghar. Over seventy insurgent fighters were killed with no Canadian casualties. Along with the CO and many anxious Battle Group Headquarters staff, I followed the battle from the Battle Group Command Post at Kandahar Airfield. Situation reports (sitreps) came in over the radio and we could watch parts of the battle in real time from video feeds provided by Canadian and US Unmanned Aerial Vehicles.

In the following week Taliban fighters attacked both 1 and 2 Troop as they transited through Ambush Alley on Highway 1 to improve the defences at Patrol Base Wilson. Cpl Austin, the Squadron's storyteller and blogger, describes these events in the chapters named "Ambush Alley" and "Mortar Attack on Patrol Base Wilson." Because of the condition of our own heavy equipment, we attempted to hire civilian contractors to perform force protection works at Patrol Base Wilson. None would accept the very lucrative contracts offered due to Taliban threats of retribution and the intense violence in the area.

As part of the planning for Op Medusa, another helicopter recce was conducted, this time focusing on Pashmul. Masters of using camouflage and concealment, no enemy was seen and there was no pattern of life detected within the entire three-kilometre-wide strip of land between Pashmul and Highway 1. Pattern of life is a term used to describe the civilian population's activities within a certain geographic area. In the months previous, the Taliban had evicted all the civilians within that area in order to prepare defensive positions in and around the existing compounds. This action on the Taliban's part created the unintended consequence that the coalition forces no longer had to discriminate our fire, as they were all targets. Essentially, it became a free-fire zone and if it had two legs and moved, we could and did kill it.

Formal orders for Op Medusa were received from Regional Command South Headquarters on or about August 21st, via e-mail. Curiously though, considering this was the largest NATO combat operation in its history, the only face-to-face meetings involving all force commanders occurred at the back-brief a few days later. On August 24th, I issued a Warning Order to the Squadron, detailing as much as possible the probable tasks for each field troop and specialist section. Along with the other OCs, I received orders from the CO on August 27th. Despite almost two weeks of preparation there were still substantial gaps in the engineer portion of the plan. By this time we had borrowed a D6 armoured dozer from the UK and the German-made Zettelmeyer (pronounced "Z-L" for short) front end loader was finally repaired and outfitted with steel plating (ad-hoc up-armour), however, that was the extent of my "breaching[5]" capability.

'Mad Maxed' Zettelmeyer Front End Loader with welded-on steel plating.

My staff continued to pursue other options, including shaming the Afghan National Army into lending us their D7 dozer and possibly renting another. Furthermore, we were waiting for word from the US if they would send two Route Clearance Packages in support of the mission. A Route Clearance Package is a suite of vehicles designed to detect and neutralize IEDs. The Battle Group still hadn't received any real quantity of either Afghan National Army or Police personnel and we still did not have a great appreciation for the ground and the enemy disposition. The most comprehensive and accurate intelligence brief that we had received came from the Special Operations Forces community, and their bleak assessment was that in August of 2006, ISAF was losing the war in Kandahar.

Formal Squadron orders were delivered on August 30th. Since much of the detail had already been passed on to the Troops, these orders were confirmatory in nature. The Squadron was broken down in to four task-tailored groupings. 1 Troop was detached to Bravo Company, who would be operating out of Patrol Base Wilson and attacking from the north. 2 Troop was detached to Charles Company, who would secure Ma'sum Ghar, act as a feint, and then attack Pashmul from the south. Sgt Houde's Recce Section, 31 Bravo, was attached to A Company who was tasked to secure the town of Bazar-E-Panjwaii and protect our southern flank. The remainder of the Squadron would deploy under my direct control and act as the engineer reserve.

At the eleventh hour, one of the two Route Clearance Packages arrived and we received word that the Task Force Engineer had obtained authorization to use the Afghan National Army D7 dozer and had found a contractor willing to rent a D8 dozer. It had taken an incredible amount of arm-twisting to get the Afghan National Army to release their civilian pattern D7 dozer to us. As it turned out, they were justified as their fears were realized when their dozer was severely damaged in an IED strike later in September. However, such are the risks in war – and after all it was their war too.

The acquisition and deployment of the rental D8 dozer was an unlikely story. I do not think that the owner had any idea that we would weld on steel plates ('Mad Maxing' as we called it) and use his yellow civilian dozer as our primary combat breaching vehicle. All is fair in love and war, and he was paid handsomely for his services. Donald Rumsfeld, the former US Secretary of Defence once remarked, "You go to war with the Army you have." Although the dozers were effective they were ersatz engineer armour - an armoured dozer does not a Badger Armoured Engineering Vehicle[6] make.

And so August ended as it began – hot, dusty, busy, chaotic and tense. Orders had been given and soldiers had made the most of the time allotted to prepare. It was time to take the fight to the Taliban and evict them from their stronghold in Pashmul.

Operation Medusa

Iacta Alea Est (The Die is Cast)
— Julius Caesar

Combat Operations

September 1st, 2006: Depart Kandahar Airfield

All Squadron elements departed Kandahar Airfield on September 1st, 2006. Sgt Houde's section was with A Company, Lt Anthony Robb's 1 Troop with Bravo Company, Lt Justin Behiels' 2 Troop with Charles Company and the Squadron reserve as an independent convoy. The Zettelmeyer and the UK D6 Dozer were scheduled for delivery to Ma'sum Ghar by lowbed once that location had been secured.

By mid-day, all the Squadron's sub-elements had made it to their respective assembly areas. The Squadron reserve took routes through the desert south of Kandahar City and, despite a couple of wrong turns, eventually linked up with A and Charles Companies. The rendezvous was in Assembly Area Three, which was located to the north of Route Fosters, approximately 10 kilometres east of Bazar-E-Panjwaii. All was going according to plan until Lt Jeremy Hiltz's LAV struck a mine while backing up. There were no injuries but since I was within in the danger area of the explosion, I counted it as the second of my nine proverbial lives. Our mine map showed the limits of the nearest Soviet-era minefield to be 600 metres away. Either the map was wrong or the strike was a fluke attributable to mine migration that can be caused by inclement weather. Heavy rains in particular can wash mines from one area to another and repeated freeze-thaw cycles can push buried mines towards the surface. Luckily my reserve had a US Route Clearance Package, which cleared a path back to Route Fosters so A and Charles Companies could move safely to another assembly area.

My engineer reserve along with the Charles Company LAV Captain, Capt Trevor Norton, and the remainder of Lt Jeremy Hiltz's 8 Platoon remained at the scene awaiting a recovery vehicle to be dispatched from Kandahar Airfield. As we occupied our position we witnessed a surreal scene begin to unfold on Route Fosters.

Canadian military convoys continued to roll down Route Fosters, pouring combat power into Bazar-E-Panjwaii while simultaneously, hundreds of civilians from the town were fleeing in the opposite direction, seeking refuge in Kandahar City. These people had whatever possessions they could carry on their backs, and were crammed on motorbikes and in cars, vans, buses, horses and donkey-drawn carts.

After a tense night of covering our arcs, the LAV was recovered in the early hours of September 2nd. At daybreak we moved towards the A Company leaguer where we refuelled and ate breakfast.

Throughout the 1 RCR Battle Group, many Combat Service Support assets had been removed, centralized and then migrated to the National Support Element. The predicament for 23 Field Squadron was that we were not manned or equipped to run a Quartermaster (logistics) function outside of Kandahar Airfield. This model had been adopted for the Balkans and Kabul, where operationally and geographically it may have made sense, and had been maintained in Kandahar where it was assumed that sub-units would always be well within resupply distance from Kandahar Airfield.

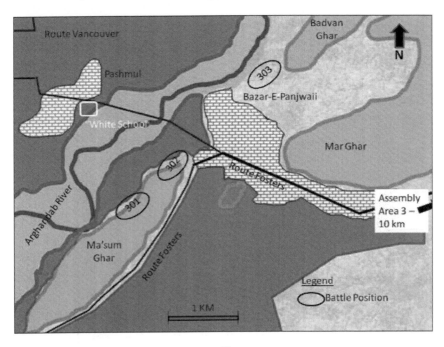

While work-arounds and *ad hoc* solutions were implemented, it was a poor setup for a full battle group conducting combat operations. Thus, since the Squadron had no deployable logistics echelon of its own, we had to get combat supplies (fuel, water, rations, generic ammunition) from the respective infantry companies within whose areas we were operating or transiting. Soon the Squadron was on the move again as the town of Bazar-E-Panjwaii and the surrounding high ground (Ma'sum Ghar and Badvan Ghar) had been secured, without the use of force, by the forward elements of A and Charles Company and ISTAR Squadron. There were three Battle Positions overlooking Taliban-controlled Pashmul - two (301 and 302) on the northern slopes of Ma'sum Ghar and one (303) on Badvan Ghar. Due to space limitations the reserve was positioned at Battle Position 303 and I joined Niner Tac (the group of people that he travels around with tactically) at the more crowded Battle Position 302.

SEPTEMBER 2ND, 2006: OCCUPY MA'SUM GHAR

Upon arriving at Ma'sum Ghar, 2 Troop immediately started working on friendly force mobility tasks. These tasks included the clearing[7] of two lanes in order to reach the south bank of the Arghandab River from Ma'sum Ghar. These lanes would allow Charles Company ease of access to the river as well as the enemy defences in Pashmul, once the order was given to attack. The actual clearing of these lanes involved the use of explosives to remove some trees because they were so hard that our small chainsaws could not effectively cut them down.

We also had to use our heavy equipment to doze a lane through the adjacent grape fields. These grape fields presented some of the most challenging terrain that we as an Army have ever seen. Someone had commented that the terrain in the Panjwaii was akin to the bocage[8] in Normandy during the D-Day invasion - times ten. Almost everything in the region was surrounded by walls. Every home or building had a tall mud wall around it. Most roads were very narrow, just wide enough for a small car, and lined with drainage ditches and/or mud walls. The fields consisted of two to three metre tall marijuana plants, wheat crops or grapes. The grape fields were by far the most difficult to cross because of their construction. As with everything in Afghanistan, a mud wall bordered each field. Each field consisted of repeated rows of parallel, tapered, one-metre thick, one-and-a-half-metre high mud hedgerows spaced at two-metre intervals. The grape vines grew out of the sloped sides of these hedgerows. In essence, these grape fields provided the Taliban with successive trench lines, with the foliage from the vines providing excellent cover from overhead observation. The only way across was as a dismounted soldier. The only way through was a dozer; not a tank and certainly not a LAV.

Aerial view of a vineyard in the summer.

In light of these realities, the terrain posed significant mobility concerns. There was, however, some good news as my headquarters at Kandahar Airfield, in conjunction with the Task Force Engineer, had managed to obtain two more civilian-pattern Caterpillar dozers. An Afghan National Army D7 and a rental D8 were in the process of being fortified with metal plates for operator protection, a process jokingly referred to as being 'Mad Maxed.' These vehicles would soon be brought forward to join or replace heavy equipment already supporting the fight.

The "3 Horsemen" at Patrol Base Wilson on September 7th, 2006. From left to right: The rented D8, UK D6 and the borrowed Afghan National Army D7 Caterpillar Dozers.

In the early afternoon of September 2nd, 2006 during the first of four days of preparatory bombardment of enemy positions, the Commander of Regional Command South flew into Ma'sum Ghar to talk to LCol Lavoie. I was present when, in a near Damascene reversal of the original plan, he told LCol Lavoie, "Omer, I need you to go now. Do you understand what I am asking?"

Regardless of the rationale, that order accelerated the plan by more than 48 hours and led to a suspension of preparatory bombardment and a hasty crossing by ground forces on the morning of September 3rd, rather than a more deliberate manoeuvre planned for several days later. No one will ever know if going with the original plan would have changed the final outcome of the battle, or who lived and who died.

In conjunction with the Battle Group's artillery, Offensive Air Support continued to strike known and suspected Taliban targets throughout the area. It was an awesome demonstration of the lethal effects available as we watched everything from 155mm howitzers to 1000 lb bombs to HIMARS missiles pound the targets not one kilometre across the river to the north, where Charles Company, along with many of my engineers, would be attacking the next morning.

Top: HIMARS Missile Strike against a Taliban position in Pashmul as seen from Ma'sum Ghar.
Bottom: 500 lb bomb strike as seen from Patrol Base Wilson.

Like Caesar crossing the Rubicon, once the orders were given there was no turning back and at approximately 6:00 am on September 3rd, 2006, the first wave of the assault force based on Charles Company Combat Team with 2 Troop, heavy equipment and Afghan National Army troops left the relative safety of Ma'sum Ghar and crossed the Arghandab River.

Their crossing and breach of the enemy bank was unopposed. It appears, in retrospect, that the Taliban waited for our lead elements to almost reach the White School before they started to engage, at which point they surrounded the Charles Company Combat Team on three sides. The White School was to the front, marijuana fields were to the left and wadis and mud walls were to the right. From my vantage point at Ma'sum Ghar, some 1200 metres away, it was difficult to see the detail of what was occurring. As soon as Charles Company came under fire, the LAVs on Ma'sum Ghar, including my own, commenced firing at suspected positions in the vicinity of the White School. While scanning for other targets, my gunner picked up movement on the left flank. At 2375 metres the High Explosive rounds fired from our cannon were killing Taliban reinforcements moving between two compounds. Their movements were hidden from view, except for a ten-metre gap. We kept our cannon trained on that gap for the next two days. At final count we had twelve unconfirmed kills. We were lucky in the sense that the distance made those kills somewhat impersonal. It was like a video game looking through our sights as those enemy foot soldiers were killed over two kilometres away.

There were various radio networks throughout the 1 RCR Battle Group. Among the 'nets,' as they are known in short hand, there was the Squadron net for all the engineer call signs. I tried to raise 2 Troop on the Squadron net, but they were fully engaged in the pitched battle raging around them. In hindsight, I should have operated with a third radio installed to listen to the Charles Company net, a deficiency which my gunner sorted out later.

Then the sitrep came in over the Battle Group Net: the White School was a heavily defended position. Fire was coming in from three sides. Four Canadian soldiers had been killed in action and many others were wounded. Two vehicles had been destroyed and the situation was untenable. The OC, Maj Matt Sprague recommended a withdrawal.

The CO instructed Matt to retrieve the dead and wounded and pull back. Minutes later, on the Squadron net, we received word that 32 Delta had been hit, killing Sgt Shane Stachnik and wounding MCpl Greg Murray. MCpl Dwayne Orvis, the 32 Delta Second-in-Command had taken over and led his men out of the kill zone. Orvis was awarded a Mention-in-Dispatches for his actions that day. The Zettelmeyer had also been hit, injuring MCpl Lance Hooper. From my turret, I looked back into the back of the LAV at my sergeant-major, MWO Brad Montgomery. We nodded our heads in sad acceptance of the news.

After what seemed to be an eternity, the mauled Charles Company Combat Team withdrew from contact, back to the centre of the riverbed. The post-attack consolidation took place there, focusing on the evacuation of the dead and wounded. In total, three vehicles had been abandoned in the enemy kill zone: The Zettelmeyer, a G-Wagon and the LAV that Cpl Clinton Orr had unsuccessfully tried to extricate from a ditch with his dozer – an action for which he would later be awarded the Medal of Military Valour. Sensitive communications equipment left inside necessitated the targeting and destruction of both the LAV and the G-Wagon by coalition aircraft. At 14,000 feet and 670 kilometres-per-hour, all our vehicles, which were in very close proximity, must have appeared the same to the pilot, so a Royal Air Force Harrier using 500-pound bombs destroyed the Zettelmeyer along with the two targeted vehicles.

I joined the CO and his Tac as he went forward to see the Charles Company Combat Team. The scene was tense and busy, but by no means chaotic. The signs of the first of the five stages of grief (denial) were plain and visible. Anger, bargaining, depression and acceptance would follow and for some that would take mere days, while for others the cycle is still, to this day, not yet complete. Most were still in shock and the events of the day had not fully registered. I particularly wanted to speak to two people individually: The 2 Troop Commander, Lt Justin Behiels, and the 32 Delta Second-in-Command, MCpl Dwayne Orvis. I saw Justin first and he was visibly shaken. I wanted to get his story of what had happened and also to get his assessment of the combat effectiveness of his troop for the next assault. Despite all that had transpired, there was still an enemy objective to seize, and although the day's events were tragic, we had to quickly recover from the setbacks and resume the offensive.

The remaining members of 32 Delta were huddled next to their LAV. I looked directly at Orvis and said, "They're your soldiers now. I need you to take care of them." The gravity of the situation and the weight of his new responsibility were evident in his eyes and on his face. He nodded in solemn acceptance. I shook his hand and let him to tend to his men.

We all returned to Ma'sum Ghar to recuperate from our wounds, brief higher headquarters and revisit the plan, while at the same time maintaining overwatch positions onto Pashmul. For me, that meant pulling 31 Delta out of the Squadron Reserve forward to Ma'sum Ghar to replace 32 Delta. September 3rd would mark the day when, individually and collectively, we grew up as men and women both, and above all as soldiers.

The remnants of MCpl Hooper's Zettelmeyer after taking a hit from a Taliban fired Rocket Propelled Grenade and a Coalition Force 500 lb bomb. Ma'sum Ghar is in the background.

SEPTEMBER 4TH 2006: A10 FRIENDLY FIRE

Just prior to dawn, my gunner and I were in the turret of our LAV. I was scanning for targets with binoculars, while he was keeping his eyes on the sights; ready to fire on any Taliban trying to cross the open area identified the day prior.

Out of the corner of my eye, 15-20 metres to the left, I saw a flash of light. It was like a bunch of sparklers igniting at a fireworks display. At first I thought we had come under attack from Taliban-fired rockets. Then, delayed by a second or two, I heard the loud, deep, burping sound that was the unmistakable signature of 30-millimetre high-explosive rounds fired from the main cannon of a US Air Force A-10 Thunderbolt II fighter. It was a sound we had all heard many times over the last 48 hours as the A-10s had been constantly engaging enemy targets. This time, however, it had hit us.

It came over the Artillery net very quickly that it had been pilot error, and an inquiry later determined that the pilot had mistaken Charles Company Combat Team's garbage fire for a burning enemy position. The CO then called back to the Battle Group Command Post at the Kandahar Airfield that we had a mass-casualty situation and would need significant air assets in order to extract the numerous wounded. He also called on the artillery to fire a smoke mission to prevent Taliban observation onto Ma'sum Ghar. My gunner, who was Tactical Combat Casualty Care Qualified or "T triple C" in our parlance, Cpl Shannon Fretter (the Squadron Medic) and my sergeant-major were all dispatched to the Casualty Collection Point to assist. I remained in the turret scanning my arcs. This incident qualified as the third of my nine lives.

With the smoke screen in place, and the triage and first aid occurring on the ground, all we could do was wait for the 'Dust-off,' which was the call sign given to all US medical casualty evacuation helicopters, to arrive. Coordination of the sequence of casualty evacuation was being handled on the Battle Group net between the Doc, Major Erin Savage, OC of Health Service Support Company and the Casualty Collection Point. Two US 'Dust-Off' Black Hawks were inbound for the most serious casualties and a 'Dust-Off' Chinook would arrive third to pick up the rest. The Black Hawks arrived and departed without incident. However, the Chinook mistook the smoke screen on the far side of the river as the Landing Zone marking and nearly landed completely exposed to Taliban fire. Once called off, the pilot corrected and landed at Ma'sum Ghar to load up the remaining casualties. The strike resulted in one killed and close to 35 wounded. Four of my soldiers were evacuated with wounds of varying severity, including two Dragoon crew commanders and the 2 Troop Commander's vehicle crew. Lt Behiels was also wounded, but not seriously enough to warrant a return to Kandahar Airfield. Charles Company had lost two Platoon Warrant Officers on the 3rd, and the friendly fire had wounded, among others, Maj Sprague and his sergeant-major. With its leadership severely depleted and over a third of the sub-unit made casualties, Charles Company was now combat-ineffective. My own 2 Troop as well was close to being physically and emotionally spent.

Mass casualty situation – aftermath of the A-10 friendly fire incident at Ma'sum Ghar. At the Casualty Collection Point, the wounded await the arrival of the medical evacuation helicopters.

SEPTEMBER 5TH-7TH, 2006: REASSESS AND REORIENT

With the majority of a company out of the fight, and the disposition and size of the enemy presence in Pashmul ascertained, a reassessment of the plan was sorely needed. During this time frame, the Bravo Company Combat Team in the north continued to develop the enemy positions and executed crossings over the first wadi, which was nicknamed Cracked Roof. At Ma'sum Ghar we continued our overwatch of the far side of the river. It occurred to me, as I watched our LAVs parked on the slope, shooting Taliban that were unfortunate enough to expose themselves, that we were engaged in a sort of 'Human Safari.' Troops would be having casual conversations in and around the back of their LAVs while their comrades up in the turrets were shooting and killing Taliban. Then on whatever pre-determined schedule existed, they would switch positions to keep the killing machine going 24/7. We could rarely see the enemy, but fired on them whenever we did.

They could always see us, as the LAVs, which the Taliban referred to as "The Monster" in communications intercepts, were parked plain as day on the forward slope of Ma'sum Ghar. They could not, however, hit us. Not, that is, until they started lobbing indirect 82-millimetre anti-armour recoilless gun rounds at our position. The first such shot landed not ten metres behind my LAV, constituting the fourth of my nine lives. The debris found in the crater confirmed what we had suspected from the death of Sgt

Stachnik: the Taliban had recoilless anti-tank guns.

New orders were issued on or about September 6th that would see the Battle Group redistribute the majority of its combat power, including the newly arrived US Humvee-mounted infantry company (call sign 'Mohawk'). The remnants of Charles Company had been incorporated into ISTAR Squadron, and those elements were detached to US Task Force Grizzly. That grouping would remain on the south side of the river and keep the pressure on Pashmul from there. In order to support this shift in axis, the majority of the Squadron's elements were also shifted to the north. Our mission continued to be the provision of mobility support to the 1 RCR Battle Group with a combination of centralized and decentralized, full-spectrum, task-tailored combat engineer capability to all manoeuvre elements. EOD Team 1, commanded by PO2 Paul 'Knobby[9]' Walsh and 'Rock 26,' a US Route Clearance Package, remained in the south in support of Task Force Grizzly.

It would be an extremely busy and demanding operation for 1 and 2 Troop, as they had to support three leap-frogging infantry companies in the advance. The Squadron Reserve, comprised of the remnants of 32 Delta, EOD 2, heavy equipment assets and US Rock 47, would continue to provide mobility and force protection along the Battle Group's line of communication between Patrol Base Wilson and the front line. MCpl Thompson and Cpl McDonald would take over 2 Troop's Bison Armoured Personnel Carrier and act as a forward Quartermaster out of Patrol Base Wilson.

I returned to Kandahar Airfield with LCol Lavoie to coordinate with our higher Headquarters and sort out some other details of the new plan. After the Ramp Ceremony[10] for Sgt Shane Stachnik, WO Frank Mellish, WO Richard Nolan, Pte William Cushley, who were killed on September 3rd, and Pte Mark Anthony Graham who was killed on September 4th, I sat down and undertook the unenviable task of writing Shane's fiancée and parents. I had no idea what to tell them other than what Shane meant to us as a soldier and a man in the hope that these sentiments would give them some solace. In certain respects these letters are written to ease the author's burdens and I beg the family's understanding in that regard.

Left: Ramp Ceremony at Kandahar Airfield. Members of the Squadron carry Shane's casket onboard the awaiting Hercules. *Courtesy of DND Combat Camera.* Right: Sgt Shane Stachnik.

SEPTEMBER 8TH-13TH, 2006: REPORT LINE CRACKED ROOF TO OBJECTIVE RUGBY

The events of September 8th-13th, 2006 are as numerous as they are diverse. There were many moving parts, with engineer field troops being attached and subsequently detached from different infantry companies, sometimes on a daily basis. On the line of advance from Bravo Company's bridgehead there were four wadis that needed to be crossed and Report Line Cracked Roof was the first. The area in between these wadis primarily consisted of vineyards or compounds, and the wadis themselves were lined with mature trees. Route Comox, which served as the centreline for our attack, generally ran north – south, however it had many sharp bends. It was a single-lane dirt road with concrete slab bridges over the wadis. There was a 500-metre swath of open country between the fourth and fifth wadi, known as Wadi St John's as it paralleled a route of the same name. There was a series of compounds at the intersection of Routes Comox and St John's. This area was known as Objective Templar. The stretch from Objective Templar down to our final objective in Pashmul – known as Objective Rugby – was all vineyards.

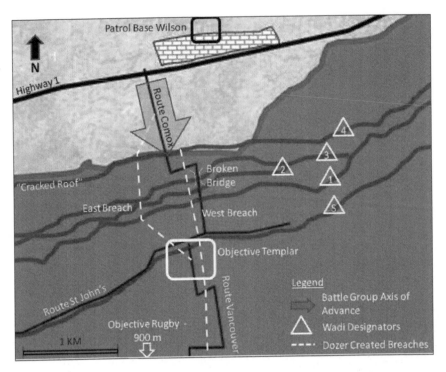

The advance south was conducted with conventional tactics. We would fix the enemy with direct and indirect fires, including Close Air Support, while dismounted infantry supported by combat engineers would clear the vineyards and compounds out to 300 metres, which was the effective range of enemy Rocket Propelled Grenades. Often my sappers would create 'mouse holes' in the compound walls with explosive satchel charges. These holes allowed the infantry to enter without going through possibly booby-trapped doorways. This tactic, initially devised by the Loyal Edmonton Regiment's Capt Bill Longhurst, was used by Canadian Soldiers with great effect during the street-to-street and house-to-house battles in Ortona, Italy in World War 2[11]. Then the dozers would breach a lane through the vineyards to connect open areas and thus allow the LAVs to move forward and link up with the dismounted soldiers. Once that bound was secure, the Route Clearance Package would clear Route Comox to allow for resupply. ISTAR assets would then secure our flanks as our line of communication extended to the south. These steps were conducted repeatedly as we advanced south towards our ultimate goal of securing Objective Rugby. At night, recce patrols would scout forward of the front line and the infantry companies would send out raiding parties to disrupt Taliban operations.

The casualties of war are not only physical. Emotional, spiritual and psychological injuries are often insidious and tougher to accept and to treat. In an unfortunate turn of events, a Squadron member succumbed to a combat stress reaction and was returned to the Kandahar Airfield. Hindsight suggests that there were others in a similar situation, but based on their rank and position within the organization it was not obvious. In any event, if it was obvious to some, it wasn't to me. Ultimately, war is a human endeavour and it is in this regard that we had the most to learn, and that we learned the most.

This phase of Op Medusa was going smoothly and according to plan, albeit slowly. With three companies keeping pressure on the Taliban, they could not react to our overwhelming force. Additionally, the freedom of movement provided by the dozers completely dislocated the enemy, as we were no longer restricted to the existing routes that were riddled with pre-placed IEDs. Our use of dozers to circumvent the enemy's kill zones had not been seen before in theatre (since the Soviets withdrew - at any rate) and was certainly not expected by the Taliban. Communications intercepts indicated that the enemy was short on rations, medical supplies and ammunition. They still, however, had some 82-millimetre rounds. Enemy resistance decreased as we moved south. While the Taliban were squeezed on their northern and southern flanks, there were few NATO forces hemming them in east and west of our thrust and thus, many escaped to fight another day.

Truth is often stranger than fiction and I certainly could not have imagined many of the events that I experienced in Kandahar. One day a report came over the net from A Company to the Battle Group Command Post. Their Second-in-Command, Capt Jordan Schaub, was quoted as saying, "Zero this is One, You're going to find this far-fetched but there is a lion in front of our position. I say again a lion. Not sure if it wild or tame… wait it's a large dog, disregard."

While we are on an animal theme, when we had secured Waiting Area 7, the boys found a goat on which they promptly spray-painted "Black Sheep". When we rolled out, the goat was loaded in a LAV. Eventually, it was given to a family in the village of Kolk as a good will gesture. I'm not sure if they got the joke.

On September 13th, the now historic linkup between LCol Lavoie and

Col Williams of Task Force Grizzly occurred at Objective Rugby East. Over the next day-and-a-half we would clear the remaining cluster of compounds that made up Rugby Central and West. Not a shot was fired as all the Taliban had fled. If the materials left behind were any indication, they left in a hurry but as with any protracted conflict, we would all meet again.

Top: D7 Dozer breaching Wadi #4 at Report Line Cracked Roof. *Photo is courtesy of Graeme Smith of the Globe and Mail.*
Bottom: Dismounted Sappers gaining entry to a compound by explosively breaching a 'mouse hole'.

Top : US Mohawk Company elements survey a Taliban-blown bridge (aka "Broken Bridge") on Route Comox

Bottom: Soldiers patrol between rows in a vineyard.

Top: US Col Williams (Task Force Grizzly) links up with LCol Lavoie prior to the eventual clearing of Objective Rugby.
Bottom: A LAV driving on the breached "Route Summit Extension", through a 10-foot-high marijuana field east of Objective Rugby East.

Top: A sapper conducts a door breach using a shotgun.
Bottom: Sappers taking a break during Op Medusa. Photo courtesy of DND Combat Camera.

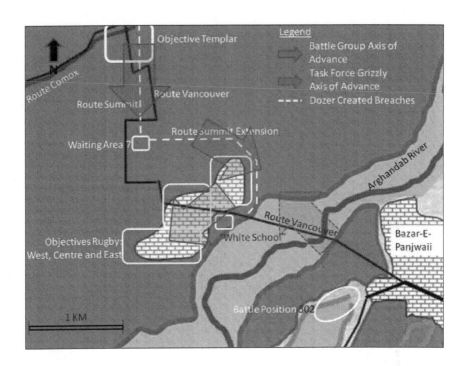

A Dangerous Peace

Sounds of terror are in his ears;
While at peace the destroyer comes upon him.
— Job 15:21

September 13th – 16th: Consolidation

The clearance of Route Vancouver began in earnest on September 13th, 2006. In total four IEDs were found that day – three by detection and one by detonation. The former were discovered and rendered safe, or blown in place by EOD 1. All three were pressure plate[12] IEDs. The latter was a strike by Rock 26's Husky vehicle. Post-blast analysis revealed that it was at least a triple-stacked mine strike, likely Italian-made TC-6 all-plastic anti-tank mines. Luckily there were no fatalities, although the US Husky driver received a severe concussion from the immense blast. There would be many more IED finds and many more IED strikes to come, not only on Route Vancouver but throughout our recently-secured area. Several tunnel and trench complexes were found. Once exploited for intelligence value they were blown up, often using the ordnance from the defused IEDs.

> On or about September 13th, 2006, we finally moved across to the north bank of the Arghandab River, setting up our vehicles in our standard formation in a cleared leaguer 100 metres northeast of Route Vancouver. PO2 Scott Elson donned the bomb suit, as he was the first to go down range in order to clear Route Vancouver. After his first search he removed the bomb suit due to the incredible heat and resulting loss of functionality. He then proceeded to work on the first of the many IEDs. Next came my turn. I advanced over Scott's cleared path and located a partially buried 107mm rocket with a detonator packed into the fuse-well. Digging it out was a task requiring my hands, a bayonet, and a bottle of water. After removing the detonator, I hooked on and pulled the

rocket head out enough to expose an Italian anti-tank mine under it. With some more digging and pulling the ordnance was finally cleared and removed to our storage area. Next in was PO1 Knobby Walsh. While he was in the breach, the rest of us discussed our next move with the American Route Clearance Package element that had joined us. When Knobby was finished rendering another IED safe, the American Husky vehicle pulled out to perform a confirmatory sweep of the area we had just manually cleared. It was not more than 40 metres away from us when a terrific explosion ripped the air. The smoke, dust and debris were everywhere and you couldn't see your hands in front of your face. The Husky had driven over a triple-stacked anti-tank mine IED, literally blowing it to pieces. Once we had determined that everyone was OK, we moved to what was left of the driver's compartment and pulled the driver out. In less than 10 minutes the driver was evacuated by helicopter back to the hospital at the Kandahar Airfield. He recovered, joining up with his teammates several weeks later. The IED was right under the path we had been taking all day. It was now a 2-metre deep by 3-metre diameter crater. Dusk was approaching as we completed the post-blast analysis of the scene and we moved on to clearing and neutralizing two Taliban bunkers that had been located on the perimeter of our leaguer. To assist us with the disposal, we used the ordnance from the IEDs discovered that day. Again, as with every time we blew things up, the dust and dirt would hang in the air lending a surreal look to everyone and everything. We then settled in for the night.

  — LS Bruce (EOD 1)

Upon our consolidation throughout Objective Rugby, we started to dig in around the White School. While dozing LAV run-up positions we unearthed a TC-6 anti-tank mine. This find, coupled with a similar discovery in the vicinity of the soon-to-be FOB Zettelmeyer dictated that the troops

Top: Taliban trench system.
Bottom: EOD 2 clearing Route Vancouver with their TEO robot.

conduct a Level 3 clearance of all digging sites. Level 3 clearances are repeated Level 2 clearances, whereby you scan the ground with a mine detector before digging. Then you only dig as far down as the mine detector can scan.

The clearance of Route Vancouver continued in addition to the many bunker and trench systems in the area. On September 16th, while scraping off the top 4-6 inches of soil on Route Vancouver, MCpl Hooper's D7 Dozer hit a very large IED. Post-blast revealed another set of deep-buried triple-stacked all-plastic anti-tank mines, again likely Italian-made TC-6. This incident earned MCpl Hooper his second wound stripe. Luckily the nature of the mines and the emplacement technique forced most of the blast straight up, thus saving the dismounts, which were close by. Still, MCpl Hooper and Cpl Reid were evacuated back to Kandahar Airfield for treatment. This was the second strike on Route Vancouver that involved deeply buried IEDs. Since there was little assurance that our clearance procedures had detected all explosive threats beneath the road, I closed the road to all Coalition traffic and we pursued bypass options. Route Summit was beginning to take shape without us really knowing it at the time.

I returned to Patrol Base Wilson for some rest and refit. War changes many of your points of reference, and reinforces the notion that everything in life is relative. After Op Medusa, Patrol Base Wilson seemed like an oasis, where I felt safe, able to relax and to clean up. I even did laundry on an old-fashioned washboard and yes, I know what you are thinking, but as a Generation X'er, I had only ever seen them on vintage TV shows. The CO told me that the barber was in. I told him that I had already been to see the barber requesting an 'eight' back and sides, only to be told that my hair was not yet long enough, and to come back later. It was all bullshit of course as I had no intention of seeing the barber, but you have to love The RCR for their by-the-book consistency.

September 17th – 28th: Clearing to the West

Three main activities occurred during the waning weeks of September 2006: patrolling into peripheral towns such as Kolk, Siah Choy and Sablaghay, the commencing of the construction of protective works at FOBs Zettelmeyer and Ma'sum Ghar, and the continued clearing of existing routes and responding to IED events.

MCpl Hooper's D7 Dozer IED Strike.

By this time Mohawk Company had received orders to return to the US area of operations, in Zabul Province. We said goodbye to our American brothers-in-arms and proceeded to clear territory to the west. Task Force Grizzly assumed control of Pashmul and surrounding area in our absence. It was during this expansion to the west that a suicide bomber pushing a bicycle targeted A Company. 32 Delta, which after the death of Sgt Stachnik was now being temporarily commanded by Sgt Neil Coates, was supporting Maj Mike Wright's soldiers on a dismounted patrol at the time. The bomber achieved devastating effects with his suicide vest, killing four soldiers and wounding many others. Among the wounded engineers were MCpl Dwayne Orvis, Cpl John Lalonde, Cpl Denver Williams and Spr Mike McTeague. While very lucky to be alive, Orvis and McTeague were in serious condition. All would require surgery and some multiple surgeries over the course of the next year.

Between the events of September 3rd and September 18th, 32 Delta was combat ineffective with only one engineer and her Dragoon crew left in theatre. Upon reconstitution with replacements to be sent from Canada, the new section would be assigned the 32 Foxtrot call sign – 32 Delta would be retired until the end of tour. Many members of the Troop wanted it retired forever. It was an understandable sentiment, but in the end it was decided that that would not be a good idea. Retiring every call sign that is destroyed or rendered combat ineffective is not a sustainable practice for an Army.

Niner Tac returned to Kandahar Airfield to visit the wounded and attend to some administration. At various points over the next three days I managed to see all of my guys at the Multi-National Hospital at the Kandahar Airfield. I found it to be an incredible facility and one of the biggest morale boosters that a soldier or commander could hope for. LCol Lavoie said it best when he described the moral and societal contract between the state and her soldiers. Soldiers accept unlimited liability in the conduct of their duties in the profession of arms. The state, which ultimately sends those same soldiers off to fight its wars, owes them the clearest mandate, the best protection and equipment available, and every effort to treat them and restore them to good health should they become injured.

The suicide bomber's vest was designed to inflict horrendous injuries. McTeague was intubated, but could respond with his eyes. His body was Swiss cheese except for the area protected by the ceramic ballistic plates on his flak vest. Lalonde was in good spirits and was telling stories. Williams was all smiles despite the fact that his body was visibly broken. Orvis' arm had been shattered but was now stable. He had seen and been through so much. We had played soccer together back at our home base, CFB Petawawa, so I knew Dwayne fairly well but strangely did not know what to say to him. Not knowing how he would react, I did not want to bring up the event and I did not want to feed him a bullshit line that everything would be all right, because it was not looking like it would. In the end I thanked him for everything that he had done, that it was not his fault and to look after himself.

I talked to Col Denis Thompson, the Commander of 2 Canadian Mechanized Brigade Group, which was our higher headquarters in Petawawa. Col Thompson was visiting his troops in theatre and he told me to just ask them what happened. More often than not, he said, soldiers will want to tell you, and will do so. Maybe. I still don't know. I took part in the ramp ceremony for the four soldiers killed by the suicide bomber. At this point I had lost count of the number of ramp ceremonies that I had attended and despite their unfortunate frequency they did not get any easier.

Throughout Op Medusa, the Battle Group was working with the Afghan National Army's 201 Kandak. A Kandak is roughly the equivalent of a battalion, and they were a fantastic unit, albeit severely under-strength and poorly supported logistically by their own chain of command. Their CO had been trained in the United States and his English was impeccable. He was pivotal in the provision of security in Bazar-E-Panjwaii, a stability which aided in the resettlement of the town and helped to win the locals over to our side. He told the elders of that town and the surrounding villages to take note of the destruction unleashed on Pashmul. Furthermore, he intoned that if they did not rid themselves of the Taliban then their towns would suffer the devastation of Pashmul. When the issue of the exact command relationship between the 1 RCR Battle Group and his Kandak came up he told us, "You have come thousands of miles from beautiful Canada to help us rid our country of evil-doers. I don't worry about doctrinal terms like TACOM, so we work together." TACOM, which is shorthand for 'Tactical Command,' is a NATO-defined command relationship where one unit is attached, and therefore subordinate, to another unit within the confines of a specific mission assigned by the attached unit's higher headquarters.

Afghan National Army "Assault" Ford Ranger.

That aside, we were sorry to see his Kandak rotated out of our area of operations. Sadly, they were not immediately replaced due to a severe shortage of Afghan National Army units in Kandahar Province, and their absence affected our own abilities to conduct successful counter-insurgency operations during the remainder of our tour.

The area between Pashmul and Patrol Base Wilson now contained a web of criss-crossing civilian-built roads and military-cleared paths. Realizing that Routes Comox and Vancouver were the Coalition Forces' only mobility corridor and supply line, and thus our centre of gravity in the strategically important area, the Taliban re-infiltrated Pashmul in the later half of September and began emplacing IEDs. Up to and including September 28th, Canadian Forces struck four non-legacy[13] and three legacy IEDs along that mobility corridor. Including Rock 26's and Hooper's D7, the Squadron would claim four of the seven. It is my belief that the Battle Group, 23 Field Squadron and myself included, was developing a *laissez-faire* approach when traveling the roads. In many respects the LAV made us lazy and we relied on it far too much for its perceived inherent protection.

To counter the threat of IEDs, the Squadron was tasked to perform daily clearances of the routes. To assist with these clearances the Squadron had two US Route Clearance Packages (call sign 'Rock') attached in support. These Route Clearance Packages did not have their own integral EOD assets, therefore Canadian EOD teams were embedded during route clearance tasks.

On September 22nd, Rock 47 struck an IED while performing clearance operations along Route Vancouver. The driver, Specialist West, was injured and evacuated to Kandahar Airfield for medical attention. The Husky vehicle was damaged beyond field repair and was eventually sent back to the Kandahar Airfield using US recovery assets.

While the ISTAR Squadron Sergeant-Major was traveling on Route Vancouver during the night of September 27th he struck an IED. His LAV suffered only very minor damage to one of the tires – more akin to a flat. As we would discover later the next day, the damage was due to the small explosion caused by the device's initiator. The main charge had failed to function.

EOD 2, commanded by PO2 Jimmy Leith, was sent out in conjunction with Rock 26 the next day to conduct an investigation of the probable IED site. While enroute, EOD 2's Bison struck an IED 300 metres short of the intended investigation site. The blast ripped a massive hole in the bottom of the back end of the Bison. The EOD robot housed in the back of the Bison was thrown against Cpl Jimmy Lightle's leg, breaking it. To this day it has never properly healed, however, he is lucky to be alive. Oddly enough, EOD 2 was fourth in the order-of-march, therefore, the Route Clearance Package did not pick up the IED and the other leading vehicles did not detonate it.

Along with Rock 26 we left Patrol Base Wilson, around 5:30 am, to clear Route Comox. The night before, we were all playing cards and chatting, and I turned to Parker Krantz and said, "It's shitty you're staying back watching the kit and not coming with us. Hope no one goes skydiving [blown out of the vehicle by an IED] tomorrow."

He replied "No more talking about going skydiving, as every time we say that, something happens to our crew!" PO2 Jim Leith was crew commanding and Cpl Jimmy 'The Savage' Lightle was in the rear sentry hatch, and I was driving. We were fourth in the order-of-march. Typically, in order to keep it light, we were always laughing at each other. Strangely however, as we traveled to Route Comox no one was saying much. I remember Jim Leith came on the radio and asked, "Isn't anyone supposed to be out here doing over-watch on this route?"

I flicked my radio switch and said, "There should be, I saw two RGs a little further back." As we kept driving there was an unsettling quiet. PO2 Leith always liked to keep the C6 pintle-mounted machine gun right above my head, so every time I looked from side to side I would hit it. So I came on the radio and asked "Hey Jimmy just push the C6 to the side - I keep whacking my head on it." He laughed, and moved the C6 accordingly.

We were driving and I saw a hole in the road, so instinctively I swerved around it. As I stated earlier, we were fourth in the order-of-march, following Rock 26's Husky, a Humvee and our team's other Bison. The next thing I knew, we were in the air and it was like some giant had grabbed me and whacked me from side to side in my driver's compartment. Still to this day I am not sure if I blacked out when it first happened but I remember being tossed from side to side and I knew that we had hit an IED.

As we landed I was stuck in between my seat and the steering wheel. Trying to get unstuck, I turned to make sure PO2 Leith was all right. As I looked back at him he was trying to stand up. I yelled at him to make sure he was OK.

"Fucking cock-suckers got us!" he replied. Then I yelled for Jimmy Lightle but heard no answer. I finally got myself unstuck and preceded to get out of the Bison. The dust and the smoke were still settling and as I was running back to get Jimmy I could finally hear him calling back to me as I shouted to him. I got to the air sentry hatch and incredibly the only spot that wasn't totally destroyed was the spot where he was standing. By the time I got there, Rock 26's Greg 'Robbie' Robinson and Adam Free (a US Medic) were already there tending to Jimmy. Robbie helped him up as I grabbed him and laid him on me while Robbie and Adam worked on his foot. My main task was to ensure that he didn't pass out. I also took the chewing tobacco out of his mouth and proceeded to remove the shrapnel from his armpit.

While all this was going on he looked up and said, "Mikey, did you check yourself over? How's my foot?" I told him not to worry about me, that I would be fine and that his foot was in pretty bad shape. Once his foot was bandaged he was loaded into a LAV bound for Patrol Base Wilson, where he would then be taken by helicopter back to the hospital at the Kandahar Airfield.

— MCpl Mike Maidment (EOD 2)

The EOD Bison was heavily damaged and the majority of the EOD equipment (all remote investigation tools including the robot) was destroyed. As part of the IED strike scene management, PO2 Leith cleared the area of possible secondary devices and began an initial post-blast forensics search. PO2 Leith and Cpl Maidment were then sent back to Patrol Base Wilson for a medical assessment and to wait for the Counter-IED specialist personnel to arrive by helicopter.

Approximately an hour later, upon returning to the scene with the Counter-IED personnel, PO2 Leith began to investigate the suspected anti-personnel mine strike that had been reported the night previous on Route

Vancouver, 300m south of the current IED strike. During the course of the manual investigation, he discovered that there was much more than a single detonated anti-personnel mine. Instead, it was a partially-detonated and therefore inherently unstable IED. This IED consisted of two anti-tank mines coupled with home-made napalm (fuel and soap mixture). Knowing that Canadian forces had suffered many IED strikes and that, to date, we had not uncovered any non-legacy ones intact, with other EOD teams unable to deploy to the scene in a reasonable timeframe, or if they did, that Kandahar City would be without any EOD coverage, and finally with all of his equipment destroyed, PO2 Leith courageously set out to dismantle the IED by hand – aided only by his bayonet.

The results of PO2 Leith's actions were twofold. Firstly, Route Vancouver was immediately reopened to Coalition traffic, ensuring vital mobility (patrolling, resupply, ground casualty evacuation, etc.) on our only route through the area. Secondly, he alone provided the first pre-detonation find of a non-legacy IED in the Pashmul region. His discovery and the subsequent forensic analysis led to a flash report to all Coalition forces in Afghanistan on the use of, not-seen-before-in-theatre, home-made napalm but more importantly, contributed significantly to the identification and eventual targeting / elimination of that prolific IED cell. Prior to their elimination, that cell would be responsible for five more IED strikes, one of them claiming the life of a Canadian soldier and three of them severely wounding three more.

Once complete, all Squadron elements returned to Patrol Base Wilson. All of EOD 2, less PO2 Leith, subsequently returned to KAF that evening for refit. He remained due to a requirement to support the insertion of a sniper detachment that night into a high threat area, such that they could overwatch Route Vancouver for insurgents emplacing IEDs. For his actions that day, PO2 Leith was awarded the Star of Courage.

These incidents precipitated the order to build Route Summit. In keeping with LCol Lavoie's mission command style, I was given a broad intent and endstate (military shorthand for 'the why'). He told me to build a road that would connect Patrol Base Wilson with Ma'sum Ghar with the view to permit an infantry company to dominate the area and not his entire Battle Group. The details of the *Who, What, Where, When* and *How* were left up to me.

Top: EOD Team 2 Leader, PO2 Leith.
Bottom: A Field Section performing a route clearance using a mine detector.

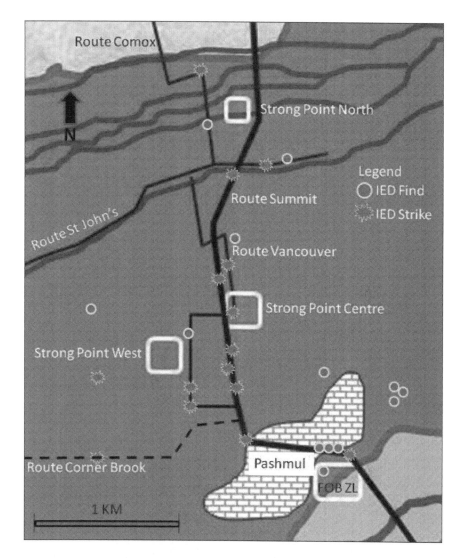

This sketch depicts all of the IED finds and strikes that occurred on the Route Summit and Vancouver / Comox corridor during Roto 2. Therefore, it shows some IED events that occur later on in the book. All but one incident involved members of the Battle Group.

Route Summit
and the FOBS

To every thing there is a season,
and a time to every purpose under heaven:
A time to kill, and a time to heal;
a time to break down, and a time to build up;
— *Ecclesiastes 3*

This chapter attempts to depict the Squadron's activities between September 29th and December 16th, 2006. At times, even for the author, it is a confusing story to tell, as there were up to five different Squadron elements working in distinct and sometimes changing areas. The only way to accurately portray these events in time and space would be to break the information down into daily summaries. However, since that would turn this into a rather pedantic and dry account, I have chosen not to do it that way. Instead, this chapter is divided into three general segments based on blocks of time where my troops' locations and/or tasks remained somewhat constant. They are September 29th – October 22nd, October 23rd – November 6th, and November 7th – December 16th. This chapter ends with the 1 RCR Battle Group preparing for the resumption of offensive operations under the aegis of Op Baaz Tsuka.

SEPTEMBER 29TH – OCTOBER 22ND, 2006

The 1 RCR Battle Group's disposition during this timeframe had A Company, supported by 1 Troop, at FOB Ma'sum Ghar. Bravo Company, supported by Sgt Houde, moved back to FOB Martello. Charles Company, supported by Sgt Clucas, was co-located with other Coalition forces at FOB Spervan Ghar. ISTAR Squadron and 23 Field Squadron(-)[14], augmented with various infantry platoons, worked around and on Route Summit. And finally, E Battery provided indirect fire support from various locations. I would be remiss not to mention that, after holding the fort for the entire Battle Group in Spin Boldak for the previous 6 weeks, the "King of Costall," MCpl Thomas, returned to Kandahar Airfield on September 30th.

Sadly, no one ever took a picture of the Afro he had grown after a month of fruitless requests for hair clippers to be sent to him.

The initial intent for 1 Troop was to construct a small FOB at Ma'sum Ghar for A Company and a large one in the vicinity of Pashmul for the Afghan National Army garrison. By the end of the month, Maj Mike Wright and I managed to shift the priority from the construction of FOB Zettelmeyer to that of focusing our efforts on simply improving the natural defensive features offered by Ma'sum Ghar, arguably the Battle Group's vital ground. Why build a wall when Mother Nature has built one for you? 1 Troop was dedicated to that task - a task that would take them the better part of four months to finish. In force protection works, 'completion' is a relative concept, whereby you never seem to finish upgrading the defences of a FOB or battle position. For this particular job, 'completion' refers to the basic force protection measures and living arrangements: hardened ob-servation posts, overhead cover, LAV/tank run-ups, internal roads, multiple access routes, protective barriers and wire fence, ablutions, and storage areas (ammunition, fuel, food, stores). Capt Anthony Robb, who was awarded a Meritorious Service Medal for his actions during Op Medusa and his efforts at FOB Ma'sum Ghar, details these activities in his chapter in Part 2.

FOB Ma'sum Ghar, a week following Op Medusa. Notice the road to a run-up is al-ready complete.

On September 29th, Bravo Company[(-)], with Sgt Houde and MCpl Debagheera's 31 Bravo section, returned to FOB Martello. Bravo Company conducted a relief-in-place with the Dutch soldiers who had occupied the FOB in order to free up Canadian troops for Op Medusa. Upon completion of the handover, Bravo Company assumed security for the FOB and began patrolling the surrounding area. Sgt Houde and his section assisted with both those tasks. With very few engineer tools to work with, he improvised, turning a forklift into a front-end loader in order to fill Hesco walls with gravel. They also built bunkers and emplaced Texas barriers[15].

Sgt Houde's 31 Bravo Recce Section posing, with their RG-31 in the background, at FOB Martello.

FOB Spervan Ghar is located approximately 15 kilometres southwest of FOB Ma'sum Ghar. Both FOBs are on the south side of the Arghandab River. Spervan Ghar is a large dirt hill protruding out of the tabletop flatness of the desert. A school, built by the UN, is situated on the main plateau. Spervan Ghar completely dominates the surrounding area and because of its tactical significance, this promontory had been the object of many previous battles.

Initially, 2 Troop was in support of Charles Company (now commanded by Capt Steve Brown) as they manoeuvred in the vicinity of Spervan Ghar on the south bank and the village of Siah Choy directly opposite on the north bank of the Arghandab River. On September 28th, Sgt Clucas' section and Rock 26 remained to provide engineer support as the remainder of 2 Troop departed to commence the construction of Route Summit. The first priority at Spervan Ghar was to improve the entrance and exit routes to the FOB. Unable to get any civilian contractors to the site, and because at the time we did not have any hauling capability, Sgt Clucas used Rock 26's lone dump truck to move rock from the river to the FOB. It was a tremendously inefficient means of delivering material to the site as the narrow and serpentine route had to be cleared for IEDs each time. Moreover, river rock is an inherently poor choice for use on roads because it contains very little fine material and the rocks are smooth. Both of these characteristics do not allow for proper compaction and thus the effort only produced one dump load of poor quality road-grade aggregate at a time. This operation continued for a couple of days until the steep and rutted in- and out-routes had been covered with stone. Due to the overwhelming amount of 'moon dust,' the talcum-powder-like dirt that was ubiquitous in Kandahar Province, Spervan Ghar would remain a dusty and dirty place until we could haul in enough gravel to cover all the routes and the large, centrally located Helicopter Landing Zone. Even with the eventual graveling of the FOB it would always remain a dangerous place to live as the Taliban often emplaced IEDs on the approaches and the FOB came under frequent small arms, mortar and Rocket Propelled Grenade attacks.

On October 1st, Cpl Chris Ashton with his backhoe was dispatched to the FOB to assist with the construction of the defensive works (bunkers, berms, Hesco walls, LAV run ups, etc). The first to rise and the last to sleep, Ashton would spend almost the entirety of the remainder of the tour at Spervan Ghar. In the words of Maj Andy Lussier, OC ISTAR Squadron, who would eventually relieve Charles Company there, Spervan Ghar is the FOB that Chris Ashton built. For his efforts, Cpl Ashton was awarded a Canadian Expeditionary Forces Command Commander's commendation.

Cpl Chris Ashton digging in bunkers at FOB Spervan Ghar with his backhoe.

Between October 8th and 15th, Sgt Louis Proulx's section relieved Sgt Clucas'. Clucas and his men had been in continuous contact, or the threat of enemy contact, for over 30 days[16] and they badly needed a break. They returned to Kandahar Airfield for a few days of R&R and to conduct vehicle and weapons maintenance. The Squadron had instituted a minimum of 72 hours back in camp but often the end date was predicated on the convoy schedule. Once Sgt Clucas had returned to Spervan Ghar it was Sgt Proulx's turn for R&R at the Kandahar Airfield.

Sgt Clucas' return coincided with the arrival of a civilian contractor delivering gravel and a large shipment of defensive stores such as lumber, plywood, Hesco, and sandbags. Despite it being a partial order, with some of the stores arriving not exactly as ordered (4"x4" instead of 8"x8" beams), this enabled Clucas and his troops to finish off many bunkers with overhead protection. By mid-October, E Battery had begun its move to Spervan Ghar. This necessitated the construction of additional bunkers, ammunition storage points and protective berms.

Back side of FOB Spervan Ghar with one of the M777 guns in the foreground.

After EOD 2 had struck an IED on September 28th, the Squadron was short a suite of EOD equipment and a vehicle. This capability gap was quickly rectified as the United States Air Force EOD teams stationed at Kandahar Airfield agreed to backfill our team outside the wire. This arrangement remained in effect until we could reconstitute EOD 2. Initially the team was forward in support of Rock 26, but when that Route Clearance Package returned to Kandahar Airfield on October 4th, they remained at Patrol Base Wilson acting as the EOD component of the Quick Reaction Force until October 15th.

EOD 3 was attached to 1 Troop throughout and stationed at Ma'sum Ghar. EOD 1 remained at the Kandahar Airfield as the airmobile team. On October 1st, Sgt Wayne Vickers, our Australian Electronic Counter Measure team leader was seconded to the Joint Task Force Afghanistan Counter-IED Cell. This ended the multi-national aspect of the Squadron's composition.

There were several IED strikes and finds during this period, which were all investigated by the EOD teams. On October 14th, PO1 Walsh disabled a suicide vest that had been obtained from the Afghan Secret Police.

ROUTE SUMMIT PHASE 1: SQUADRON COMBAT TEAM

Route Summit (Phase 1) construction occurred between September 29th and October 21st, 2006. Phase 1 activities consisted of grape hut demolition and vineyard removal in order to broaden the initial combat road to a 100-

Top - Bottom: Bunker construction.
Bottom: The 2 Troop Command Team of Capt Dan Clarke and WO Scott Clucas inspect the force protection works at FOB Spervan Ghar.

metre wide swath. This widening would enable us to straighten out and flatten the centreline, thus allowing for continuous and complete observation of the route from the FOBs and the Strong Points. In its 6.5 kilometre entirety, Route Summit consisted of six sectors, running from Patrol Base Wilson in the north to Ma'sum Ghar in the south. Early in the process we attempted to get government input into the location of the route, especially in and around Pashmul. In the absence of any direction I then decided upon the centreline.

It was a pivotal time for the 1 RCR Battle Group as we fought weekly battles with the Taliban in order to secure and consolidate our Op Medusa territorial gains. The Battle Group also began to fan out from its original Patrol Base Wilson / Ma'sum Ghar-centric concentration. ISTAR Squadron, with additional attachments, was given the task of dominating the northern sectors (1 - 3) of the planned Route Summit[17]. In the end, the only sustainable way to achieve this task was the actual construction of Route Summit.

The initial two-week period of Phase 1 was unique as it saw the creation of an engineer squadron combat team whose sole task was to build the road. LCol Lavoie had given me my orders and had attached two infantry platoons to the squadron to enable me to achieve success. I can't speak with any historical certainty that manoeuvre elements have never been attached to an engineer squadron during combat operations, but personally I have never heard or read about it. Based on mutual agreement, these platoons were a shared resource between OC ISTAR, Major Andy Lussier, and myself. This occasion proved to be the most challenging and rewarding two weeks I have ever had in command. It also highlighted several flaws in my plan and the inherent structural weaknesses of a contemporary and therefore non-doctrinally based engineer squadron.

Orders were issued to the Squadron on September 29th. Due to the combination of possible deep-buried legacy and newly-emplaced IEDs along the Patrol Base Wilson / Ma'sum Ghar mobility corridor, the 1 RCR Battle Group had to change its intended post-Op Medusa scheme of manoeuvre. The Squadron's mission was to provide mobility support to the 1 RCR Battle Group throughout the area of operations with our main effort being the construction of Route Summit.

At the time, only the previously dozed lanes were known as Route Summit, named by Captain Chris French in the Plans Cell because he lived on Summit Trail in Petawawa. The local road network that was used in the

Patrol Base Wilson - Ma'sum Ghar mobility corridor was known as Route 'VCDS' (Routes Vancouver, Comox, Desperado and St John's). Route Summit was to be constructed wide and straight to reduce the surveillance bill, but also in a manner that would minimize damage. Make no mistake though, Route Summit's final chosen alignment resulted in the complete destruction of the landscape. The idea, however, was to limit that destruction to the extent possible, to the landscape that had already been destroyed during Op Medusa.

My concept of operations saw a mix of centralized and decentralized combat engineer support to the 1 RCR Battle Group. The Squadron Combat Team consisted of 2 Troop, EOD 2, Heavy Equipment Section, Rock 26 and a rotating combination of 3 Platoon from A Company, 4 Platoon from Bravo Company and 9 Platoon from Charles Company.

Route Summit's start point – an Op Medusa combat road. Looking south with Ma'sum Ghar in the background.

Tragically, and hours before Rock 26 was to clear that section of Route Summit, Cpl Josh Klukie of Bravo Company's 6 Platoon was killed when he stepped on a massive IED. Rock 26, commanded by 1st Lt Jason Webb, responded to the site within minutes. Already dismounted, I met him there shortly after. Webb's US combat engineers cleared the scene, attended to the wounded and assisted with the recovery of the remains.

Those US sappers had seen more combat throughout their careers than most Canadian soldiers. For this reason, they had a very calm and professional demeanour when conducting their tasks. The violence, the destruction and the setbacks were all taken in stride. Individually and collectively they were battle-hardened. I learnt much from them and despite our initial interoperability issues, working with them afforded a remarkable experience.

Route construction operations over the next few days witnessed the substantial completion, with only some cleanup and debris removal remaining, in Sector 3. This was done with only one serviceable dozer – the rented D8 that was scheduled to be returned to its owner. All the others were either destroyed or in need of repair. Essentially, 2 Troop's heavy equipment had cleared 1300 metres of vineyards and grape huts. 2 Troop, now under the very capable command of WO Roger Perrault, was also becoming expert in the explosive removal of grape huts using 200 to 250 blocks of C4 plastic explosive, placed in 10 block borehole charges within the grape hut walls and initiated from the inside out. The grape huts were of mud-wall construction and there were slits in the vertical walls, evenly spaced both horizontally and vertically. It was in these slits that the demolition charges were placed. There is no thrill like overkill and once the charges detonated there was nothing left of the grape hut, not even to clean up.

Word of our activities had reached the Governor of Kandahar Province. Apparently, he was not pleased with the building of the road. As a Battle Group, we were not happy to be in the road-building business either. Ironically though, in a few days' time, the Governor sent us a replacement D5 dozer for the D8 that the civilian contractor was clambering to get back. I am not sure if the contractor had become aware that we were using his dozer in a combat zone rather than working in Kandahar Airfield. It was moved back to Kandahar Airfield, the up-armour was taken off and it was eventually returned to him - no harm, no foul.

One day we needed to remove a tree that was in the way. 2 Troop set out its cordon and proceeded to rig the tree with explosives that would be initiated non-electrically. This involves activating an igniter that is attached to a one-metre length of time fuse and the detonator. One metre is the minimum length of time fuse as directed in our Range and Training Safety Manual. Due to necessity, the Squadron had used much shorter lengths during the combat phases of Op Medusa for wall- and door- breaching charges. Without getting too technical, a metre of time fuze can take a couple of minutes to burn down. In the past three days we had not seen one single

Top: WO Roger Perrault, the 2 Troop Commander / Warrant Officer issuing direction to Sgt Rob Kennedy during the construction of Route Summit.
Bottom: D8 Dozer destroying a grape hut.

Top: Demolition charge preparation.
Bottom: Explosive removal of a grape hut.

local anywhere near Route Summit. In the two to three minutes that we were conducting the demolition, two locals had walked unnoticed past our cordon and were just 100 metres away from the demolition site when it went off.

My gunner saw them through his sights just seconds prior to the explosion but it was too late to warn them. We did a search of the area after the explosion. They were nowhere to be found and there were no signs of injury (i.e. body parts or blood trails). All that was left was an abandoned bicycle that one of them claimed two days later. Luckily, we didn't kill them. Thankfully they didn't have the telephone number of the Canadian Forces' Ombudsman. From then on, all demolitions, other than those on dismounted recce patrols and specifically approved by myself, were initiated using electric means, thereby ensuring positive control right up to the moment of detonation. The lesson to be learnt is that *Threat + Endstate = Tactics, Techniques and Procedures selection.* What was prudent and applicable during the combat phase, use of the time fuse for example (and even then, time fuse cut short), was no longer acceptable in terms of risk when the situation changed and became more permissive. This, I believe, is a general lesson that the Battle Group could have profited from. It seemed to me that we had become prisoners of our own experience in the sense that the very robust procedures used during Op Medusa and still being used extensively during the post-combat phases may have been counter-productive to the accomplishment of the counter-insurgency campaign

The ISTAR leaguer was located at the intersection of Sectors 2 and 3 – the old Op Medusa Objective Templar. From that 100-metre by 100-metre area, ISTAR Squadron could observe all of Sector 3 and part of Sector 2. My squadron's road-building assets were co-located there as well. It was set up as an all-around defence with the non-fighting vehicles in the middle.

At mid-afternoon we received an imminent-threat warning that insurgents were preparing to attack Coalition forces in the vicinity of Zehdanan with "mortars, rockets and small arms." On the map that was close to our present position. Often nothing would ever come of these warnings and it seemed as if they originated from a random threat generator. For some unknown reason, I took this one seriously. I gave the order to mount up in preparation to move half a kilometre to the north, and to start a show of force with our 25-millimetre cannons. Within a minute of giving that order, explosions started going off around us. Based on the warning, I had it in my mind that we were experiencing incoming mortar fire. I was dead wrong as the explosions were caused by incoming Rocket Propelled Grenades being fired from a series of compounds 70 metres to our east. Not appreciating this reality, I told the crew to go hatches down and ordered a 'crash harbour,' which basically means all vehicles in the leaguer are to depart ASAP, and proceeded to leave. While grabbing the rear hatch a round exploded just behind our vehicle spraying MWO Montgomery with dirt. I stopped the LAV on Route St John's just 100 metres north of the leaguer. From there I witnessed a direct hit against the ISTAR Observation Post located on Route Comox to our north. I remember thinking, "They are very accurate with their mortar fire." Then our vehicles at the leaguer started to open up with cannon, grenade and machine-gun fire against the compound to their east. No one else had responded to the crash-harbour order. It was only then that I realized that direct fire and not mortars were targeting us. So whether the right or wrong manoeuvre was executed is debatable, but without question it was done for the wrong reason.

Suddenly, there was a large explosion. The US EOD's Humvee trailer carrying all their explosives had taken a direct hit from a Rocket Propelled Grenade. Luckily it had only low-ordered, which meant it had not detonated to its full potential. Andy Lussier was controlling the fight from the leaguer and his appraisal of the situation was exact. He confirmed that his Observation Post on Route Comox had been hit, that the large explosion was a low order from an initial Taliban-fired Rocket Propelled Grenade round, and not newly incoming fire, that we had eventually won the fire fight and that there were three injuries – all Rock 26 personnel. Additionally, Strong Point Centre to our south had also come under attack. Being already on Route St John's and not knowing if we would have to fight our way to Patrol Base Wilson, I told Rock 26 that once they had gathered their wounded (two Priority 1 and one Priority 2 casualties) to proceed to my location where I would lead them to Patrol Base Wilson via Route Comox. This occurred within minutes and my LAV with the 2 US Humvees raced off to Patrol Base Wilson. I dropped them off at the entrance then returned to the scene. They entered the base and proceeded to the medical station to stabilize the casualties before they were evacuated by helicopter to Kandahar Airfield. In the end Private First Class Peters and Staff Sergeant Robinson were repatriated back to the US via Germany - Robinson had his foot amputated. Specialist Denkins was released before long. The remainder of

Rock 26, less two of their broken/damaged vehicles and one of their sergeants returned to Patrol Base Wilson shortly after.

It was getting close to nightfall when I returned to the leaguer. It was decided that this area was not defendable so ISTAR Squadron set up a new Observation Post and defensive positions to provide overwatch on the road. We had a US Humvee stranded in the leaguer and a US Husky broken down

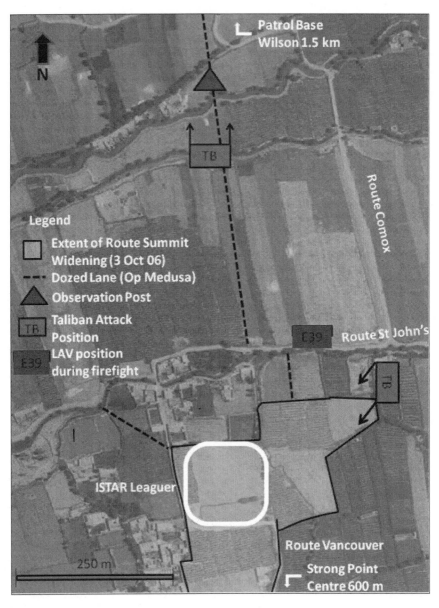

on Route Comox. My first inclination was to set up an all-around defence in vicinity of the Husky until morning while we continued to watch Route Summit. In reality though, we were sitting ducks in that location, as we could neither dominate the surrounding compounds, nor the infiltration routes through the nearby wadis. Communications were in disarray as some vehicles were on the ISTAR Squadron net and some on my squadron net – a mistake never made again as I finally had my third radio installed and then always set to the frequency of the manoeuvre unit whose Area of Operations we were working in or traveling through. My sergeant-major had dismounted to liaise with the other crew commanders and platoon commanders to piece together a plan. It was only after seeing the ISTAR Sergeant-Major drive by me while conducting a recovery operation of the destroyed ISTAR Observation Post (Sgt Gillam and Cpl Mitchell were killed in that attack) that I decided to conduct a recovery operation of our own on the Husky and the Humvee.

I remember thinking, "He is crazy, if he could do it in a lightly armoured truck then we could with our LAVs." After re-issuing orders, we hooked up the Humvee and the Husky and proceeded back to Patrol Base Wilson. I led the convoy back, bounding ahead to cover the next vulnerable point until we reached our destination. It is true, an order followed by a counter-order usually means disorder. This case was no different. In the end, though, the right call was made but it was extremely ugly getting there.

Based on the repeated Taliban attacks and the lack of serviceable dozers (armoured or otherwise) the completion of Route Summit had already stalled and was in jeopardy of failure. In fact, it was becoming clear that the Taliban were directly targeting our dozers. As a result we stopped using the un-armoured D5 dozer after the October 4th battle. In conjunction with the 2 Troop Commander, it was decided to leave Sector 2 until we could get an armoured dozer and concentrate on Sector 1, working north to south. With the heavy equipment situation we were forced to take many risks in order to complete the mission. Every day that we postponed our work meant the infantry platoons had to guard the incomplete road. One of those risks was attempting to pull out trees with LAVs. It worked, but at a cost of a LAV transmission. As we discovered, it was much better to do it in reverse due to the gear ratios than by driving forward. The mechanics did not approve of the abuse to the vehicle, and from their perspective they were absolutely right. I did not like having to resort to this either. I accepted the risk and like most risky decisions it came at a cost.

Unlike the other sectors, some of the locals had returned to Sector 1. I had a 'shura' (Pashtu for meeting) with them to discuss the layout of the road and compensation for the impending destruction of their vineyards and grape huts. As it turned out they were very grateful to be consulted and one landowner wanted his fields to be ploughed, rather than his neighbours so he could get the compensation. I do not know how much the Canadian Kandahar Provincial Reconstruction Team paid each owner but given that the smallish area on the south bank of the Arghandab River alone garnered a combined $200,000 USD plus payout, I am sure that it was well above fair market value. In the end the amount was not the issue, but rather the timeliness of the payments as all the money was disbursed through the district government. Afghan face, Afghan pace as it has been remarked.

Because of a lack of progress in several key areas, it was necessary that I return to Kandahar Airfield to raise the issues with the key Route Summit players within the Task Force. A meeting was convened with the Joint Task Force Afghanistan Deputy Commander, Col Fred Lewis, the Task Force Engineer, the PRT Commander, LCol Simon Hetherington, and an ISAF Engineer representative. My concerns were the lack of armoured dozers to finish Phase 1, the sad state of all of our heavy equipment in general[18], the inability or more likely the unwillingness of local contractors to support the construction (gravel and equipment) due to the security situation, and the amount of time it was taking to line up funding for the ultimate paving of the road. In terms of equipment, I was assured that soon we would have Canadian armoured D6 dozers ready to deploy and that the Badger (Armoured Engineer Vehicle) would be arriving shortly from Canada. Furthermore, Canadian Expeditionary Forces Command had a plan to replace all of the heavy equipment in theatre by the end of November with equipment from garrison stock. This would certainly help even if the "new" equipment was the same age as the "old" equipment that we were sending home. I was told that up until then, no amount of money could convince any of the contractors to send equipment or gravel. I am not sure how they finally addressed that issue but it was eventually sorted out.

With respect to the financing, ISAF became involved at the political level. Three countries had come to the table with an intention to fund – Canada, the US and Germany. Based on the ISAF Engineer's recommendation it was agreed that Canada would fund Sector 6, USAID would fund

Sector 5, which was the bridge across the Arghandab River, and Germany would fund Sectors 1-4. The Canadian cash was released relatively quickly and that sector was paved by January. The Germans eventually released their funds, but the delay cost the Battle Group an extra two months guarding the road. Sectors 1-4 were paved after we left theatre in March 2007.

To this day, I still do not know why USAID never did fund the bridge. It took another two rotations for the engineers from 5^{ieme} Régiment du Génie de Combat, commanded by Maj Walter Taylor, to build a permanent causeway over the river. I still find it perplexing that Task Force Headquarters denied my and my successor's request for bridging. Allegedly the commander did not want to turn the Panjwaii into an engineer playground, whatever that meant.

In the early hours of October 7th, an ISTAR RG-31 struck an IED on Route Comox. The strike resulted in the death of Tpr Mark Wilson. It would also presage the events that would occur later that same day. The only good news was that the armoured D6 dozer had arrived at Patrol Base Wilson for use on Route Summit.

Due to the October 3rd Taliban attack, 9 Platoon was dug into Wadi 1 just east of Route Comox and 3 Platoon was dug into Wadi 1 just west of Route Comox. From there they could dominate Route Comox heading north to the highway and Sector 2 of Route Summit. Upon completion of dozing for the day, the 'Nomads' from 4 Platoon along with 2 Troop would occupy a defensive position in the open area north of Wadi 4 in order to watch Sector 1. There were also other ISTAR Observation Posts in the area. At night the dozers and other non-fighting vehicles would return to Patrol Base Wilson.

The plan for October 7th was to work on punching Sector 1 through the last Wadi (to an initial width of only 15 metres) in the morning then move on to the choke point in Sector 2 (intersection of Sector 2 with Route St John's). Based on the October 3rd battle, I wanted to have dismounted forces clear the compounds to the east and west of that choke point before sending the dozer in. 9 Platoon, commanded by Lt Ray Corby, would act as the clearance force and 3 Platoon, commanded by Lt Duncan Redburn, would act as a firebase should the clearance turn into an assault. Justifiably, Ray was worried about the repeated clearing of the same compounds. He wanted to prepare the position with speculative fire, which, after some deliberation with CO, I denied. By mid-afternoon his platoon had swept

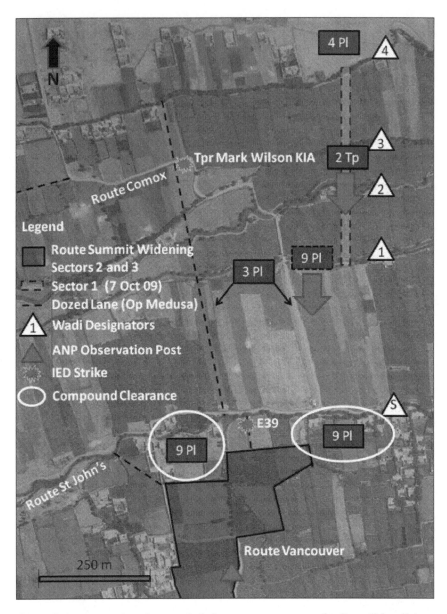

through unopposed and occupied the target compounds. Ray did call in a contact with unidentified persons carrying weapons on a rooftop further to the south, but I told him to hold fire unless fired upon and to continue to observe until I could confirm if they were Afghan National Police. And, in fact, they were. It would have been so much easier if they had only worn their uniforms.

The work in Sector 1 was running behind schedule. It was getting late in the afternoon and I did not want to jeopardize Ray's soldiers by having them clear the same compounds yet another day. So I was pressuring Capt Dan Clarke, the commander of 2 Troop, to speed things up and cut corners if necessary. Once the D6, driven by Cpl Parker, was clear of Wadi 1, I latched on to him and told him to follow me. Since there were no radios in the dozer, I gestured to him to doze Sector 2 starting at Route St John's moving south and off he went. Realizing that there were no LAVs protecting the dozer to the south, I attempted to catch up to Parker by taking a previously dozed path – a path that I had driven not three hours prior.

Then my LAV struck an IED. The third wheel on the driver's side had initiated the device. The hull was not breached but the wheel and the up-armour on the left side were badly damaged. The explosion was so loud I didn't hear it. I am not sure how many seconds it took to recover from the concussion but I remember yelling at my gunner, "What the fuck was that?" Pause two, three, "Fuck me, IED strike."

I had felt the blast wave travel through the vehicle and up through the turret. My legs felt like they had just had a vigorous massage and I remember feeling a swish of air up and into my helmet. Being 'T-Triple C' qualified, my gunner proceeded to check on Foley in the driver's hatch, then Kravjar and Haggarty who were in the back. Everyone was fine although shaken up. It was only then that he realised that he had suffered flash burns on his left arm and his face. The blast had blown off his goggles and glasses as well as the entire contents of his bustle rack. He received first aid in the back and by then the dust had settled. The vehicle was still running and the radios still worked so I sent in an initial sitrep on both the Squadron and Battle Group nets. Before getting on the radio I took a few seconds to calm down and collect my thoughts by practicing the tactical breathing technique that LCol Grossman had taught us back in Petawawa. Breathe in for four, hold for four, and breathe out for four. Breathing is one of the few autonomous bodily functions that can be consciously controlled. In doing so, one can regain control of one's subconscious and revert the mind back to functioning in the cerebral cortex from the stress induced limbic system. Then sitting on the top of my LAV, and in a purposely monotone voice, I sent in an initial sitrep.

Ray Corby came up to my LAV. He reported that two dismounts had sustained non-life threatening injuries and had already been evacuated. I told him to hold their positions for the recovery operation that would soon follow. Dan Clarke reported that his sappers tried to conduct a clearance of the path so that we could recover the vehicle back to Route St John's but that there were too many metal fragments throwing the detector off. My gunner was then offloaded from the non-blast side of the LAV and subsequently sent to Patrol Base Wilson where he would be transported back to Kandahar Airfield with the other casualties. I sent in a rather poor 9-line medical evacuation request to the Squadron Command Post. Even with the format in front of me I just gave them the situation and the casualties' information in plain language. I summed up that transmission with, "Sorry for the lousy 9-liner but it is a bit of a shit show here right now. I trust that you have the info required to sort it out"

My gunner recovered his eyesight after several weeks. The 2 Troop Warrant Officer, WO Roger Perrault would eventually require repatriation to Canada due to serious injuries sustained to his back. He had been blown back off his feet some five metres and had landed very hard. To this day he suffers a great deal from his injuries.

Once the scene had settled, Dan, Ray and I came up with a recovery plan. Since the LAV was only 20 metres south of Route St John's we would hook it up to another LAV and pull it back to the safety of the road. This way if there were any secondary devices no one would be in the towed LAV. If it were driveable then we would drive it the two kilometres back to Patrol Base Wilson. If not then we would tow it. Since the clearance around the vehicle was unsuccessful, and not wanting to step on the ground around the LAV, MCpl Steve Matte did his best monkey impersonation to hook it up. He also picked up a rifle that had been blown out of the bustle rack and had ended up underneath the LAV's front tire. Angered by the turn of events Parker wanted to keep dozing. While I appreciated his warrior spirit I told him that we were done dozing for the day.

By nightfall the LAV was ready to be driven back to Patrol Base Wilson. So, with one wheel crooked and immobile, we proceeded back. Because of the noise generated by the other wheels rubbing against the damaged one, the locals came out to see what was going on. Taking on the aura of a freak show Mardi Gras parade, I waved from the turret of my LAV at the wide-eyed spectators. The three platoons and 2 Troop readopted their defensive positions and settled in for another night of watching the road. Sector 2 was turning into our Achilles Heel and my worry was that if the Taliban had suc-

Top: An armoured D6 dozing Route Summit Sector 2.
Bottom: MCpl Haggarty and Cpl Kravjar survey the damage to my LAV from the IED strike on Route Summit.

ceeded in emplacing the device that I had just hit right under the noses of two watching platoons, then we could be in real trouble. The platoons were doing their best but the ground was extremely difficult to cover and the Taliban operating in the area were highly skilled at infiltration. I have no doubt that anti-personnel mines covering the approaches to Route Summit would have stopped some of these Taliban attacks, but that is no longer an option since Canada signed the Ottawa Accord in the 1990s that banned the use anti-personnel mines that could not be command-detonated. Sadly, we have never replaced that capability, so now we just go without.

Just prior to returning, I sent a final sitrep on the Squadron net. Jokingly, I told Monty that the blast had blown my boot bands right off and that I had looked everywhere but still couldn't find them. Boot bands are used to keep your combat pants bloused above your boot tops. I am not a big fan and therefore, did not use them – much to the chagrin of the CO and the RSM. Monty, who as my sergeant-major usually travelled with me, was back in Kandahar Airfield taking care of some business. He then joked that I couldn't go out without him any more as he didn't trust me not to wreck the family car. When I got back to Patrol Base Wilson, the CO and Maj Greg Ivey greeted me. They shook my hand and asked if I was okay. I told them the story and finished with the boot bands comment. The CO just shook his head and walked away. Could he really yell at a guy with only three of nine lives left?

I no longer had my LAV. So not only was I without a vehicle but also without a command and control platform. There was no structural redundancy for engineer squadron level command and control, something that had not caused us any issues until we started to reengage in combat operations. Military command structures are always done in parallel and thus seem inefficient, however, all of those redundancies are crucial when vehicles, equipment and personnel casualties are likely. Fortunately, the Squadron Combat Team's operations were within one to two kilometres of Patrol Base Wilson. Haggarty and I set up in a Battle Group Signals Platoon Bison that was re-broadcasting my squadron's radio transmissions back to Kandahar Airfield. Along with a man-portable radio on the Battle Group net, I commanded the Squadron from that static location for the next three days. Foley and Kravjar returned to Kandahar Airfield with the LAV in a National Support Element convoy. 2 Troop continued to doze Sector 1, eventually widening it to the required 80 to 100 metres.

Col Lewis was out for a visit and introduced me to a reporter from the American National Public Radio, somewhat akin to our own Canadian Broadcasting Corporation. During the interview I talked about my experience of getting blown up. I assumed that since she was from the States, it was safe to divulge, without it getting back to my family. I wasn't going to tell them until the end of tour so they wouldn't worry. Well, my youngest sister who worked in the US happened to hear the interview on her way to work. She downloaded it and sent it to the entire family. Shortly after the incident, I called home from Kandahar Airfield. My wife asked me what I was doing back so early because it had only been a few days since my last call and I was scheduled to be out for a while. I told her that I needed to change a tire on my LAV and left it at that. The next time I called she asked me how my LAV was doing. I replied with, "You know, don't you?" They always know.

Post-blast exploitation and analysis had revealed that my LAV had struck an anti-tank mine linked to a Russian flechette round. The flechette round, which is filled with small darts, had not detonated because the Talib emplacer had put the explosive charge on the cone. Luckily for us, they did not know that it was a base-detonating round, otherwise many of the dismounts around the LAV at the time of detonation could have been killed.

One night Capt Piers Pappin, B Company's 4 Platoon Commander, suggested that he send out an ambush patrol in the hopes of engaging Taliban infiltrations along the wadis to the east of Route Summit. It was an uneventful operation but I was nervous the entire time as I listened to the progress on the net. I would return to Kandahar Airfield the next day. It would be my last operation as a combat team commander. It had been quite an honour and I would gladly work with Duncan, Ray and Piers again. As I told Piers, the Nomads (4 Platoon's nickname) were welcome with 23 Field Squadron any time. For the record any of the three infantry platoons that supported the Squadron over those two weeks would be welcome.

ISTAR Squadron had swapped locations with Charles Company in Spervan Ghar. 2 Troop would continue to work on Route Summit but now they were attached TACOM to Charles Company. On October 14th, the Taliban once again attacked our forces building the road, killing Sgt Tedford and Pte Williamson at Strong Point Centre. Dan Clarke's LAV engaged and destroyed an enemy 82-millimetre recoilless rifle crew during that battle.

Throughout the dozing operations we would unearth caches comprising

Top: Strong Point Centre with its commanding view of Route Summit Sector 3. Bottom: Memorial to three of the soldiers killed protecting road building operations. Sgt Tedford and Pte Williamson were killed at that spot. Cpl Klukie stepped on an IED a few hundred metres north of there.

weapons, ammunition, rockets, mines and IED-making material. Due to our lone dozer working at 50% capacity because of over-heating, it took 2 Troop until October 17th to complete Sector 2 and until October 22nd to complete all the necessary clean up on Sector 3 and improve the defences at the strong points. It was an incredible relief that the road was now through and just in time as by then all of our dozers were once again inoperable. MCpl Lance Hooper was involved in his third explosive incident when the Canadian Armoured D6 Dozer he was operating struck an IED. No injuries were sustained and the dozer was only slightly damaged. Meanwhile, a civilian contractor had started to dump gravel along Sector 1. The intent was to have a gravel stockpile in case we needed to spread it in key areas should it ever rain. I also believed that it would assist us in winning over the locals, as they would start to believe that we were actually going to build a road connecting the Zhari and Panjwaii District Centres. After only one week of deliveries the contractor refused to honour the contract due to unspecified security concerns. Maybe the Taliban had threatened him or his workers, or maybe it was a ploy to get us to give him more money.

Modern Canadian history occurred on October 21st when one Badger was finally transported to Patrol Base Wilson. The Squadron now had an unprecedented capability to influence the battlefield. Furthermore, it was one that did not put my soldiers at undue risk. In a remarkable logistical feat, in only a matter of weeks, the Canadian Forces had prepared and transported an entire squadron of Leopard tanks and a troop of Badgers to Kandahar Airfield. While I am not sure who was chiefly responsible on the

The Badger (Armoured Engineer Vehicle) pulls down a grape hut with its excavator arm on Route Summit.

Canadian side, it deserves mention that Maj Carla Harding and the rest of her cell made it possible on the Afghan end.

One of the many high-ranking visits that we received was by two brigadier- generals from ISAF Headquarters in Kabul – the ISAF Chief of Operations (US) and the ISAF Chief Engineer (UK). They were down to see first-hand how the progress on ISAF's main effort, post-Op Medusa reconstruction, was going. Both the CO and I briefed on the situation, warts and all. Paraphrased, this was the US general's response:

> Omer, Op Medusa was a huge success. It is now over. We are on to Op Baaz Tsuka *(at the time, something I had never heard of)*. Kandahar City was in jeopardy and now it isn't. You did a fantastic job! You are working miracles down here – You're a god damn miracle worker, Omer. You are world famous for it. Don't beat yourself up over what happened. The overall success or failure of this mission is not on your shoulders; it is on the government's and ISAF's. You have done what you could and more...
>
> Omer, so what you are telling me is that the bureaucracy is stalling combat operations. Some accountant with a stubby pencil is holding up the construction of this road. Is that what you are telling me? Well we are now on a personal crusade to see this road through...

American officers have a real knack for rousing speeches. It seems when we Canadian officers try to imitate that same delivery it often just comes off as forced enthusiasm. It was just what the Boss needed. He needed to hear those words from a superior who had been in combat. It was through no fault of their own, but it was something his Canadian bosses couldn't offer. As Canadian soldiers we were all in this for the first time and none of us had a point of reference from previous combat experience at a lower rank to rely on.

We are taught that the priority is always *mission, men, equipment, self.* Like all things in life, one must adopt a holistic approach. If you do not take care of yourself eventually you can't take care of first three. From what I have witnessed there is an inherent dichotomy. Junior commanders tend not to look after themselves physically. They won't eat or sleep while an operation is ongoing. Senior commanders tend not to look after themselves emotionally. Life is lonely at the top, where the notion persists that being the rock that steadies your unit requires the suppression of all emotion – at least publicly. However, as it has been said, too long a sacrifice makes a stone of the heart.

OCTOBER 23RD – NOVEMBER 6TH, 2006

With the completion of Phase 1 of Route Summit, the Battle Group and by extension the Squadron changed its scheme of manoeuvre. The Battle Group was postured as follows: No change to A Company as they continued to fortify FOB Ma'sum Ghar and patrol in vicinity of Pashmul and Bazar-E-Panjwaii. No change to Bravo Company's location or operations in FOB Martello. Charles Company did a switch with ISTAR Squadron guarding Route Summit by occupying Strong Points Centre and North. ISTAR Squadron moved down to Spervan Ghar; co-locating with the entire Artillery Battery. For this period 23 Field Squadron operated in a completely decentralized manner – that is to say that all of our elements outside Kandahar Airfield were detached to one of the manoeuvre sub-units.

The Squadron's updated priority of work was: 1 - Strong Points. 2 - Route Summit Sector 4. 3 - FOB Ma'sum Ghar. 4 - FOB Spervan Ghar. 5 - Route Summit Sector 6. This was all to be accomplished in the midst of the military's generous leave schedule that gives all troops roughly three weeks leave, and the ongoing requirements to get the troops some time off the line. Based on those priorities and the leave requirements, the Squadron was organised as follows: 1 Troop with heavy equipment and EOD was anchored at FOB Ma'sum Ghar in support of both A and Charles Companies. Sgt Houde remained at FOB Martello. 2 Troop returned to Kandahar Airfield for their R&R and to incorporate their replacement section – 32 Foxtrot. And at FOB Spervan Ghar, Sgt Clucas' section would be augmented by and then handover to Sgt Neil Coates' section.

By now the Squadron had settled into the routine that comes with an overall defensive posture. Our focus then shifted from day-to-day reaction to events on the ground to long-term planning. Thus, in conjunction with the Task Force Engineer Cell, my staff and I were coordinating the details of Route Summit gravelling, paving and culvert fabrication with the Specialist Engineer Team from PRT and the host of civilian contractors who would eventually start the work. By the beginning of October this project was already weeks behind schedule, however, the arrival at FOB Ma'sum Ghar of Sgt Wayne Tripp from the aforementioned Specialist Engineer Team greatly assisted in getting the project started. On October 31st, Canadian funding for Route Summit Sector 6 was finally authorised and released. The Task Force Engineer Cell was also working on purchasing and stockpiling engineer resources because as a principle, just-in-time delivery is not advisable in a war zone. They also endeavoured to contract Explosive Detection Dogs and to rotate all of our heavy equipment with replacements from Canada. The replacement of our own equipment could not have come soon enough as the Governor's D5 dozer suspiciously suffered a blown engine and the UK D6 dozer was returned to its rightful owners. If construction and friendly force mobility were our strong suits, then admittedly Intelligence Preparation of the Battlefield persisted as our weakness. As you will read, the Squadron failed to plan for a change in the weather and failed to accurately predict the location and timing of further IED emplacements.

The work at FOB Ma'sum Ghar was progressing well. Projects that relied on specific but either unavailable or slow-in-coming materials were postponed and other tasks were completed in their place. By the beginning of November, 1 Troop had completed the majority of the Observation Posts and LAV/Tank run ups, perimeter fencing, gravelling and construction of the internal routes and Helicopter Landing Zone, widening of the in-route and construction of an alternate entrance, storage and maintenance sites, levelling of the sleeping and working areas, drainage projects, and installation of showers and ablution facilities. These projects were greatly assisted by the arrival of civilian heavy equipment and the surge of construction engineers from the Engineer Support Unit. All the locally-contracted equipment came with its own operators who lived at the FOB during the week with the interpreters. Our Heavy Equipment Section Commander, Sgt Ron Dix was in charge of the day-to-day operations at the FOB and over the course of the tour he developed a close working relationship with these local operators.

The hardest-working and most talented of them all was our excavator operator named Mohamed. After he completed the switchback road to Observation Post 4 at the top of Ma'sum Ghar, he was affectionately known as "Mohamed on the Mountain." For his services we acquired some money to give him at Eid, a significant Muslim holy festival, effectively doubling his salary that month.

The Heavy Equipment Section Commander, Sgt Ron Dix overseeing the work at FOB Ma'sum Ghar. Mohammed's excavator is in the background working on Observation Post 4 at the top of mountain.

The extensive progress already achieved at Ma'sum Ghar allowed the Squadron to shift 1 Troop's efforts to construction tasks at FOB Zettelmeyer and to backfill 2 Troop at the Strong Points during their four-day R&R. With the recent addition of the Badgers, the work went more quickly at the Strong Points. The finding of a legacy IED slowed the progress at FOB Zettelmeyer, as a manual Level 3 clearance was required to mitigate the explosive threat.

After a few harrowing weeks building Route Summit, it was now 2 Troop's turn for some well earned R&R. Since I needed to get back to Kandahar Airfield to conduct some coordination with the Task Force Engineer, my LAV joined their packet. Instead of travelling back through Kandahar City, I decided that we would take the scenic route and try to find a suitable alternate route back using the little-used roads south of the city. I led the convoy back as I had travelled in that vicinity once before. After a few navigation checks, impassable defiles (or at least impassable to the Dragoon-crewed LAVs in the convoy) and "checking of laterals," an amusing term Sgt Rob Kennedy introduced me to, meaning that you took a wrong turn but did so in order to confirm where the incorrect road led. For the record, we were never lost. We made it back to Kandahar Airfield in three times

Top: Gravel being dumped at FOB Ma'sum Ghar.
Bottom: WO Rouzes walking up to Observation Post 2 at FOB Ma'sum Ghar

Top: A bunker under construction at FOB Ma'sum Ghar.
Bottom: Mohammed's excavator building the road up to Observation Post 4.

A panoramic view of FOB Ma'sum Ghar in the foreground with the town of Bazar-E-Panjwaii and Mar Ghar in the background. Taken from Observation Post 4.

the time but no worse for wear – although the troops had a laugh at my expense based on my route planning skills. Unfortunately no suitable route that by-passed the city (where the suicide bomber threat existed) was found.

During their time at Kandahar Airfield, Capt Dan Clarke incorporated 32 Foxtrot into the Troop. 32 Foxtrot was led by Sgt Solomon "Sammy" Ross who had deployed as Sgt Shane Stachnik's replacement. The remainder of the section was comprised of the four remaining members of 32 Delta: MCpl Greg Murray, Cpl Dave Layton, Tpr Jason McDonald and Cpl Andy Exham. Replacements from Canada included Cpl Richard White and Cpl Greg Caissie and some internal switches, including newly-promoted, MCpl Scott Thompson as the Section Second-in-Command and Cpl Carl Desjardins. Upon returning to the front, 2 Troop resumed the provision of combat engineer support to Charles Company in vicinity of the Route Summit Strong Points.

There was no change for 31 Bravo as Sgt Houde and his small section of sappers continued to provide combat engineer support to Bravo Company in the hinterland of FOB Martello. Life at FOB Spervan Ghar was much more fluid as 32 Echo commanded by Sgt Neil Coates would take over from Sgt Scott Clucas' 32 Bravo. 32 Bravo was subsequently disbanded. Scott Clucas was promoted to Warrant Officer and resumed his place in 2 Troop as their Troop Warrant – a move that was meant to restore some stability after all of their combat losses. WO Clucas would be their fourth and final troop warrant. The remainder of 32 Bravo's crew would augment the newly arrived 37 Bravo – 1 Combat Engineer Regiment's Sgt Ted Peacock, from Edmonton.

Sgt Ted Peacock – 7 Troop's Recce Sergeant.

NOVEMBER 7TH – DECEMBER 16TH, 2006

Until the latter half of this time period, there was little change to the overall Battle Group scheme of manoeuvre or to its disposition. For several reasons, some planned, others not, that continuity did not apply to the Squadron. The major known factor was that the headquarters element for 7 Troop and its remaining Badgers were ready to deploy. Furthermore, it was Sgt Houde's turn for leave so his section had to be replaced at FOB Martello by an *ad hoc* and partial section made up of sappers taken from throughout the Squadron (given the call sign 31 Foxtrot). Two other series of events would test the flexibility and ingenuity of the Squadron – the 'Rains of November' and continued IED strikes against Coalition and civilian targets within our sector.

The Squadron's disposition was as follows: 1 Troop was at FOB Ma'-sum Ghar in support of A Company. 2 Troop was roving between FOB Ma'sum Ghar, when conducting centralized operations on Route Summit Sector 6, and the Strong Points when in support of Charles Company. 7 Troop was at FOB Spervan Ghar in support of ISTAR Squadron. 31 Foxtrot was at FOB Martello in support of Bravo Company. And, after almost two months of absence, an EOD team, commanded by the quiet and unassuming MCpl John Valois, returned to Camp Nathan Smith in order to react to the suicide vehicle-borne IED threat that was prevalent in the city.

Unlike the previous two timeframes (where the paragraphs were structured based on tactical groupings), this time frame will be broken down by category of event/project, as follows: IEDs and Minefields, the Rains of November, Routes Summit and Brown, the FOBs / Strong Points, and Send in the Clowns.

IEDS AND MINEFIELDS

After a two-week lull in enemy IED activity, things picked up again in early November. IED emplacements had largely shifted from the Route Summit corridor to the vicinity of FOB Spervan Ghar and Route Fosters. This could be attributed to the 1 RCR Battle Group's then complete dominance of a practically IED-proof Route Summit. In that respect the insurgents were extremely adept at manoeuvre warfare in that they consistently avoided our strength and attacked where we were weaker. It is not that we lacked the combat power at FOB Spervan Ghar to deal with any Taliban threat, but the routes in and out were problematic from a surveillance perspective. However, as you will read, the threat from suicide bombers and legacy IEDs and mines remained high throughout the entire Area of Operations.

There were several IED strikes on the roads leading to FOB Spervan Ghar. Largely due to the armour protection afforded by our vehicles, the several strikes that involved Canadians resulted in minor to moderate injuries, while the ones on US Forces and civilians frequently resulted in death and catastrophic vehicle destruction. These strikes had two consequences - the requirement to build a Summit-like in-route to FOB Spervan Ghar and the refusal of local contractors to continue to haul gravel to that FOB at any price. Unfortunately, the latter affected our ability to fully complete the former. Until the Battle Group could replicate the safe and secure environment, by Kandahar standards, that existed in Bazar-E-Panjwaii, progress would remain slow. The expansion of those conditions a mere five kilometres to the west to include Spervan Ghar would take until late November. On December 5th an infantry platoon LAV struck an IED on Route Fosters and two days later, not far from that incident, Sgt Coates' 32 Echo LAV struck an IED. 32 Echo along with Badger 1 (commanded by MCpl

Kris Schroder) were conducting an initial recce for Route Brown. In total, Sgt Neil Coates, MCpl Kris Schroder, Cpl Steve Nason, Cpl Shannon Fretter (the medic) and Spr Ryan Kendall were evacuated due to their injuries. Fortunately, they all eventually returned to duty, although some of these soldiers are still affected by their wounds.

Work was progressing well on the morning of November 21st. I had lent my LAV to Capt Dan Clarke as all the LAVs in 2 Troop were in need of repair. I was riding in the back, as I needed to have access to both Battle Group and Squadron radio nets. The Sergeant-Major remained at Patrol Base Wilson so he could take care of some administration there. We were located at Strong Point North and Dan's sappers were conducting flood remediation work and clearing fields of fire, consisting largely of grape hut demolition. Fifteen minutes after Sgt Ross' section had completed the first demolition there was an unexpected explosion. My initial fear was that someone from that section had blown themselves up setting up for the second grape hut demolition. Along with two other Charles Company LAVs, we immediately rushed the 500 metres to the scene and stopped at the intersection of Routes Comox and St John's. The first report that came back was that the first detonation (probable IED) had triggered a secondary explosion of the M-72[19] that a soldier was carrying on his back. As with most reports, the first one is typically incorrect or only partially correct and this one was no different. The explosion was caused by a victim-operated IED, in this case an anti-personnel mine linked to a small mortar round, that Cpl Barnewall had stepped on. There was no secondary explosion, however the M72 was damaged and would eventually need to be disposed of. Due to his 'T Triple C' qualification, my gunner was dispatched from the turret to assist with the first aid. Dan then instructed Cpl Randy Duggan to jockey the LAV such that it was turned around and facing the direction of Patrol Base Wilson, which was the nearest Helicopter Landing Zone.

Waiting the few minutes that it would take to stabilize the casualties and move them by stretcher back to the LAVs (Route St John's east of Comox was impassable to vehicle traffic), I had the foresight to rearrange the right side of the back of the LAV so that a stretcher would have the width to fit inside. When the casualties were being brought out, I motioned to the second stretcher bearer crew and they loaded up one casualty into the back of my LAV. The Company Medic joined the injured soldier and me for the trip to Patrol Base Wilson. Although we had the width to fit in the stretcher, it still would not fit lengthwise. When closed, the LAV ramp angles up and out slightly. We lifted up the stretcher in the hopes that the ramp would close but that was still not enough. I then remembered how to chain off a partially closed ramp (the only benefit from the handover abandonment incident). We then began the journey to Patrol Base Wilson. At that time Route Summit was still very rough and all the bumping was causing the casualty tremendous pain. He had lost his right foot to the IED. His thigh was in constant contraction due to the pain. The air in the LAV was heavy with the smell of cordite and burnt flesh. Other than the actual ground evacuation, the only comfort that I could offer was to tell Duggan to slow down and then to cradle the injured soldier's right leg in my arms to cushion it from the bumps. Hearing on the net that the helicopter was inbound, I told him, "The bird is in the air now."

Upon arriving at Patrol Base Wilson, he was unloaded at the Medical Aid Station. I had never met this soldier before and the next time I saw him was when Cpl Michael Barnewall's photo appeared on the cover of the March 26th, 2007 edition of Maclean's Magazine, entitled "Coming Home." While sudden, loud noises don't bother me too much anymore the smell of cordite still evokes strong emotions, bringing me back to that day.

On November 22nd, the entire Tank Squadron (B Squadron or Call Sign Tango 2), led by Major Trevor Cadieu, was set to deploy from Kandahar Airfield destined for FOB Ma'sum Ghar. Their routes had been meticulously planned based on the known minefield data, likely IED and ambush sites and in order to avoid going through the heart of Kandahar City. I had returned the night previous and was hanging out in the Battle Group Command Post when a contact report came in over the net: *minestrike, Tango 29's tank (Maj Cadieu's), no injuries, just southwest of Kandahar Airfield.* We looked on our map and the latest version of the minefield database known as IMSMA, which stands for 'Information Management System Mine Action', and it did not show any minefields in that area. Since it was very close to Kandahar Airfield we would react with forces from there. Our Kandahar Airfield-based EOD airmobile team, consisting of my second-in-command, Capt Rich Busbridge and PO2 Jim Leith were already on 30 minutes notice to move. Notice to Move is a state of higher readiness whereby the actual number of minutes denotes the maximum allowable time it would take that organization to deploy in reaction to an event. So they were dispatched immediately by ground to link up with the Tango 2

Squadron Sergeant Major.

The initial report stated that half of the entire tank Squadron (two complete tank troops) and their OC, had driven into an unmarked Soviet-era minefield southwest of Kandahar Airfield and that the OC's vehicle had struck an anti-tank mine, blowing off its track, with another anti-tank mine visible directly underneath the belly of the stricken tank. Furthermore, it was reported that the lead tank troops could see numerous exposed or surface laid anti-tank and anti-personnel mines.

Tango 29 disabled tank. Notice the anti-tank mine just in front the vehicle.

Based on Rich's assessment of tasks, more combat engineer assets would be required in order to extricate the tanks by last light. Instead of having an entire field troop return from the Panjwaii, we formed an *ad hoc* section made of sappers from the Squadron Quartermaster shop and the Engineer Support Coordination Center, all led by MWO Brad Montgomery. They departed in my LAV within the hour. I stayed back in the Command Post in order to backfill the corporals who were required to go forward, and frankly, Rich had it under control. The Battle Group also dispatched a liaison officer to the Kandahar Airfield Air Control Tower, as our recovery operation would no doubt interfere with air operations because of our proximity to the runways.

The plan was simple but the execution was methodical and slow. Rich goes into the detail of the recovery in his chapter in Part 2. Plough tanks created lanes to each of the tanks believed to be in the minefield. Sappers and EOD operators would clear the lanes and their verges of any residual mines. One anti-tank mine had to be blown in place as it was found in the spoil of overturned earth in of one of the lanes. All the tanks were recovered from the minefield by 5:30 pm that evening and subsequently returned to Kandahar Airfield. To his credit, Trevor Cadieu had his tank repaired that night and his squadron departed the next day for FOB Ma'sum Ghar.

On November 27th, my driver, my gunner and I, were to be departing on leave the next day. Rich was the acting OC in my place and was set to depart from Kandahar Airfield with Niner Tac to go forward. I met the crew that morning (Rich, Monty, Duggan, Winnicki and Vomastic) to say goodbye. Monty was the only veteran of the original crew. I then went to the Command Post to sort out some last-minute paperwork prior to going back to my room to pack. I then heard the fateful words; "Zero this is Niner, contact IED strike, grid … Echo 39 can you check on Niner Charlie (the RSM's call sign) who has been hit."

In the midst of all the frantic radio traffic, I thought that Rich had been hit but then it became clear that the RSM's vehicle had been the target. The two Priority 1 casualties were then changed to Vital Signs Absent. The ZAP[20] numbers were then transmitted – CWO Bobby Girouard, the Battle Group RSM and Cpl Albert Storm had been killed. It was as if the temperature dropped instantly in the Command Post. The change in mood was palpable. As shock and disbelief set in an eerie silence overtook the Command Post and the radio net. I went over to shake MWO MacRae's and the Deputy Commanding Officer, Major Marty Lipcsey's hands in condolence. It was "the day the music died" and I had never hated that place or the war more than I did that day.

Once the recovery operation was in place and the scene stabilized, I then departed for the Personnel Support Programs tent, where Rich's wife Kishara worked. I wanted to tell her that he was all right before any rumours of the tragedy spread. She asked me what she could do. I told her just to be there for him. When Rich showed up, my parting words to him were to talk about it. I then went to find Monty to see how he was coping.

Along with MWO Montague, Monty was the first responder to the RSM's Bison. He went to give first aid to the RSM while Montague went to check on Cpl Storm. At first, Monty believed that the RSM had died in his arms. After speaking to the medical staff he now believes that he was killed instantly and that what he thought were his last breathes was the last vestige of air leaving his lungs during CPR. Both Monty and MCpl Valois, who conducted the post-blast investigation, describe their actions at the scene in their respective chapters in Part 2.

Rich didn't see the explosion but remembers driving through the massive fireball that emanated from the suicide vehicle-borne IED, engulfing the convoy as it drove by. Large pieces of shrapnel from the bomb and the car carrying it embedded themselves in the LAV. Remaining at eyeball defilade in the LAV turret likely saved Rich from injury.

There was very little left of the vehicle including the engine block, indicating that the IED consisted of a large amount of explosives. The bomber was completely shaved, which is fairly common for suicide bombers as part of their preparations, and had been cut in two by the blast.

THE RAINS OF NOVEMBER

For the previous eight years, there had been a severe drought in Southern Afghanistan. There was no real precipitation data to be had, or if there was we couldn't find it. That being said, in early November 2006 the long-term forecast called for the possibility of rain. As early as November 9th, I was telling anyone who would listen about the threat that rain posed to the movement of any traffic on Route Summit. To be honest, I think that collectively we hoped that nothing would happen. On November 15th the rains came and by the 16th flooding started to occur all over Kandahar Province. As an Unmanned Aerial Vehicle circled high above the ground, I watched the video feed at the Battle Group Command Post as the water broke the banks of the previously dry wadis and began to flood Route Summit and the Strong Points. The desert soil does not absorb water very well and thus all the water cascaded off the hard ground until it pooled in low lying areas or escaped into a river or wadi. Since we had filled in all the wadis bisected by Route Summit, this torrent of water began to back up at those points and eventually started flowing down Route Summit to the south trying to get to the Arghandab River. Had it not been for 2 Troop's actions and the ability of the Badgers to operate in those conditions we would have lost a major part of Route Summit and at least two of the three Strong Points.

Over the next week all three Troops were engaged in full-time flood-mitigation projects. 2 Troop was tasked to construct a berm around Strong Point North and to dig a trench on the east side of Route Summit that would connect the northernmost Wadi (Wadi 4) to the southernmost one (Wadi St John's). This would divert the water into the fields to the east of Route Summit and eventually south into the Arghandab River. Because the mobility corridor had been bisected by "Lake Summit" and we no longer had any confidence that Routes Comox and Vancouver were IED free, there was no longer any connectivity along the route. Therefore, 1 Troop had the task of shoring up Strong Point Centre, diverting water away from the southern parts of Route Summit and eventually building an expedient causeway over the Arghandab River, as the river was becoming impassable even to LAV traffic. While not related to Route Summit, flooding was an issue in and around Spervan Ghar, so 7 Troop also had its hands full with flood mitigation tasks. After a week "Lake Summit" turned into the "Summit Bog" and by November 29th all parts of Summit had been reopened to traffic.

This incident had many lessons for me. They are: It rains in the desert. When it rains there will likely be flash flooding. No matter where you are,

Flooding on Route Summit as viewed from Strong Point North. The flow was estimated at 3 metres / second.

Top: A Badger performing flood mitigation work on Route Fosters in the vicinity of FOB Spervan Ghar.
Bottom: 1 Troop building an expedient causeway over the Arghandab River.

water flows downhill. Just because you told someone about a problem does not mean that you cease to have any responsibility to fix it, especially if you alone own the equipment necessary to enable the solution. Accepting *risk*, especially in war, really means something. And finally, *hope* is not a valid Course of Action. So, I should have solved the issue even if the rest of the Battle Group was not interested in the potential problem and I should have had a plan to mitigate the risks of rain instead of relying on chance. I rolled the dice without insurance and Mother Nature made us pay.

The final plan for the paving of Route Summit had the local contractors build concrete culverts where the road crosses the wadis. I am told that the design for these culverts was insufficient for the flow and that flooding east of Summit and drought west of Summit, as of the Spring of 2009, is still an issue.

ROUTES SUMMIT AND BROWN

This section deals with the non-flood-related activities as they pertain to road construction during this timeframe. Prior to the rains, the Squadron's work on Route Summit progressed very well. Between November 7th and 11th, with 2 Troop working under centralized control of the Squadron, we cleared all of Sector 6. While this was the contractor's responsibility, his sense of urgency was not in line with our timelines, so we put two Badgers to work to help things along. Work was interrupted twice: once to exploit a sizeable weapons cache that had been unearthed and the second time to realign the centreline in order to avoid some ancient graves. On November 19th, the contractor started hauling in gravel. At some point the truckers informed us that certain elements of the Afghan National Police were charging tolls of 30 Afghanis (the local currency) on each truck. Through the local Afghan National Army Commander we quickly put a stop to the extortion.

As previously mentioned, at the ISAF level it had been decided that Canada would fund Sector 6, USAID the bridge in Sector 5 and the German Government Sectors 1-4. On November 12th, the Germans signed the contract for their sectors with work due to begin on December 1st. On December 5th we assisted the German representative "Hans" who conducted his first survey of Sectors 1-4. While this was great, albeit long-awaited news, I wasn't going to abandon the construction of the road to the whims of civilian contractors and to the influences of the Taliban. 1 Troop was tasked

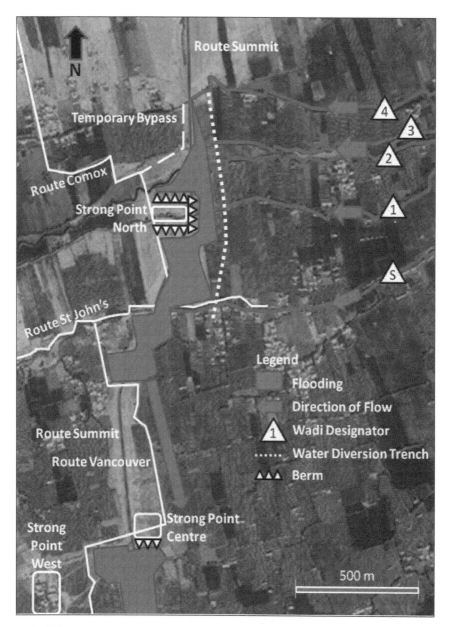

to build Sector 4 so that the contractor could simply pave over top of it. The task was given to an old heavy equipment veteran – the handlebar moustached Sgt Rene Grignon, his band of merry men in 31 Delta, and a couple of attached heavy equipment operators.

This reliance on civilian contractors and the pace at which reconstruction funds were being made available were a major source of frustration for the CO. In fact on more than one occasion, LCol Lavoie told one of our generals that, "Had the Task Force given Gasparotto two million bucks the road would be built by now." There is always a balance to be achieved. A task can either be completed on time, on budget, or in accordance with the original specifications – rarely meeting two or all of those criteria. Commanders will have to decide if they want something done based on strict timelines or if it is better to spread the money around the local population in the hope that by hiring civilian contractors there is an economic trickle-down effect. Undoubtedly, the construction of Route Summit helped the local economy but I am not convinced that it was worth keeping the Battle Group in a defensive posture for three months.

The requirement for a Summit-like in-route connecting FOB Spervan Ghar to Route Fosters has been detailed above. On November 9th, Capt Matt Arndt and his Troop Warrant, WO Luc Aubuchon conducted their initial recce of what would become known as Route Brown. CWO Brown of US Task Force-31 had been killed by an IED on one of the roads leading to FOB Spervan Ghar. Captain "Rusty" of Task Force-31 had made the request to name the road in Brown's honour through Major Andy Lussier. My initial thought was to name it 'Badger Way' in recognition of the superb work that those machines had performed for us but that idea was quickly sidelined after the request. No one in the Battle Group seemed to mind either. With one Badger initially, then with two as of November 12th, Route Brown punched through as a 60-metre-wide, 1.6-kilometre- long combat road almost reaching Route Fosters before the rains came. While I am on the topic of Badgers, it should be noted that due to force generation problems, the third Badger crew commander never did show up from Canada. Luckily we had some other qualified personnel resident in the Squadron. Initially Cpl Marc Poulin was taken from EOD to operate a Badger. When he was repatriated due to an injury and without any other qualified members (excluding some senior NCOs back at Kandahar Airfield) we needed to resort to something more drastic. Our National Treasure, Cpl Clinton Orr was taken out of Heavy Equipment Section and taught how to drive and operate a Badger. In two days he became very skilled and reluctantly remained part of MCpl "Mac" McDonald's Badger 2 crew until the end of the tour. Further progress in terms of the last leg, crossing the Fosters' Wadi, building the sub-base and gravelling would have to wait until early January – after

Top: A Badger removing trees in order to clear the way for Route Summit Sector 6.
Bottom: A civilian contractor's workers building a culvert on Route Summit at Wadi 4.

cleaning up the effects of the rain, completing Op Baaz Tsuka and freeing our road building magician Sgt Grignon from other tasks.

THE FOBs AND STRONG POINTS

Work on Ma'sum Ghar was progressing unimpeded each and every day. However, due to Ramadan and with Eid looming the local workers were increasingly absent from work. While many were from the Kandahar City region, some were Pakistani and had a long way to travel home. When they left, they took the keys to their equipment with them. I can't blame them really as they had witnessed what happened when the military used civilian equipment – it typically got blown up. So when the last local operator left, we hot-wired their equipment for use within the safe confines of FOB Ma'sum Ghar. We had the means to replace it should it have been damaged or destroyed and we simply did not have the luxury wasting two weeks or more being unproductive. We had more money than time and all is fair in love and war.

I met with a Kandak commander and his Canadian Mentor to discuss the construction of FOB Zettelmeyer. I advised them that the Afghan National Army were the owners of that FOB in the hopes of getting them to take over the plan, with my Squadron relegated to a supporting role. It was agreed that we would complete the perimeter protective walls and the gravelling and that the Kandak would sort out the interior. Within a couple of days they arrived with their own heavy equipment, Hesco walls and other construction material. I was amazed. The irony of it was that no one, Afghan National Army or coalition, ever occupied the FOB permanently. I am told that the FOB has since been completely torn down. Hopefully the material has been recycled for other use.

The Strong Points were always in a state of construction. Defensive positions can always be improved and certainly Major Matt Sprague, who had returned from Canada some seven weeks after being wounded on September 4th by the US A-10 strike, worked 2 Troop hard to push the envelope with the fortifications and clearance of fields of fire. Even at this stage the Strong Points came under Taliban attack with several substantial battles occurring in November. On November 8th, and within hours of Sgt Ross' 32 Foxtrot deploying for the first time, they were involved with Charles Company in a large gun fight at Strong Point West. Welcome to the Suck.

By the end of November, gravel was flowing again to FOB Spervan

Top: An artillery fire mission suppressing a Taliban attack on Strong Point West. Bottom. Badger 2 breaching a lane through the grapefields around Strong Point West. Photo taken from the turret of Tango 29's tank.

Ghar. In that short time, 7 Troop transformed that dust bowl into a sustainable and liveable FOB, all the while under threat of contact with the enemy, in the form of Taliban rocket, mortar, Rocket Propelled Grenade, small arms and IED attacks.

SEND IN THE CLOWNS

It was not always death and destruction as we certainly had a sense of humour in the Squadron. The following anecdotes provide a glimpse of the lighter side of the tour.

Before we built the switchback road up to Observation Post 4 at the top of Ma'sum Ghar we decided to acquire a donkey in order to haul up the construction materials. Anthony Robb convinced me, so I convinced the CO to tell the PRT to give me the money. No doubt we were grossly over-charged, but the $300 was more than worth it for the morale and the story - and you can never underestimate the value of a story. So on November 7th we took possession of Regulator 1. I am not sure who gave her that call sign but soon she would be named Tina – after someone's ex-wife I am told. The Parade State was amended from "Officers, Non Commissioned Officers and Other Ranks" to include another column for "Four-Legs." The boys built a pen for her, fed her pop tarts and took her for walks in the camp. There is video footage of Rene Grignon riding her and possibly there are others who managed to get on as well. One day Tina escaped from her pen. Rene managed to persuade our truculent beast to return with him. He is now known as the 'Ass-Whisperer.' At the end of our tour, and after having not worked a single day for us, we gave Tina to a local family.

While not humorous, the Tina story serves as segue to the Squadron's other four-legged members. On December 14th, ten Explosive Detection Dog teams were deployed to the various FOBs in support of military search operations. The Task Force Engineer Cell negotiated this contract on our behalf, with the handlers and their dogs coming under the Squadron's control. It was one of these handlers who painstakingly spray-painted and arranged all the rocks on the side of Ma'sum Ghar that make up the massive maple leaf that commemorates Canada's contribution to the war.

Sgt Neil Coates had a rough tour; however, one of his injuries was the result of an unusual incident. In the back of his LAV at Spervan Ghar one evening, he was making tea. The steam from the kettle set off the fire suppression system, which then turned the same kettle into a projectile as it was located in front of one of the discharge vents - a very British injury indeed and entirely apropos as Sgt Neil Coates is an ex-Royal Engineer and a veteran of the 1982 Falkland Islands War. After that he insisted on wearing his 'sumo' protective suit.

In the same week, but this time at Ma'sum Ghar the smoke grenade

Top: Sgt Rene Grignon riding Tina.
Bottom: A contracted Handler with his Explosive Detection Dog assists Canadian soldiers with searches of the area for explosives and weapons caches. *Photo courtesy of DND Combat Camera.*

dispensers malfunctioned on a Bison one evening. I happened to be present at the time and initially I thought that we were experiencing incoming rocket fire. Naturally I hit the deck but unwittingly decided to take cover under a canvas camp cot. Apparently Darwin is still alive and well. The phosphorus in the smoke canisters started small fires in and around the rest

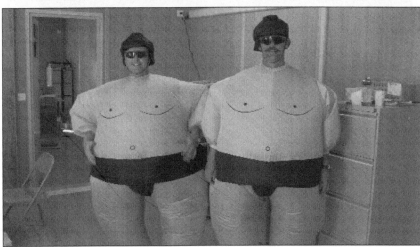

Top: The Canadian flag at FOB Ma'sum Ghar. *Photo courtesy of DND Combat Camera.* Bottom: Sgt Neil Coates (left) and MCpl Justin O'Neill (right) sporting their new Sumo protective suits.

of the vehicles. When one soldier reached into the back of a LAV to grab a fire extinguisher another soldier simultaneously hit the manual button for the vehicle's fire suppression system, which effectively blasted the first soldier out of the back. All the fires were quickly extinguished and no one sustained any serious injuries.

I was travelling on Route Summit as it was still drying out from the rains. Cpl Randy Duggan was driving in order to get familiarized with the LAV and the Area of Operations in order to take over from Foley during his leave. I gave the order "Gun Left" for my gunner to traverse the turret to the left. Duggan mistook that order for him to "Turn Left," which resulted in our becoming stuck in a still-wet part of the road. This is exactly why the Armoured Corps preface every command with either "driver" or "gunner." Naturally it was close to the 'witching hour', an hour or two before sunset, which was the typical time for a Taliban attack. They would infiltrate during the day, sometimes pretending to be farmers, attack close to the end of the day then egress under the cover of darkness. Fortunately Badger 1 was operating close by and extricated us quickly.

On another occasion, I was approached by Major Erin Savage to see if we could assist with the removal of some unused equipment and structures at the Kandahar Airfield's Hospital in order to make room for a new addition. Always wanting to ingratiate myself with the medical community, I said that we could assist. The task would require the use of a crane. Since ours was broken, the excavator arm on our spare Badger was a suitable alternative. The task, therefore, fell to the only two Kandahar Airfield-based Badger- qualified operators – WO Derek Marcoux and Sgt Mike Mazerolle. They would have to do it during their spare time as they already had 12-16 hour shifts to pull in the Engineer Support Coordination Centre. I sold them the task based on a promise that they would be invited to a nurse-rich party. The task, completed in the usual thoroughly professional way entailed more work performed than was asked for and required the use of liberated materials from around Kandahar Airfield. It was all for a good cause. The boys were invited to a medical BBQ, which turned out to be a gathering of predominantly male nurses. It was not at all what they had in mind. They took one for the team and I still owe them.

This Chapter ends with the Squadron, under Rich's capable command, preparing to support the Battle Group's resumption of offensive operations – Op Baaz Tsuka Phase 2c. It also coincided with the closure of FOB Martello and the Relief-in-Place of Charles Company at the Strong Points by Bravo Company. In that vein 31 Foxtrot returned to Kandahar Airfield and was disbanded and when 31 Bravo returned from leave, Sgt Houde and his men were then deployed to live with Bravo Company at Strong Point Centre.

Op Baaz Tsuka
and the Relief-in-Place

They walk amid strange faces in strange places
Thousands they have saved from their own fanaticism
Often with poor reward
— Unknown

Op Baaz Tsuka Phase 2C

From my understanding, Phases 1 through 2b of Op Baaz Tsuka actually equated to Phases 1 through 2b of Op Medusa. For the purposes of perception, ISAF wished to transition away from Op Medusa's war-fighting connotations to Op Baaz Tsuka's emphasis on reconstruction and Afghan National Security Forces involvement. In preparation for Op Baaz Tsuka ('Falcon Summit' in Pashto) Phase 2c, Niner Tac conducted a helicopter reconnaissance and 2 Troop conducted a ground reconnaissance of the village of Howz-e-Madad. This village is located 10 kilometres to the west of Patrol Base Wilson on Highway 1. The operation itself was designed to expand the presence of both coalition and indigenous security forces to the west of our traditional area of operations in Zhari and Panjwaii, and to attempt to separate Tier 1 and 2 Taliban from the lower level fighters who were often forced to fight.

The continuation of the various road building (Summit and Brown) and FOB construction (Ma'sum Ghar and Spervan Ghar) projects would occur in the background. My personal recollection of these series of distinct, small and spread-out operations is quite vague. The Squadron's daily sitreps suggest that it occurred in two official Phases (2c and 3), however there were some changes to the Battle Group's scheme of manoeuvre during Phase 3.

The initial disposition of the 1 RCR Battle Group had A Company supported by 1 Troop at Ma'sum Ghar. Bravo Company, supported by Sgt Houde, had just taken over from Charles Company and secured Route Summit, the Strong Points and Patrol Base Wilson. Charles Company, supported by 2 Troop, staged out of leaguer locations that changed daily. ISTAR

Squadron was supported by 7 Troop at Spervan Ghar. Finally, B Squadron's tanks were split between the companies with their headquarters at Ma'sum Ghar.

The operation commenced on December 17th with 7 Troop's Badgers cutting a combat road from Spervan Ghar to Zangabad Ghar, several kilometres to the west. Four days later Charles Company Combat Team, which included tanks, engineer assets and a sizeable contingent of Afghan National Army troops, deployed to Howz-e-Madad to construct an Afghan National Police Vehicle Check Point as part of our securing of that area. Aided by our Badgers, the checkpoint was constructed by UK Royal Engineers. It was during this period that I returned from my leave and was delivered to Howz-e-Madad by helicopter on December 24th, 2006.

Rich, in Howz-e- Madad, commanding the LAV during Op Baaz Tsuka.

Several IED incidents occurred during this timeframe, including a strike on an Operational Mentoring Liaison Team vehicle and a suicide vehicle-borne IED to which the Kandahar Airfield-based airmobile EOD Team responded.

The Squadron Quartermaster staff remained very busy as the replacement heavy equipment from Canada began to arrive and the first ever Canadian Multi-Purpose Engineer Vehicles were deployed. These vehicles had been more than a decade in the making. As it would turn out, the wait was not worth it. The Engineer Support Coordination Centre staff was performing its usual miracles, coordinating the many tasks and keeping the

Op Baaz Tsuka's opening act – the dozing of Route Dwyer. This combat road connected FOB Spervan Ghar to Zangabar Ghar to the west.

Squadron moving forward. Through the Task Force Engineer, they managed to secure another US Route Clearance Package to assist the Battle Group in the clearance of routes. Due to the circumstances surrounding the casualties suffered by a previous Route Clearance Package under my command during the Taliban attack on October 3rd, this one was placed under command of US Task Force 31 at FOB Spervan Ghar. To my Operations Officer, Capt John Hayward's relief, the Afghan National Army D7 Dozer that had suffered an IED strike in mid September was finally recovered.

Top: The Squadron Quartermaster, WO Ted Gombert.
Bottom: Multi-Purpose Engineer Vehicle (MPEV).

Top: The CDS visiting the troops on Christmas day at FOB Spervan Ghar. Notice his and my lack of boot bands.

Left: Rick Mercer with the "King of Costall," MCpl Thomas. Photo taken Christmas Day at FOB Spervan Ghar.

He now no longer owed them $400,000 USD.

Because of the Muslim holiday of Eid, work on Routes Summit and Brown was progressing slowly but surely. On December 15th, Capt Rich Busbridge and Capt Anthony Robb assisted the USAID reconnaissance of Route Summit Sector 5, which was the proposed bridge location over the Arghandab River. Rich went on to assist the ISAF Chief Engineer's Route Summit inspection and subsequently the Clerk of the Privy Council's visit. On December 25th, replicating Sgt Grignon's work on Route Summit Sector 4, Sgt Houde began work on Sector 3b. The next day we dozed 3 compounds in Pashmul, expanding the width of the road at the intersection of Sectors 3 and 4. These three compounds were the only homes destroyed in order to build Route Summit and we did not proceed with their removal until the village elder granted us permission.

On Christmas Day, 2006, the Chief of Defence Staff (CDS), General Rick Hillier and comedian Rick Mercer arrived at FOB Spervan Ghar with three Members of Parliament for their Christmas visit with the troops. Their presence was a morale boost for the soldiers and was genuinely appreciated. One of the sappers from 7 Troop, a Newfoundlander, invited Rick Mercer into their bunker for tea, cards and some stories. After 20 minutes someone came looking for him because it was thought that he had wandered off and was lost.

As for the CDS it was not what he brought as a Christmas gift, but what he did not bring. Maj Greg Ivey and I asked LCol Lavoie if he could take a picture of us with the CDS, considering the fact that the he was not wearing boot bands. We were promptly told to "Fuck off." He later added something to the effect that the CDS could do what he wanted but that this was Lavoie's Battle Group and what he said goes... that I would look good in a cowboy hat (I immediately went searching for one) with no boot bands.... and when I was a PRT commander I could then, and only then, dispense with the wearing of boot bands. Funny stuff – he made me laugh. If I had a dollar for every time he half-jokingly told me to "Fuck off," I'd be rich.

OP BAAZ TSUKA PHASE 3

The preparations for Phase 3 started on December 27th, however the final regroupings did not occur until December 31st. The CO had organized the Battle Group as follows: A Company Combat Team supported by half

Top: The commanding view from the top of Ghundi Ghar.
Bottom: The 1 Troop Command Team of Lt Anthony Robb and WO Earl Rouzes at the base of Ghundi Ghar.

Left: 1 Troop's unofficial historian, Cpl Matt Austin posing atop Ghundi Ghar. Bottom: The OCs at Ghundi Ghar– Majors G, Mike Wright, Matt Sprague, Andy Lussier and Capt Tim Spears, the acting Battery Commander. Majors Geoff Abthorbe and Trevor Cadieu are absent as they were conducting operations elsewhere.

of 2 Troop operated in the far western portion of Kandahar Province. There was no change to Bravo Company on Route Summit. Charles Company relieved both ISTAR and A Company, and was split between FOBs Ma'sum Ghar and Spervan Ghar. Sgt White's section and 7 Troop supported them respectively. ISTAR Squadron initially conducted reconnaissance and surveillance tasks throughout the Area of Operations and then on January 8th, 2007, with 1 Troop in support, secured Ghundi Ghar while B Squadron Combat Team supported by the other half of 2 Troop operated in western Zhari district. The operation continued in its fullness until January 22nd when it was scaled back in preparation for the relief-in-place with the 2 RCR Battle Group, from Gagetown, NB.

Until ISTAR required a field troop in order to secure Ghundi Ghar, 1 Troop remained under squadron control. For the first half of January, I was detached from Niner Tac and commanded the Squadron Reserve. Much like Op Medusa, this was done to ensure that the Battle Group's lines of communication could be re-opened, should it be required. Furthermore, a UK Royal Engineer Search Team was attached to the Squadron to assist with the search and clearance of the cemetery area just west of Strong Point West. The Taliban always returned to that area and it was believed that there was a large cache of weapons, or something else of importance, located there. With their specialized equipment, the 'Brimstone' call signs searched the area for two days but found nothing of any significance. After a week with us they returned to their base in Helmand Province.

While we are on the topic of 'The Cemetery' there is a lesson to be learnt with respect to naming conventions. It may seem obvious to name geographic locations based on what they actually are (i.e. Cemetery or White School), however when you are being attacked from those locations and you refer to them by those nicknames during a call for fire, it can result in that fire support being refused based on optics alone. Moreover, for cultural sensitivity reasons, not every one agreed with the choices. In the lead-up to Op Medusa, for example, direction was passed from Regional Command South Headquarters to stop referring to the White School as the 'White School' and instead to call it 'The Saw-Toothed Building.' There was a concern about the optics of attacking a school. In a similar vein, our own Task Force Headquarters doggedly refused to call Patrol Base Wilson 'Patrol Base Wilson' as it had not been named following the Canadian Forces naming conventions, and insisted on calling it the 'Zhari District

Centre.'

To be honest, I relished the opportunities to break away from Niner Tac and become a manoeuvre commander in my own right. Once I had tasted that freedom it was difficult to relinquish command of all my troops by attaching them to the other companies and acting solely as the CO's engineer advisor. I am eternally grateful to LCol Lavoie for giving me the opportunity to command my own troops. He saw the benefit of having an additional sub-unit commander to task and trusted me to accomplish the mission. Unfortunately, many infantry COs have not, and will not, operate this way and insist, at best, on holding their engineer OC close solely as an advisor, and at worst wasting them as just another vehicle and crew for Niner Tac.

Ultimately, that CO is not employing all of his assets to their full potential and that engineer OC does not get the command and tactical experience he or she needs to develop fully. No engineer squadron in Kandahar, before our rotation or since, has provided the same level of support to its battle group. This has nothing to do with the other squadrons' capabilities but mainly on the opportunities afforded to the squadron by the CO. It is my belief that as engineers we have sold our soul to the concept of close support, relegating many of our traditional and technical skill sets. One day we will all pay the price for this neglect.

IEDs continued to plague the Battle Group right up until the bitter end. Suicide strikes persisted in the city, and in a worrying trend, there were several command-initiated IED incidents along Highway 1 in the vicinity of Senjaray. Command-detonated means that someone is watching the IED site and essentially presses a button when they want it to go off. One struck an American heavy transport truck, one missed its target and one was found and neutralized by EOD.

In the early morning darkness of January 12th, 2007, a sniper, MCpl Jody Mitic, stepped on an IED while conducting dismounted operations west of Route Summit. He lost both of his lower legs to what was determined to be an anti-personnel mine stacked on top of two rockets. How he even survived a blast of that magnitude is miraculous. The extraction took almost an hour as two groups raced to treat and ultimately evacuate him. Recce Platoon, commanded by Capt Steve MacBeth rushed back a kilometre on foot to secure the scene. MCpl Steve Matte, who was attached to Recce Platoon, was awarded a Commander's Commendation for, among other things, his actions to clear the site that night. 2 Troop with a Badger was the other group that rushed to the scene.

Within 15 minutes of the explosion WO Clucas and his troop departed Ma'sum Ghar for Strong Point West. The Badger was then used to doze a path through the grape fields to where MCpl Mitic was being treated. This combat road enabled the ambulance to come forward and then rush back to Patrol Base Wilson where a helicopter picked him up. If it hadn't been clear to everyone after Cpl Barnewall's IED strike that all the lateral routes leading up to Route Summit were likely targeted by IEDs, it became so then. It is my belief that these roads and paths had IEDs emplaced in them in order to protect fleeing Taliban from pursuing Coalition ground forces after the conduct of ambushes and attacks on the Strong Points and Route Summit.

A few days later Sgt Houde's sappers found what appeared to be an anti-personnel mine on a similar path, this time east of Route Summit. They took cover behind a nearby mud wall before blowing it in place. However, they barely escaped being showered with red phosphorus as the mine was linked to a mortar round containing that chemical. The wounds from such a device would have been devastating.

Later in the month 7 Troop was involved in supporting Task Force-31, who had located a large cache of weapons and explosives west of Spervan Ghar. MCpl Marc Barrette's Badger 3 was used to excavate the area.

On January 5th, in keeping with the saying that "no good deed ever goes unpunished," Sgt Grignon and his section were sent to Spervan Ghar to assist with 7 Troop's construction of Route Brown. It was my intent to complete all current road projects prior to the relief-in-place. We needed him to reproduce the same engineering feats that he had pulled off when he built Route Summit Sector 4. By the end of the month, all 1600 metres of Route Brown had been shaped and a third of it graveled. On February 6th, the road was complete, connecting the FOB to Route Fosters with a two-lane, completely observable road. I remember visiting the project one day. As I approached the site I could see Sgt Grignon, in full combat gear, riding a bicycle. Due to the perceived IED threat, a new camp commander had forbidden the use of ATVs outside the FOB. The sergeant had a 1600-metre road to build and inspect, and walking was not a viable option. He was clearly not amused. It was my assessment that if he used the ATV strictly on Route Brown, the risk of striking an IED when this road was under per-

Top: Sgt Rene Grignon and his civilian contracted road crew pose on a grader at the base of FOB Spervan Ghar and the start point of Route Brown.
Bottom: 7 Troop Commander, Lt Matt Arndt drinking Chai with one of the local heavy equipment operators.

sistent and unimpeded surveillance was extremely low. I overruled the decision and he got the ATV back. On the next rotation, three soldiers were killed when the ATV they were riding struck an IED. The difference was that the road they were on was not under the same level of observation.

January proved to be a significant month for Route Summit. For our

Building up of the sub-base, surveying and gravelling of Route Summit Sectors 3b and 4.

part, Sgt Houde with military and civilian heavy equipment completed the shaping and graveling of Sector 3b. Due to the collective efforts of 31 Bravo and MCpl Hooper's heavy equipment crew, work was completed on January 22nd. I want to make special mention of Cpl Glenroy Warner, a reservist, who used his extensive Ministry of Transportation of Ontario background during the surveying of that sector. Civilian contractors working on the northern sectors eventually linked up with the Squadron's completed work. On January 18th, contractors started paving Sector 6 and completed that work by the end of the month. Paving of the other sectors would not begin until we had departed theatre under the watchful eye of Roto 3 soldiers. Progress on the remaining aspects of the road was now completely in the contractor's hands.

After having completed FOB Zettelmeyer and in preparation for the impending handover, we began to scale back our presence in the forward areas. On January 22nd, 1 Troop handed over their tasks at Ghundi Ghar to an element from 2 Troop, who would then be responsible to provide emergency engineer response coverage to the entire area. While en route back to Kandahar Airfield, 1 Troop stopped at Ma'sum Ghar in order to conduct

A paved Route Summit as it passes through Pashmul heading south.

some re-supply. It was recorded in the Daily Sitrep that Capt Anthony Robb and Capt Dan Clarke climbed together to the top of Ma'sum Ghar to take some photos. The guys back at the Squadron Headquarters had some fun with this, eliciting such comments as "Jack and Jill went up the hill" and "Ma'sum does not mean 'Brokeback' in Pashto." I am not sure who played the role of Jill, but I am sure that the photos turned out well.

A week later, 1 Troop returned to Ma'sum Ghar and performed a last relief of 2 Troop, who then returned to Kandahar Airfield in order to support Charles Company, now based from there. 7 Troop continued to provide support from Spervan Ghar. In essence, during this time frame, the Squadron was limited to providing emergency coverage of the forward areas with elements staging out of Ma'sum Ghar and Spervan Ghar only.

Every member of 2 Troop returned to Ma'sum Ghar one last time in order to erect a sign dedicated to Sgt Shane Stachnik at 'Stachnik Crossing.' However, because of the sensitivities of another sub-unit, the 'Stachnik Crossing' sign was only erected long enough to take a 2 Troop photo. For some of the other sub-units who had suffered casualties, singling out one of the fallen, by naming a landmark for that soldier, was deemed to be in-appropriate and insensitive to others. I must admit that at the time this dis-agreement created a great amount of ill will between the Squadron and the other sub-unit. It also highlighted how tired and emotionally spent we had become, as individuals and as a group. The Deputy CO, Major Marty Lipc-

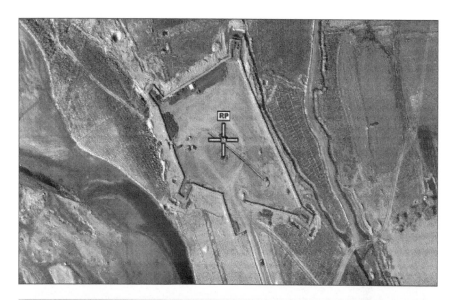

Top: Imagery of FOB Zettelmeyer.

Bottom: The OC and Sergeant-Major posing next to the Afghan flag for their own 'Jack and Jill' photo at the top of Ma'sum Ghar (Monty was Jill).

sey, did a great job keeping the peace. His wise handling of this incident and sage advice throughout the tour helped immeasurably to calm me on various occasions. He was there to diffuse my near-poisonous anger and to facilitate my understanding of other points of view. He, along with the Operations Officer, Major Jay Harvey, and the Adjutant, Capt Kyle Keffer and the rest of the Kandahar Airfield-based Battle Group Headquarters were the unsung heroes of the mission.

The Stachnik Crossing sign at FOB Ma'sum Ghar. It was repatriated after our tour and is located within the 2 CER lines in Petawawa.

RELIEF-IN-PLACE (HANDOVER)

In early February 2007, the lead elements of 42 Engineer Squadron from 4 Engineer Support Regiment in Gagetown, NB, began arriving in theatre as part of the Relief-in-Place. 1 RCR was being replaced by one of its sister units, the 2 RCR Battle Group. Once the first of 42 Squadron's field troops were declared operationally ready they were split between providing support to the 2 RCR companies at FOBs Spervan Ghar, Ma'sum Ghar and at Kandahar Airfield. While I was still in command, Maj Jake Galuga, 42 Squadron's OC, was involved in all the decision-making, as most of the issues became what was known as an "R3P" (Roto 3 Problem).

The Area of Operations tour was scheduled for February 12th. Having learned the lesson from my handover, Jake was not in the turret with me but in another LAV. We visited every major Canadian installation in the city and thankfully it was an uneventful tour. I had two more days in command, by which point every last 23 Field Squadron member was to return to Kandahar Airfield. On the morning of February 14th, I officially handed over command. What should have been a relief for me turned into a very tense day, as Lt Matt Arndt, who was leading the last Area of Operations familiarization tour, was involved in a major traffic accident with 42 Squadron's LAVs in the convoy. I spent the day at the Hospital waiting for everyone to be discharged and then went to the Command Post to wait for word that the final 23 Field Squadron call sign had returned to Kandahar Airfield. Once the last sapper was in, it was then a matter of staying out of the way. It was now someone else's war and time to kick off Op Sapper Bronze. This was a sun-tanning exercise in the days before embarking on our decompression trip to Cyprus. As usual, our adopted sapper, PO1 Knobby Walsh set the standard by proudly wearing a Speedo in public.

Incidentally, on the day I handed over, the gates of the Dala Dam up in Shah Wali Kot were opened, flooding the Arghandab River. With no bridging assets and open hostility at the Task Force Headquarters to acquire any, 42 Squadron spent a large portion of their tour trying to restore the crossing site. If they were willing to forgo mobility across the river, then so be it. However, the implication was that forces north and south of the river could not support each other except for a 60-minute drive back around through Kandahar City. As engineers we often repeat the lamentable refrain, "If only manoeuvre commanders would understand our capabilities and use us to our full extent." I have arrived at the opinion that we give the boss the advice and he or she can disregard it at their own peril.

The sun had set on 23 Field Squadron's mission in Kandahar. As fate would have it, our tour of duty occurred during Roto 2 and Op Medusa. In the heat of those battles and the killing fields of Zhari and the Panjwaii, we joined the ranks of the Old Breed.[21]

Top: Engineers from 42 Field Squadron attempt to re-establish a causeway made of large bolders across the swollen Arghandab River – Roto 3.
Bottom: Roto 4 designed and constructed permanent causeway.

Epilogue

I have fought the good fight, I have finished the race,
I have kept the faith.
— II Timothy 4: 7

POST-DEPLOYMENT

Upon returning from our post-deployment leave, we were fortunate to have several months of Squadron integrity prior to the summer posting season. That is to say that the majority of the original core of 23 Field Squadron remained together. The members of other Squadrons within 2 Combat Engineer Regiment, 7 Troop (1 Combat Engineer Regiment), the Dragoons, naval clearance divers, Electronic Warfare operators, reservists and other individual augmentees all returned to their parent units. Out of necessity, the Army uses a plug-and-play approach for force generation. The obvious downside to this approach is that those who fought together do not necessarily benefit from a collective healing process. This physical distancing from the group also affected the wounded soldiers who had been repatriated and who were convalescing in the major hospitals of Ottawa and Toronto. We kept close tabs on those soldiers, most of whom have made remarkable recoveries.

It was a difficult time as some members cried out for help and struggled to contain and face the demons within. My own anger would not bubble over until many months later. I remain eternally grateful to our 'Madre,' Padre Jean Johns as she spent, and continues to spend, countless hours assisting our members in the matters of the mind, heart and soul. I struggled on a personal level as how to best assist the individual soldiers while still providing the requisite leadership to the Squadron as a whole.

Ultimately, I was completely overwhelmed by the situation and as the OC had to adopt a utilitarian approach that provided the greatest good for the greatest number. This meant that I had to balance the needs of the collective with a certain individual's requirements for help.

Several major ceremonies and events were organized to commemorate and recognize the soldiers of Roto 2. The night prior to the Medals Parade, the Squadron with all of its attachments, except those from Edmonton, gathered at the Petawawa Yacht Club. All the non-engineers were then inducted into the Order of the Pukka Sapper[22]. Senior Generals, along with many other dignitaries were there to present the Battle Group and the Task Force with its medals. A month later, at 2 Combat Engineer Regiment, we gathered for the Canadian Military Engineer Day to unveil a memorial stone. Finally we were united one last time in June, on Gibraltar Island in the Ottawa River, at the conclusion of the Squadron's weeklong canoe trip.

The first recipients of honours and awards gathered in Ottawa on a cold and rainy day in October 2007. MCpl Dwayne Orvis and PO1 Paul Walsh each received a Mention-In-Dispatches. The ceremony was held at the Museum of Civilization and was presided over by General Rick Hillier. The next day, with our families in attendance, Capt Anthony Robb, MWO Brad Montgomery, MCpl Lance Hooper, Cpl Clinton Orr and I assembled at Rideau Hall, with the other recipients, to receive our medals from the Governor General. Cpl Orr was awarded the Medal of Military Valour. The others were presented with Meritorious Service Medals. On separate occasions, Capt Dan Clarke, WO Ted Gombert, Sgt Scott Clucas, MCpl Steve Matte and Corporal Chris Ashton all received Commander's Commendations. At the time of publishing, several honours and awards have yet to be issued.

Left: Cpl Clint Orr, receives his Medal of Military Valour from the Governor-General. Right: MCpl Lance Hooper receiving his Meritorious Service Medal at Rideau Hall.

I have spent many hours reflecting upon my time in Kandahar and what it meant to have led in combat. During the course of that contemplation, perhaps as a coping mechanism, I have become somewhat philosophical as I attempt to process not just the violence, but the amazing successes of that tour. I have tried to measure and record the current and long-term effects of those singular experiences, the intensity of which will change a person. The trick is to attempt to make those changes positive ones. As soldiers we have witnessed and lived the best and worst the world has to offer. Thus, we tend to view life through the paradoxical lenses of cynicism and hope.

The ultimate determination of enduring success in Kandahar Province and Afghanistan will be as a result of Afghan actions: the Government of Afghanistan's actions, the Afghan National Security Forces actions, the non-state power brokers' actions and of course the people's actions. For despite our best efforts and intentions, we will always be strangers in a strange land.

At this point in our ephemeral history of involvement in a centuries-old struggle, it is far too early to judge success or failure. For our rotation, it is my belief that we won the tactical battle, at least militarily. How that has actually influenced the campaign is open to debate. The question that keeps getting asked, especially amongst some in the media, is, "Is it worth the cost in blood and treasure?" In essence, was it a Pyrrhic victory? For the soldiers who were there, and for those who continue to fight, the belief that the sacrifices were not made in vain is an essential part of the coping process. It is that belief that provides the rationale for those who continue their struggle to reconcile their current emotions with the experiences of war.

How do we determine success? What are the criteria? What are the metrics and how are they measured? In a counter-insurgency it is often extremely difficult and traditional military measures such as body counts mean very little. Even by the end of our tour I do not believe that we knew how successful we had been, for we had no real understanding of our effects on the enemy. If this information was in fact known, then I was ignorant of it. So we were successful based on our Boss's and his boss's belief that the Task Force was successful. This conflict, like all conflicts, is a struggle of wills, and as I have come to understand, battles can be won or lost sometimes entirely within the minds of the commanders.

I believe that it is fitting to end this story with the last words that I delivered to the Squadron. This occurred on a cold but sunny day in May of 2007 at 2 Combat Engineer Regiment in Petawawa, as we gathered for the last time for the unveiling of the memorial rock with Sgt Shane Stachnik's name inscribed upon it.

We gather here today, not only to pay our respects to Sgt Stachnik and offer our continued condolences to Shane's family, but also for some closure for ourselves. Life is for the living, so my hope is, that not only will I be telling you things that you already know, but that you have already acted upon.

When I addressed the Squadron at KAF in August of 2006, I told you many things:

• That the mission would be like running a marathon.

• It would require the flexibility of mind, body and spirit.

• Hence: A bullet-proof mind, physical fitness and strength of spirit – well, that is our focus today.

• I told you that I had confidence in all of you. Your actions not only proved me right, but also to a country that was hoping, and to a world that was watching.

• And finally about the Finish Line – well, here we are. Now we are in the post-race recovery. A recovery that is important, as we will all be called upon to fight again, in support of Canada's national interests.

We have been to hell and back, losing one of our brothers along the way. Whether you were injured physically, mentally or emotionally, no doubt there are still good days and bad. And some of us still walk through our own valleys of darkness. However, know this: unless a personal choice, none of us need walk alone.

What is done is done, and it is what it is. We did our best, and what we were trained to do. Accept what has occurred, be better men and women for it, and do not be troubled by decisions past. I am reminded of Robert Frost's poem "The road not taken". At Ma'sum Ghar one night, remarkably, WO Earl Rouzes recited it to me off the top of his head...

I shall be telling this with a sigh.

Somewhere ages and ages hence:

Two roads diverged in a wood, and I –
I took the one less travelled by,
And that, has made all the difference[23].

I will finish off with a modified passage from Shakespeare's, Henry V. I read this to the Orders Group prior
to launching on Operation Medusa. The words are as
valid today as they were in September 2006, or for that
matter since time immemorial, when man first took up
arms. And there are days when I am still haunted by the
prescience of those words. They sum up what it means to
me to have gone to war with the elite group of sappers
from this Regiment and throughout the Canadian Forces
- The men and women of 23 Field Squadron who have
contributed to the writing of modern history, not only in
Afghanistan, but here at home.

From this day to the ending of the world,
But we in it shall be remembered.
We few, we happy few, we band of brothers.
For he today that sheds his blood with me,
Shall be my brother; be he never so vile.
This day shall gentle his condition.
And gentlemen now a-bed,
Shall think themselves accursed they were not here,
And hold their manhoods cheap, while any speaks,
That fought with us, upon that day[24].
CHIMO.

Squadron Honours and Awards

If I have seen further,
it is by standing on the shoulders of giants.
— Sir Isaac Newton

Star of Courage

Petty Officer 2nd Class James Anthony Leith, S.C., M.S.M., C.D.

On September 28th, 2006, Petty Officer 2nd Class James Leith risked his life to prevent the loss of civilian and military lives by dismantling an IED on a road in the Pashmul area of Afghanistan. After his vehicle had been struck, Petty Officer 2nd Class Leith discovered an unstable IED. As his equipment had been destroyed in the original blast, he dismantled the IED using only his bayonet. His courageous actions enabled the reopening of a vital route for coalition forces.

Medal of Military Valour

Corporal Clinton John Orr, M.M.V.

Corporal Orr was a member of 23 Field Squadron, 1st Battalion, the Royal Canadian Regiment Battle Group, in Rotation 2 of Operation Archer, in Afghanistan. On September 3rd, 2006, he was operating an armoured vehicle attached to 2 Troop during an assault in Pashmul. Amidst intense combat action and under direct enemy fire, he placed himself at great risk by manoeuvring to recover one light armoured vehicle and only ceased his relentless attempts to extract a second one when informed that the vehicle's crew had withdrawn to safety. His focus on the mission and his courage in the face of danger have brought great credit to the Canadian Forces and to Canada.

Meritorious Service Medal

Major Mark Anthony Gasparotto, M.S.M.

Major Gasparotto was deployed as officer commanding 23 Field Squadron, 1st Battalion, the Royal Canadian Regiment Battle Group, in Afghanistan, from August 1st, 2006, to February 15th, 2007. With force protection as his priority, he effectively transformed forward operating bases and battle positions into highly defendable locations that enabled effective enemy engagement. Under continuous contact with the enemy, he led his squadron through the construction of Route Summit, a critical enabler for battle group operations. Major Gasparotto's innovative thinking, dedicated efforts and exceptional leadership under enemy fire made a strategic impact on the battlefield of Afghanistan that enhanced battle group operations and saved the lives of Canadian soldiers.

Master Corporal Lance Thomas Hooper, M.S.M., C.D.

From August 1st, 2006, to February 15th, 2007, Master Corporal Hooper, a combat engineer with 23 Field Squadron, 1st Battalion, the Royal Canadian Regiment Battle Group, in Afghanistan, demonstrated exceptional dedication to duty. During three separate incidents, either enemy fire or explosive devices destroyed the engineering vehicle he was operating. On two of these occasions he was wounded and required medical evacuation. In spite of being hit, he eagerly returned to duty each time. Master Corporal Hooper's remarkable dedication and professionalism in combat set an inspiring example for all ranks of the battle group.

Master Warrant Officer Bradley William John Montgomery, M.S.M., C.D.

Master Warrant Officer Montgomery was deployed as the Sergeant-Major of 23 Field Squadron, 1st Battalion, the Royal Canadian Regiment Battle Group, in Afghanistan, from August 1st, 2006, to February 15th, 2007. His professionalism, leadership and experience were critical to the development of roads and forward operating bases during intense combat situations. The selfless commitment he demonstrated to his fellow troops was an inspiration. During four separate incidents, he readily placed himself in harm's way to aid soldiers who had been targeted by enemy attacks. Respected by many, Master Warrant Officer Montgomery is the embodiment of a soldier: professional, selfless, loyal, relentless and dedicated.

Captain Anthony Peter Robb, M.S.M.

Captain Robb, then Lieutenant, was deployed as a troop commander with 23 Field Squadron, 1st Battalion, the Royal Canadian Regiment Battle Group, in Afghanistan, during Operation Archer, from August 1st, 2006, to February 15th, 2007. He courageously led his troop of field engineers through extremely challenging conditions to develop forward operating bases and transportation routes in support of the advancing battle group. He remained calm and focused under enemy fire, providing encouragement and inspiration for his troops. Captain Robb's professionalism and exceptional dedication greatly contributed to the success of operations in the Pashmul region.

MENTION IN DISPATCHES

Master Corporal Dwayne Robert Alvin Orvis

Master Corporal Orvis was a member of 23 Field Squadron, 1st Battalion, Royal Canadian Regiment Battle Group, in Rotation 2 of Operation Archer, in Afghanistan. On September 3rd, 2006, during Operation Medusa, his section came under intense enemy attack, resulting in the death of his section leader and the wounding of numerous others. Without hesitation, Master Corporal Orvis took charge of the section, gave sound tactical direction regarding casualty care and led his team to safety. His courage and strong leadership under extreme stress exemplified the finest traditions of his profession and brought great honour to the Canadian Forces and to Canada.

Petty Officer 1st Class Paul Joseph Walsh, C.D.

Petty Officer First Class Walsh is recognized for his courage and dedication to duty while deployed as 23 Field Squadron's Explosive Ordnance Disposal Chief within the 1st Battalion, the Royal Canadian Regiment Battle Group, in Afghanistan. During Operation Medusa, in September 2006, he risked his life to assist combat engineers in clearing a section of Route Vancouver in the Pashmul region. He personally identified five improvised explosive devices and a 450 kg unexploded bomb within a 150-metre stretch of road, and systematically disposed of them. Petty Officer First Class Walsh's professionalism and commitment to his mission potentially saved the lives of many fellow soldiers.

CHIEF OF THE DEFENCE STAFF COMMENDATION

Corporal Shannon Fretter

On September 4th, 2006 Canadian troops positioned south of the Arghandab River were strafed by a US Air Force A10 aircraft, resulting in over 30 Canadian casualties. Cpl Fretter, the medic attached to 23 Field Squadron, 1 RCR Battle Group took control of the scene and immediately established a triage area. She effectively assessed, prioritized and directed the first aid response to the injured, capitalizing on the casualty response skills of those arriving on the scene. The extremely professional actions of Cpl Fretter in the face of an overwhelming and horrific event saved the lives of countless Canadian soldiers.

CANADIAN EXPEDITIONARY FORCES COMMANDER'S COMMENDATION
Corporal Chris Ashton

Corporal Ashton deployed to Afghanistan as a Heavy Equipment Operator with 23 Field Squadron, 1st Battalion, the Royal Canadian Regiment Battle Group, from August 2006 to February 2007. Demonstrating remarkable professionalism, he built Forward Operating Base Spervan Ghar from the ground up and at an astonishing pace. He worked from sunrise to sunset, under constant enemy threat, to develop a safe and defendable position for the Battle Group. His tireless construction of the Forward Operating Base was a testament to his professionalism and leadership.

Sergeant Scott Clucas

Sgt Clucas deployed with 23 Field Squadron, 1 RCR Battle Group, Task Force Afghanistan from August 2006 - March 2007. Highly respected, he commanded the entire engineer reserve during Op Medusa, which he expertly led in providing full spectrum combat engineering support, enabling coalition elements to safely manoeuvre and fight. His outstanding leadership and calm demeanour provided crucial stability during periods of extreme turmoil and ensured the smooth conduct of operations. Sgt Clucas's stoic professionalism, leadership and devotion exemplified the best characteristics of the Canadian Forces.

Master Corporal Steve Matte

Master Corporal Matte deployed to Afghanistan with 23 Field Squadron, 1 RCR Battle Group, from August 2006 to February 2007. While on patrol with Reconnaissance Platoon his skill and diligence saved the lives of his fellow patrol members when he expertly discovered a non-detonated IED. His keen observation skills were also responsible for locating a large weapons cache. His courage and determination were essential during an IED strike when he conducted a hasty breach which led to the successful evacuation of a severely wounded Canadian soldier. Master Corporal Matte's outstanding professionalism brought great credit to himself and the Canadian Forces.

JOINT TASK FORCE KANDAHAR COMMANDER'S COMMENDATION
Capt Richard Busbridge

Captain R. Busbridge of 23 Field Squadron, the 1st Royal Canadian Regiment Battle Group in Afghanistan is recognized for his outstanding performance. On November 22nd 2006, call sign T29's tank became immobilized due to a mine strike. Captain Busbridge was immediately dispatched to the scene. Despite the ever-present danger of enemy forces in the area, he immediately took control of the situation and began commanding all of the engineering assets on the ground in order to perform the mine extraction and destruction drills. In conjunction with call sign T29 he devised the entire extraction plan in order to guide all seven trapped tanks back to safety. Later, as the acting Officer Commanding, Captain Busbridge was traveling as part of the Commanding Officer's tactical group on the morning of November 27th 2006 when a Suicide Vehicle-borne Improvised Explosive Device hit the convoy. The Battle Group Regimental Sergeant Major and his driver died in the explosion. Despite the chaos, Captain Busbridge remained calm and collected throughout the post blast and vehicle recovery.

Captain Busbridge's performances during these events were outstanding and he is recognized as such.

Sgt Rene J.D. Grignon

Sergeant R.J.D. Grignon of 23 Field Squadron, the 1st Battalion, The Royal Canadian Regiment Battle Group in Afghanistan is recognized for his outstanding level of professionalism and devotion to duty. Sergeant Grignon's leadership and expertise was instrumental in the construction of two combat roads. These routes not only brought security for coalition forces, but also encouraged traffic thereby increasing presence of local nationals, increasing employment and inspiring the return of displaced persons. His tireless efforts on both Route SUMMIT and Route BROWN greatly attributed to mission success. His professionalism and devotion to duty brought credit to the Task Force.

Sgt Steve J.A. Houde

Sergeant S.J.A. Houde of 23 Field Squadron, The 1st Royal Canadian Regiment Battle Group in Afghanistan is recognized for his outstanding level of professionalism, and devotion to duty. Sergeant Houde's leadership and actions ensured that manoeuvre elements received excellent engineer advice and support when normally affiliated Troops were not available. His credibility and influence amongst sub-unit leadership was well above what would normally be expected of a Recce Sergeant. His dedication to duty and sound judgement greatly attributed to mission success.

Warrant Officer Earl J. Rouzes

Warrant Officer E.J. Rouzes of 23 Field Squadron, the 1st Battalion, The Royal Canadian Regiment Battle Group in Afghanistan is recognized for his outstanding professionalism, innovation and devotion to duty. Warrant Officer Rouzes' leadership, initiative and outstanding technical expertise were a driving force in the construction of several Forward Operating Bases and combat roads. Warrant Officer Rouzes' consistently outstanding performance in the face of the enemy earned him the respect and admiration of all who have worked with him. His stalwart attitude and professional demeanour enabled his Troop to excel in all facets of combat, greatly contributing to mission success. A combat proven leader, Warrant Officer Rouzes' ingenuity, professionalism and devotion to duty set a superb example.

CHIEF OF THE LAND STAFF COMMENDATION

Captain Daniel Clarke

Capt Clarke deployed mid-tour as the replacement for the 2 Field Troop Commander, 23 Field Squadron, on Op Archer Roto 2. He was parachuted into a troop on the brink of combat exhaustion due to injuries and enemy action. Upon assuming command of the troop he quickly restored them to fierce and effective fighting force. Under his command 2 Field Troop completed the northern sectors of Route Sumiit, often under direct enemy fire. In fact, on his first day in the Panjwaii, he came under contact and calmly repelled the enemy attack. Over the course of the mission, he has been attached to all the Battle Group infantry companies. Every single supported manoeuvre commander had nothing but praise for

Capt Clarke and his troop. Capt Clarke's credentials rest upon the consistently superb performance of his troop – work that has had a profound impact on BG level operations. His outstanding leadership, initiative and dedication throughout the mission have exceeded all expectations, making him deserving of a CLS Commendation.

Warrant Officer Ted Gombert

In recognition of his outstanding performance in his capacity as 23 Field Squadron's Quartermaster during Task Force Afghanistan Rotation 2. Warrant Officer Gombert ran a highly effective stores organization, effectively distributing responsibilities and monitoring progress in order to ensure the Squadron was continuously supported. Warrant Officer Gombert is a gifted manger of resources who deftly controlled the Squadron's extensive Distribution Account and managed acquisition and delivery of construction materials and engineer resources and a fleet of almost sixty vehicles. As Acting Sergeant-Major, Warrant Officer Gombert was very successful and proved to be highly capable as the senior advisor to the Officer Commanding. His steadfast support to the forward deployed troops was crucial to the Squadron's ability to succeed in full spectrum operations. Warrant Officer Gombert has proven to be a driving force behind highly effective soldiers in the field.

At the time of publication, one Honour and Award remains outstanding.

PART 2

INDIVIDUAL ACCOUNTS OF BATTLE

AMBUSH ALLEY

Cpl Matt Austin

The sun starts to rise in the east, casting a red hue across the horizon. Yesterday had been quite warm, with temperatures into the high forties leaving the ground still warm to the touch. Today would be no different, with promise of yet another day in the scorching heat of the desert.

Lt Robb was up long before the sun had a chance to crest the horizon. WO Rouzes, Cpl Sit, Cpl Pleasance and Cpl Loder join him in preparing their vehicle for their first patrol – a trip out to Patrol Base Wilson in the Zhari District, west of Kandahar City. Wilson or "PBW," as it is known amongst the troops, has been under intense and effective mortar attacks recently, the latest of which occurring while 23 Field Squadron's OC was out on a recce with Niner Tac, the command element of the Battle Group.

The convoy to Patrol Base Wilson is to depart Kandahar Airfield at 8:00 am and to arrive in Patrol Base Wilson at approximately 10:00 am. The day is destined to take a turn for the worse quite rapidly, however, as the planned convoy route leads through a volatile stretch of Highway 1 appropriately named "Ambush Alley."

"This is gonna be a fucking hot day," Loder says, walking beside Pleasance to the Squadron Quartermaster's building.

"No shit," replies Pleasance. "Is it ever cool here?"

They both keep walking past the North Dining Facility where the 'cooks' are grilling up something that will be passed off as the morning's breakfast.

"It's not even seven and I'm already starting to warm up," Pleasance comments, watching as a long line of Filipino contractors arrive at the dining facility to the groan of the Australians arriving after them.

They walk past a number of odd-looking vehicles and then a few generators, finally arriving at the Squadron Quartermaster's.

"Hey Randy," Loder says, seeing Cpl Duggan walking to one of the two Canadian G-Wagons parked beside the building. "Going on a Timmy's run?"

Randy continues to the G-Wagon and opens the door, not stopping. "Yeah, what do you want?" he offers.

"I'll take a large double-double," Loder replies, starting to fish money out of his pocket.

"Actually," Pleasance jumps in, "make it four large double-doubles and a large black."

The two continue around the side of the building and enter through the 1 Troop door to find the Warrant and Troop Commander sitting at the desk facing them.

"Warrant, Sir," Pleasance says, greeting the two of them in turn, and then taking a seat. Loder does the same but remains standing.

"Hey dudes," Lt Robb retorts, not looking up from the work on his computer.

WO Rouzes gets up from his chair beside the Lt while Lt Robb continues working.

"Morning Pleasance, Loder. We'll be leaving in an hour for our first time out to Patrol Base Wilson." He rests his back against the wall and continues, "What I need from you, Sapper Loder, is to get the vehicle ready to move. Make sure the turret is ready to go and go through all your checks."

Loder nods in agreement, "Understood, Warrant."

"Also," the Warrant adds, "We will be getting Cpl Sugrim with us today from 31 Delta, have him help check over things in the back and double-check we don't leave without something we'll need. After you both are done with the back, give Cpl Sit a hand if he needs it."

"Got it, Warrant," Loder says, "how many days of rations do we need?"

"Well." WO Rouzes thinks, "Make sure we have ninety-six hours of rations, right? Just in case we have to supply some to the other sections."

WO Rouzes stands up straight, signalling that work is to be done.

"So you know what you have to do?"

"Yes Warrant," Loder replies, excited that in a couple of hours he would be outside the wire.

Loder leaves while Pleasance remains sitting in the office. He has already been outside of the camp a few days ago as the OC's driver, and even though he is a member of 31 Alpha, he will remain in camp, ready in case the OC has to move.

"So, Pleasance, are you going on a coffee run?" the Warrant asks.

"Already taken care of." Pleasance says smiling.

"Excellent, I tried the stuff at the mess and it's junk, you know?" he complains. "You'd think that they could at least make a decent cup of coffee here."

"Been there, Warrant," Pleasance agrees sitting in his chair. "Go for a smoke?"

At the vehicle lines both Sgt Grignon's 31 Delta section and Sgt White's 31 Echo Section are getting their LAVs ready for the move. Gunners are in the turrets, prepping for the two-hour ride and checking the radios while troops around the back of the vehicle place their kit inside and chat.

Approaching Loder, Cpl Loza says. "Hey, what's up Loder?"

The other troops are still working behind their two vehicles which are parked beside each other, backs to the fence with the ramps down.

"Hey Loza," Loder says, walking up to the 31 Alpha LAV driver's hatch. "How are ya'?"

Loza is beside Loder as he opens the driver's hatch and ducks his head in, turning on the vehicle.

"I'm doing good buddy, and you?" Loza asks.

The LAV roars to life as Loder hits the ignition. A cloud of black smoke belches from the right side exhaust grill.

"Could be better," Loder replies, popping back out of the hatch. "But at least we're getting out of this place today."

Cpl Sit appears around the front of the vehicle holding a white Styrofoam coffee cup.

"Sup' fuckers," he says, looking at both Loza and Loder.

"Holy shit, Tommy" Loder adds. "Look who decides to show up!"

"I was here," Tommy replies. "I was drinking my coffee over by Delta's LAV. The coffee here tastes like shit," he adds.

"No shit," replies Loza, "that's why you drink Timmy's."

Loder notices the ramp isn't down and turns to Sit. "Hey Tommy," he asks, "Can you drop the ramp?"

"Sure thing," Sit says, climbing up the side of the LAV and reaching inside the hatch.

"Ramp clear?" he shouts out to no one in particular.

Loza takes a step back from the edge of the LAV and looks back towards the ramp and fence. "Ramp clear, Shawn" he replies.

When the ramp locks are released there is a loud clunk followed by a long hiss as the ramp lowers towards the ground.

In a fluid motion, Sit backs down out of the driver's hatch and pulls out his pack of Marlboro Lights, opening the top and bringing a cigarette to his lips.

"Smoke?" he offers. Loza watches as Sit finishes lighting his cigarette. Taking one long drag, he looks off at 'Three Mile Mountain,' the closest mountain to Kandahar Airfield, the "home" to well over 5,000 coalition troops who find themselves in Kandahar. In the past, those mountains were a favourite launch-spot for rockets into the camp; now it is scoured daily for insurgents by Coalition security forces.

"Well ladies, I gotta get some work done," Loza informs them, walking off to Echo's LAV where laughter could be heard from the back, presumably over some stupid joke at someone's expense.

"Hey Tommy," Loder says, "We're leaving in a little over an hour. Warrant wants you to inspect the vehicle to make sure everything's ready. If you need help, ask Sugrim."

It is the duty of the driver to perform a Driver's Inspection before the vehicle ever leaves the camp. They can be rushed: a quick inspection of the main components, checking fuel and oil. Or they can be detailed to the point where a driver could take several hours inspecting every inch of their vehicle. In this case, Sit has already inspected the vehicle several times in the last few days, and won't need to check every inch, just the main components.

Alpha, Delta and Echo sections have already prepared their LAVs, if for any reason they need to go outside of the camp or "leave the wire." Engineering equipment is neatly packed in the benches where the troops sit, and behind them against the inside of the hull, held in place by cargo netting or string.

Each soldier is instructed to pack a day-bag and sleeping kit, the only real requirements for the field. It is necessary to bring a spare set of combats and quite a few sets of t-shirts, underwear and socks... especially socks. In the hot desert, feet start sweating almost the minute you put your boots on in the morning. Airing out your socks whenever you get the chance yields an interesting fact that sweat is made up of a considerable amount of salt, rendering your now dry sock stiff enough to almost pick up flat. Not changing your socks means Athletes' Foot for many, skin damage to others. Once continually soaked in sweat for extended periods of time, skin starts to rub off and when discovered normally results in a harsh lecture on personal hygiene.

The troops packs many pairs of socks.

Laughter erupts from inside the Echo LAV where a group of engineers have started to gather. 31 Echo is notorious amongst the field squadron for securing the largest selection of men's magazines, all strapped carefully to the roof inside the back.

Sit finishes inspecting the engine and starts confirming kit in the back of the LAV, something he has done countless times in the past.

"Hey Tommy, come take a look at this buddy," Quesnelle yells out from the back of the Delta LAV.

"Is it porn, Jeff?" Tommy yells back, "I have my own - it's much more interesting."

The troops gathered around the ramp of the LAV continue to smoke and joke. This is how the better part of a day can be spent: sitting around joking and reading magazines or books until tasked out by Higher.

Sit looks into the back of the 31 Alpha LAV and runs through a checklist in his head. Finally coming to an incomplete item, he turns and leaves to grab some rations to stock up when Pleasance appears with three boxes of them.

"Here's 24 hours, Sit. If you need any more, they're back at the Squadron Quartermaster, just ask Ted."

WO Ted Gombert is a former airborne sapper who was one of the 72 engineers attached to the Airborne Battle Group before it was changed into the Canadian Airborne Regiment. He jumped with the Regiment up until 1995, when it was disbanded. This was Gombert's fourth tour, having also served in Bosnia. Now he was in charge of seeing to it that the Squadron had everything it needed plus more - a go-to guy for any sapper.

"Thanks Shawn," Sit says, taking the boxes and setting them in the LAV. Pleasance continues over to the 31 Echo LAV and Sit turns to walk over to the Squadron Quartermaster when he stops.

"Oh yeah," he reminds himself. Turning around he yells up to Loder. "Don't forget to do a comms check, Loder."

"Yeah, yeah," is the muffled reply from inside the turret followed by a thumbs up. As the gunner Loder has both radios within arms reach, and as he is qualified on the radios, there is not a better person for the job.

Excitement continues to mount amongst the troops as the time to depart nears. This is their first real tasking outside of the wire, the first time they will be put in a situation where the enemy is real and within arms reach.

They continue to joke at the back of 31 Echo LAV.

Sgt Grignon, hailing from Rouyn-Noranda, Quebec with a passion for heavy equipment and shooting things, is the first to arrive at the vehicle lines. Sergeants usually show up last, often working in the Squadron or Troop Office preparing for a road move or tasking. His second-in-command is already at the back of the 31 Delta LAV when he arrives, delegated to oversee the preparations.

"All right, *estie*, get to work," he says. "We leave in an hour and we need to go to the convoy brief at the company lines."

Convoy briefs are required, formally or informally, before a convoy ever goes outside the wire. Drivers and crew commanders are always present to confirm the details of the route, possible threats, comms frequencies and "actions-on" when an incident occurs, amongst other important information.

Within an hour, Sit, as the 31 Alpha LAV driver, stands beside Robb and Rouzes, the 1 Troop Commander and the Warrant Officer, listening as the details of the route are listed. Sgt Grignon and Sgt White, from 31 Delta and 31 Echo respectively, are there with their drivers and crew commanders as well.

For 31 Delta and 31 Echo, their drivers, crew commanders and gunners are all armoured troops from the Royal Canadian Dragoons who have been attached to 23 Field Squadron since work-up training began.

The convoy brief ends and the troops walk back to their vehicles, which are parked in a long convoy line circling the compound. A radio check still has to be performed before the convoy can leave at 8:00 am and making sure each vehicle in the convoy can communicate is crucial if there is an incident of any type.

Troops are hanging around outside their vehicles while the radio check is done. The sun isn't as hot as it would be between 1:00 and 3:00 pm, the peak of the day, but to a troop in full kit, it feels hot enough.

Boychuck walks past 31 Delta's LAV en route to his vehicle further up the convoy.

"Good luck buddy," MCpl Oland says, looking down at Boychuck from the 31 Delta turret.

"Thanks!" Boychuck replies, smiling. Both he and Cpl Huard, another

French-Canadian engineer, are driving a Mercedes G-Wagon on this road-move. The G-Wagon is a military vehicle whose civilian counterpart has a manufacturer's suggested retail price of $81,000 US. While it is armoured, the troops prefer the protection offered by the LAV or the RG-31. Still, the G-Wagon has a role to play and today Boychuck will be in it.

Finally the time comes for the convoy to start rolling out. It is split into two packets, with the second packet of vehicles being led by engineer assets, notably 31 Alpha, 31 Delta, 31 Echo and the G-Wagon, which will depart a couple minutes after the first packet of vehicles.

The troops grab their armour and help each other fit on their equipment. Being the first time out for most troops, they are eager and fresh, wearing nearly every piece of equipment needed in the field.

Engines start up as the drivers prep to move. Within seconds there is a symphony of rumbling as troops mount up in the back of their LAVs and other vehicles and then the hisses as ramps close with the troops inside.

"Radio check, can everyone hear me?" Oland asks over the 31 Delta intercom.

"Yes Pete." Sgt Grignon replies. "And you still sound old."

MCpl Oland is a little older with a gray moustache to show it. He grew up on the East Coast before joining the forces and carries a distinguished Newfoundland accent around the Dragoons.

"Thanks Sgt Grignon," Oland quips through the intercom again. "You sound twenty-one yourself."

The first packet starts to roll forward out of the company vehicle lines and heads towards the Entry Checkpoint, kicking up a cloud of dust that can be traced across the camp.

Within a couple of minutes, the second packet starts to roll off the lines and heads towards the checkpoint, chasing the cloud of dust left by the first packet. They continue out past the inner gate as a Canadian soldier on gate-duty looks on and head towards the airfield gate manned by the Afghan National Army. Afghan contract workers are coming into the camp in their beat-up Toyotas and buses. They form a long line down the main road out of the camp and are being checked at the gate by the guards.

"That's a lot of people trying to get in," Loder notes to Lt Robb in the 31 Alpha turret.

"Yeah, looks like it," replies Robb, watching the line of cars.

"I hate it how they all stare at you when you pass," Loder says.

The second packet continues to move through the camp, heading in the direction of the Afghan National Army gate. Once they are a few hundred meters from the Canadian-manned gate the order to stop and load weapons is given.

"Alright Dudka, drop ramp," Sgt White orders over the intercom to the 31 Echo driver once the LAV is stopped. There is a hiss followed by a metallic groan as the pressure drops and the ramp lowers to the pavement. The troops in the second packet load their weapons.

Inside the LAV turrets, the gunners take their 25mm cannons off safe while the crew commanders load the 7.62mm co-axial C6 machine guns. Up top, out of the turret, the crew commanders move on to load their pintle-mounted C6's while down below the troops load their 9mm pistols. The pistol is a coveted item as it is far better choice to walk around Kandahar Airfield with one than having to lug a rifle.

Once complete, the troops take their positions back in their vehicles. The convoy waits until the last troop is loaded up then the ramps are raised with a groan and a slam, shaking loose the dust picked up on the ground. With a hiss, the air breaks are let off and one by one the second packet moves forward towards the Afghan National Army gate.

At the front there is an old MiG fighter plane, one of the last remnants of the Afghan Air Force, mounted in an upward arch toward the sky. Air Sentry troops stare at it while driving by, curious that this seemingly medieval country could have had an Air Force at one time. Just past the MiG, the convoy makes a left turn and starts heading up Highway 4 towards Kandahar City. The first packet is visible in the distance and continues through the many Afghan National Police checkpoints along the highway.

Continuing to head towards Kandahar City, the packet comes upon a mountain with the words "No Drugs" written into the side with white rocks.

"No drugs," Oland jokes over the LAV intercom. "Alright boys, lets go home."

The guys in the back of the 31 Delta LAV laugh as the convoy continues towards Kandahar City. Their trip has already taken around twenty minutes and there is at least an hour of travel left.

Finally the first packet reaches the 'Golden Arches,' which describes the archway where Highway 4 and Highway 1 from Kabul merge on the eastern side of Kandahar City. It is also a dangerous, high-threat zone for suicide bombers.

The radios in all the vehicles come alive. "All call-signs, coming up to the golden arches, high-threat level, out," Announces the convoy commander.

The first packet closes up the spacing between vehicles and enters the roundabout, coming out on Highway 1 heading through Kandahar City towards Patrol Base Wilson.

Inside the vehicles of the second packet, the engineers are a little excited at hearing their first threat warning. This will become their lives on the road moves, in packets and on the offensive – a drawn-out ride into a world they can not see. Some spend the time in the back reading, others staring at nothing, listening to what is happening over the radio and trying to piece together the world outside the LAV. Some are caught up in a memory of back home: lost in a looping remembrance, smiling, sometimes even laughing at a prior happy moment.

The vehicles of the second packet start to enter the roundabout and go through the Arches without a problem. The air-sentries, who are the troops standing in the two roof hatches of the main compartment in order to cover the rear of the LAV, are endlessly scanning the groups of people who have left their homes and compounds to come see the armour moving through their city. The sentries have a more dangerous job at times, being exposed to any potential suicide bomber or roadside bomb. As a trade-off, they are able to enjoy the sights and view an ancient city like Kandahar as their vehicles continue to roll forward towards their objective.

"Don't let anyone near our LAV, Jaworski," Sgt White cautions over the intercom. Jaworski is the section C9 gunner, carrying the section machine gun and ammo. The C9, to the Canadian version of the American M249 SAW, is a favourite amongst troops in combat. It fires linked 5.56 mm rounds at an extremely high rate and it is for this reason that Jaworski is up in the air sentry hatch.

As both packets continue to move forward, the soldiers with a vantage point are rewarded with a view of Kandahar City in its entirety. Open-air meat-markets offer large slabs of meat hanging from hooks. Bakeries, specializing in their flat naan bread are everywhere. Separated from these are mechanics, peddling their wares to the many consumers while curiously interspersed are the cell-phone dealers and providers.

Most buildings are made of cheap concrete, with the stores housed in what would appear to be long parking garages, complete with a garage door to be closed when shopping hours are finished.

The many markets, some covered by corrugated tin panels of many shapes and colours, are crowded with people and this forces the LAV crews to be extra vigilant in searching for any possible aggressor.

As well, some of the smells are unappealing.

"It really smells good out here," Foulds comments facetiously through the intercom to the rest of 31 Delta. MCpl Foulds is the section's second-in-command and prefers to be out of the air-sentry hatch.

The convoy snakes through Kandahar City towards Patrol Base Wilson, slowing down occasionally as some local drivers are forced to the side of the road by the lead vehicle. Mostly, local Afghans pull over at the sight of armour approaching from the rear and those who don't see it are given a few blasts of the horn and a frantic arm-waving to move aside by the crew commander before matters escalate.

Moving through the final neighbourhoods of Kandahar City, the buildings start to become sparse and are constructed mostly of mud. Compounds surrounding mud buildings become more frequent and to the right what looks to be a tall apartment building with the top right section blown away can be seen. Afghanistan has been through many wars in the past and this building is yet another sad reminder of the country's dark history.

"What do you think hit that?" Corbierre questions Mills over the 31 Echo intercom.

Mills keeps staring at the relic building, a magnificent icon of destruction and past battles. "I don't know, man," he replies. "Maybe a big bomb?"

"Could have been artillery," Corbierre suggests, looking back at the road.

Mills looks back down Highway 1 at the many cars that have pulled over for them. He clicks on his intercom, "Anything's possible, man, anything."

Vehicle after vehicle moves towards Patrol Base Wilson, passing numerous idling Toyota Corollas on the shoulder. The Toyota Corolla is by far the most popular choice of car in Afghanistan.

Quesnelle is in sitting in the back of 31 Echo's LAV, nodding off to sleep as Loza, Pittman and Veinot sit listening to the occasional comment over the radio. The sound of the engine accelerating and decelerating along with its continual hum is making them feel tired and Quesnelle's eyes close for the first time.

"Convoy," the radio springs to life. "We will be crossing the Arghandab River in a minute. Be advised, this is a high threat area, out."

No one in the Echo LAV is really concerned as the last threat warning didn't amount to anything. The LAVs continue to roll on and Quesnelle drifts in and out of sleep.

The first packet follows the road's curve to the right and crosses the bridge. The second packet of vehicles with the engineer assets is a short distance behind.

Crossing the bridge, the left side of the road becomes solid vegetation with numerous vineyards and endless fields of marijuana, while abundant homes and compounds occupy the right.

The second packet reaches the bridge across the Arghandab and begins to cross when the radio explodes with chatter.

"Contact, contact, contact!" someone yells over the radio.

Another person comes on. "Ambush left!" they scream.

Quesnelle is now fully awake and staring at Pittman. Pittman looks at the troops, knowing that within seconds they will be in the middle of the ambush as the first packet pushes through.

"Uh-oh, Spaghetti-os," Quesnelle utters, breaking the silence between them.

Within seconds there is gunfire and the rapid "ta-ta-ta-ta" of the Canadian C6 machine guns. A large bang is heard: Rocket Propelled Grenades being fired at the rolling convoy.

"Shit," Veinot pronounces to no one in particular, hearing the firefight occurring outside as the LAV continues to speed forward.

A loud snap is heard off the left side of the 31 Echo LAV, followed by another. Dust is falling off the roof inside the LAV with each impact, creating a haze in the back with beams of light shining in from the air-sentry hatches.

Pittman looks up at Sgt White and yells "start fucking shooting!"

Veinot and Quesnelle hear this and looking at each other start smiling. "Yeah, start fucking shooting shit!" Quesnelle yells.

"Shoot everything," Veinot adds, laughing.

"Shoot it all, man," Quesnelle yells up to Sgt White.

Sgt White continues to look for targets and seeing an opportunity lets off a couple rounds as the LAV rolls on.

Suddenly there is an abnormally large "boom" from the left side of the

Echo LAV, sending dust shooting across the back. Quesnelle looks at himself, and starts patting himself all over and then shrugs. Smiling, he affirms, "Still alive, bro."

In the G-Wagon, Boychuck is honking furiously at the LAV in front of him. Rocket Propelled Grenades have flown past and the vehicles are taking shots while Huard and he are trying desperately to pull their truck up on the right of a LAV, to protect them from the ambush on their left side.

Boychuck keeps honking, getting pissed off.

"These fucking guys won't let me move to their side!" he yells at Huard, while still hitting the horn. More shots are ringing out as the ambush continues and another "boom" of a Rocket Propelled Grenade is heard.

"These guys are fucking idiots," Huard declares in exasperation, looking at the two air-sentries at the back of the LAV they are following.

Finally, an air-sentry in the LAV understands why Boychuck is trying to get his attention. Boychuck sees him reach down for his intercom button and in a few seconds the LAV rolls over to the left side of the road, allowing Boychuck to use the LAV as cover.

In the Alpha LAV, Lt Robb is leading the second packet through the ambush and yells at Loder to rotate the turret left. The 25mm cannon swings quickly left and points out at the ambush side. Inside, Loder is staring at the landscape flying by as the second packet speeds through Ambush Alley.

Another "boom" rings out, followed by a "woosh," signalling to Lt Robb and Loder that a Rocket Propelled Grenade has come close. "Tings" and "cracks" can be heard on the left side of the hull as enemy rounds impact on the LAV.

Sugrim, a Reservist from 48 Field Squadron in Waterloo is riding as the left-side air sentry. He looks around, excited and somewhat scared, bracing his C9 machine gun against the open air-sentry hatch.

"Cpl Sugrim," the Warrant confirms over the intercom, "if you see anyone out there, you fire." Sugrim clicks on the intercom to his headset and replies, "Yes, Warrant," and continues to scan the vegetation flying past.

No sooner has he replied when an insurgent pops up from behind a rock. Seeing this, Sugrim puts him in his sights and takes the machine gun off 'safe'. The insurgent starts to drop back behind the rock but isn't quick enough and with a loud "braaat," Sugrim lets loose a burst of rounds, which impact all around the man.

The last thing that Sugrim observes is the man's head dropping behind the vegetation, leaving Sugrim in a grey area, not knowing if he has hit him.

What feels like an eternity is only a matter of a couple of minutes. Exiting Ambush Alley, both packets continue down Highway 1 towards Patrol Base Wilson.

Loder returns his turret to the forward position and stares out through the day-sight. Leaning back, he looks towards Lt Robb and catches his glance. They look at each other not saying anything both thinking the same thing. They have been outside the wire for a little over an hour and people have already tried hard to kill them.

Lt Robb stands up in the turret exposing his head outside as the convoy commander comes over the radio.

"We're now approaching Patrol Base Wilson, next right turn, out."

The vegetation has changed to open dried-mud fields on the left and right with a little vegetation and the verdant Panjwaii district about 600 metres to the south. Lengthy mud bumps on the right, almost like speed bumps, mark out where there may have been a mud wall in the past.

Vehicles of the first packet slow and make the right turn into the road leading to Patrol Base Wilson. The area was formally known as the Zhari District Center but for Canadian troops, it is known only as Patrol Base Wilson.

The second packet rolls up to the road leading north to Patrol Base Wilson and one by one the vehicles make the turn. Boychuck has since moved his G-Wagon behind an infantry LAV and makes the turn in line with the packet.

Rolling up to the front gate of Patrol Base Wilson, a chicane blocks off parts of the road so vehicles have to slow down to navigate the security obstacles before entering. Afghan National Army soldiers and a couple of Canadian troops man the gate, ready to deal with any suspicious vehicles or people.

Once inside, the second packet comes to a halt near the back wall of the white compound. Inside, many A Company soldiers are moving about and a number of Afghan National Army and Afghan National Police are talking and laughing by their buildings near the front gate. Large green modular tents, with their sides rolled up, form a green square of peaked roofs providing shade.

The engineer LAVs break off from their packet and head over to the West wall with turrets facing outwards. Boychuck pulls his G-Wagon beside the Delta LAV and shuts off the engine, finally getting a chance to get some fresh air since the reinforced windows of the G-Wagon cannot be rolled down

"I thought the drive would have been longer," Boychuck says to Huard, getting out of the driver's seat.

"Yeah," Huard replies, opening his door. "I know what you mean."

"Ramp clear" can be heard being yelled out as LAV ramps drop to reveal the soldiers inside. Quesnelle stretches as fresh air rushes into 31 Echo's LAV when their ramp lowers with a creak.

Getting out of their LAVs, the engineers are greeted by WO Rouzes who has already dismounted.

"Welcome to Patrol Base Wilson," he says to them with a grin. WO Rouzes is walking around the 31 Alpha LAV looking at the impacts of the rounds from the ambush. Looking closely, he calls out to the Troop Commander, "Sir, you should come see this."

The Troop Commander, still in his turret, calls back, "Oh yeah? Is it a good one?"

"Yeah," the Warrant replies "Hit the top of Loder's left periscope and it looks like we took a few rounds to our ramp"

Over at 31 Echo's LAV, the section is crowded around where the rounds have hit their vehicle.

"Shit," Pittman exclaims. "So that was the large bang we heard inside." The boys are staring at the solar panel on the left side of the LAV that has been destroyed.

"Hey, look at these," Dudka says, pointing at the left side of the LAV near the escape hatch. "These weren't rocks," he asserts. Down the left side, near the escape hatch, are over six strikes where insurgents had scored hits. They have left a silver/brown streak as the paint has been taken off by the impact.

At that moment, WO Rouzes walks by and looks at the 31 Echo LAV. "You took some shots too," he says to the troops. "You'll have to get that solar panel replaced."

"We'll get another one when we're back in Kandahar Airfield, Warrant" Sgt White replies.

"Alright, Sgt White and Sgt Grignon, could you bring your troops to the back of the Troop Commander's LAV in five minutes?" the Warrant asks. Both sergeants agree and in five minutes all the engineers are gathered around the Warrant who is sitting in the back of the LAV facing out.

The Warrant speaks first, "Alright boys, good job today. We reacted quickly to incoming fire and some of us got some rounds off." He nods in Sugrim's direction and continues talking. "But you need to know that this shit is real. Those bullets are real and the people shooting them are real."

Troops nod in agreement that training is over. The war is now on and the threat is real. WO Rouzes continues. "If someone starts shooting at you, you fucking let him have it. Well, it doesn't matter if it's a him or a her, you fucking shoot them."

Some troops laugh at this last comment while others just smile. The Warrant continues on this theme until they are told by Company Sergeant-Major Hooyer where to park their vehicles so they can dominate the land around Patrol Base Wilson. The three sections then proceed to move their LAVs to the south-west and north-west corners from the gate with Delta's LAV and the G-Wagon half-way between the corners facing out towards the desert.

With the LAVs moved into position, the troops begin to kit down and relax, talking about what has just happened. It is now a little past 10:30 am and the sun is growing hotter by the minute. Already troops are dressed down into their tan-coloured t-shirts, darkened with sweat from the hot ride to Patrol Base Wilson. MWO Hooyer is seen talking to WO Rouzes, instructing him on the Observation Post brief that will be happening in a few minutes. Finishing the chat, he turns and leaves for the Command Post.

The Warrant walks down from the Alpha LAV and heads towards Delta-Section. "Sgt Grignon?" he asks, looking into the back of the LAV and seeing only Foulds.

"Yes, Warrant?" comes the distinctly familiar reply from Sgt Grignon around the side of the LAV.

"Oh," the Warrant says, "I didn't see you there. Anyhow, there will be an Observation Post brief in 10 minutes at the Command Post building. You and Sgt White make sure your troops are there for that."

"Understood, Warrant," Sgt Grignon replies, going back to looking through his kit.

The Warrant repeats this information to Sgt White and then returns to his LAV up in the corner. The timing for the brief comes and the troops proceed to the Command Post building where they enter through the door facing the compound wall. An older building, the inside is marked up as if a child had been let loose with a box of crayons. Drawings decorate every available surface - images of birds, shoes and such. The troops look at these and laugh - children are the same all over the world.

Inside the building a first aid station has been set up in a couple of rooms with operating tables for troops that have been seriously wounded in the field. One room was labelled 'Pri-1' while another was labelled 'Pri-2/3'. One by one the troops file past the rooms and see all the equipment and bandages, supplies and IV bags. They then walk up the stairs towards the Observation Post on the roof.

It is a bunker made of wood with a roof holding in place three layers of sandbags to protect its occupants from a direct hit from rockets or mortars. Inside the Observation Post, a soldier has over 180 degrees of vision and could bring the machine gun to bear on any target. Each soldier is told how to conduct an Observation Post shift, at night or during the day, and given instructions for what to do if they come under contact. WO Rouzes is paying attention to the directions, while at the same time sizing up the bunker, taking mental notes.

Once the brief has concluded, the Warrant is asked to provide names for shifts and also for gate duty. The Warrant obliges and presents the names. Most soldiers don't want to be on these shifts, but given a chance to tinker with a different weapon, some of the newer troops are a little excited.

Within minutes of submitting the list WO Rouzes walks over to Sgts White and Grignon.

"Alright, Sgt White, Sgt Grignon, there are a few structures that need maintenance at the Command Post. I saw the bunker on the roof was hastily built and could be improved and when I walked past the Pri-2/3 room, I noticed some heavy stress cracks in the roof below the Observation Post up top."

"Yes, Warrant," Sgt Grignon jumps in, "I noticed those cracks too, *estie*. Maybe we could stop the cracking if we shore up the roof?"

"Exactly, Sgt Grignon," the Warrant agrees with a grin, "I noticed some wood, some six-by-sixes over by the defensive stores near the gate. The job will need some good wood and I noticed that a lot of that stuff is fucking junk... anything over eight feet seems to corkscrew over 60 degrees so I think that if we have to shore up the roof we will have to do it with warped wood."

"Understood, Warrant," Sgt White replies. "We'll make it work."

Both the Sgts take their sections and get to work on planning the shoring-up of the roof. The best pieces of wood are found in the pile and pulled out to be set aside for cutting. After a few hours of work, both sections are taking a break from the incredible heat when there is a loud "boom."

"What the fuck was that?" Veinot asks, looking at the rest of Echo Section, sitting inside the back of their LAV

"Maybe an IED?" suggests Quesnelle. "I don't know buddy."

IEDs are prevalent along Highway 1 - a growing threat to Coalition troops. Insurgents plant explosives in or alongside the road, and then detonate them by several different means when a Coalition vehicle rolls past.

The troops continue on their break when they notice a large commotion near the Command Post.

"Get under cover!" a troop yells from up on the Observation Post.

Echo section looks at each other and then back at the Command Post. Soldiers start running to their vehicles as troops shout "mortars" while running past the tent lines.

"Are we being fucking mortared?" asks Jaworski, grabbing his kit and jumping into the back of the LAV.

"Alright boys, this is no fucking joke!" Pittman says, grabbing his kit and jumping in as well. Pittman is the second-in-command of Echo section and knows most Regular Force engineers from Petawawa on a first-name basis.

Dudka, the driver for Echo Section, runs up the side of the LAV and jumps in his hatch without armour. With a growl, he fires up the systems and brings the LAV to life. Corbierre and Mills are now both in the turret, taking their seats and lighting their first cigarettes to start another long session of chain-smoking.

Down the line, Delta and Alpha have also started up their LAVs and the troops are just finishing jumping in the back.

"Ramp up!" Sgt White orders into his headset over the intercom to Dudka once he jumps in as the last guy. With a groaning creak, the ramp raises until it is fully up, then with a "clunk" the ramp locks click into place.

"Hatches down, boys" Pittman yells out to the guys in the turret as well as Dudka, signalling for them to close their hatches. Corbierre and Mills stand up and turn around, facing the rear of the vehicle and releasing their hatches so they can be closed. With a click they are sealed and the LAV is dark inside except for the glowing embers of cigarettes.

"Jesus Christ it is hot in here," Loza remarks as chatter starts to come across the radio. The LAV is sealed in over 45 degree heat. Each troop has his armour and full fighting equipment on with weapon. It doesn't take long for perspiration to start flowing down their faces.

"Hey Dudka, can you turn on the AC back here, *bye*?" Pittman shouts towards the driver's compartment.

"It *is* on," Dudka replies over the intercom. Sure enough, the AC is on full but once the air has moved about a foot, it is heated up, blowing hot at the troops.

Another loud "boom" is heard by Echo section as they sit in their LAV. Finally, Quesnelle switches on his headlamp and grabs a magazine off the roof. "Porn anyone?" he asks, holding a copy of Club International in his hand.

"Don't mind if I do," replies Jaworski, taking the magazine from him. He switches on his own head-lamp and starts flipping through the pictures.

Over in the 31 Alpha LAV, Lt Robb is cracking open his turret's hatch to let out some of the smoke as Loder scans his arcs with the turret. In the back, WO Rouzes and Sugrim are joking about the mortars while the Warrant smokes Marlboros. When their conversation dies down a bit, Sugrim asks, "Wasn't Maj G mortared here a few days ago?"

Exhaling a cloud of smoke, WO Rouzes answers, "That's correct Cpl Sugrim, two days ago."

"I heard a dud mortar landed in a G-Wagon he was taking cover beside," Sugrim adds.

"I don't know if he was beside it," the Warrant replies. "But I heard about the dud that hit the G-Wagon." That would prove to be the first of six of the OC's nine lives to be cashed in over the course of the tour. By tour's end, nobody would want to be around him or MCpl Lance "I have been blown up three times" Hooper, magnets that they were for bullets and IEDs.

"Oh," replies Sugrim and the conversation ends. No more mortars have been heard over the past few minutes and the troops continue to wait for the "all-clear" to come over the radio.

After about an hour the all-clear is given and LAV ramps begin to drop. One by one, they get out of their LAVs and a number run over to the shitters still wearing their body armour but not being able to hold it anymore.

At the engineer LAVs, the troops are out and laying down their body armour. It is now past 6:00 pm and the Warrant calls an end to the day's activities. The sun is now close to the horizon and the temperature has begun to drop. Cots are pulled out from inside and set up beside the LAVs, elevating soldiers off of the sand. Troops lay out their sleeping bags on their cots only to be used as a mattress as the nights are still far too hot to sleep inside a sleeping bag. Each section grabs a box of Individual Meal Packs or "rats" and digs in, warming them up for dinner.

"So," Oland says to Delta section gathered together heating their rations in heating sleeves. "We were ambushed with small arms and Rocket Propelled Grenades and now we've been mortared... lemme see... what's left?"

The boys laugh, excited that they have lived through so much already. Though there are some Observation Post and gate shifts to be done that night, it doesn't matter much as the troops are some of the first to see combat in the Squadron.

Eventually the sun sets and the air cools a little, though still hot enough to sleep under the stars with a thin Ranger blanket. To the troops, the stars are beautiful, every glimmering white prick in the sky flaring out, something hardly seen back in Canada. One by one, they fall asleep after the chatter dies and some start to dream.

WO Rouzes is awoken just in time to hear a troop shout "Stand-to!" He jumps off of his bench and runs outside of the LAV, waking troops as he runs by.

Finally he understands what is happening.

From the sky there comes a roaring sound and a faintly noticeable flicker heading towards the compound. "STAND-TO!" is yelled out again and the engineers are starting to roll out of their cots.

The roaring stops and the flicker dies but the Warrant knows what's coming at them.

"Get in the LAV!" he shouts at his troops, looking down the line to Delta LAV, seeing that their troops were up and moving.

The calls for "stand-to" have not reached Echo LAV in time, Pittman is still asleep on his cot when the rocket explodes outside of the compound.

Pittman rolls off his cot and lands on his stomach with a "humph." Looking around, he grabs his kit and throws it on while still lying in the sand.

"Get in the LAV!" Sgt White calls out to the Echo troops, already inside and putting on his kit. Dudka has also reached his drivers hatch and is in the process of getting seated.

Pittman just finishes putting on his kit when he starts leopard crawling to the LAV. As he gets closer, he can hear Quesnelle and Loza laughing from inside.

"Master Corporal, are you leopard crawling?" Quesnelle asks while Loza and now Jaworski start laughing.

"Shut up Sapper Quesnelle," Pittman retorts, getting to the ramp and running inside. With a creak and a clunk, the ramp is closed and locked. The hatches are down and Echo section is back again for the second time.

"Anyone know what time it is?" Loza asks.

"2345," Veinot replies, still chuckling over Pittman.

"Fuck," Loza complains, "I was just having a good dream too."

MORTAR ATTACK ON PATROL BASE WILSON

Cpl Matt Austin

The 21st of August is the day when many members of 1 Troop will state the fighting really began. With the blistering heat of the desert on their backs, the members of 31 Alpha, 31 Delta, 31 Echo as well as 32 Alpha and some heavy equipment elements continue to work in Patrol Base Wilson for the majority of the day. Their tasks include digging a pit for the protection of a fuel truck, and later a reconnaissance of a future leaguer area where troops can stage before the big September offensive that will come to be known as Op Medusa. Simple tasks can become quite complex when the chaos of insurgents is added to the mix.

Lt Robb and WO Rouzes wake up beside their vehicle inside of Patrol Base Wilson, which is located in the Zhari District of Kandahar Province, some 20 kilometres west of Kandahar City. Parked in the northwest corner of the patrol base, their vehicle is angled outwards offering interlocking fields of fire with the other LAVs stationed against Patrol Base Wilson's foot-thick concrete walls.

The troops have been pulling sentry shifts inside their LAV turrets for the past several days and A Company's infantry troops have been inside Patrol Base Wilson for over a week. Only three days ago, insurgents launched mortars at the patrol base and ambushed an incoming convoy. While there is still a lot of talk about that day, troops wait in anticipation for the chance to go out and find the mortars and insurgents who were behind these attacks.

Lt Robb stretches and swings his legs off the bench inside of his LAV. It has become a custom over the past months of work-up training for him to sleep inside the LAV with the Warrant within arms' reach for assistance.

Down the west wall of the patrol base, 31 Delta's LAV is pointing out with its turret perpendicular to the wall. Sgt Grignon was at Patrol Base Wilson for the last mortar attack and is now working on upgrading the patrol base's defences. From bracing the ceilings of the buildings in order to support the heavy Observation Posts on top to creating the long perimeter fence around Patrol Base Wilson, 31 Delta has been quite busy. Today will be no different as Sgt Grignon, a man who likes to get to the day's work early, has a task ready.

Troops continue to wake and start to pack up their kit, stowing it away inside the LAVs. In the southwest corner, 31 Echo is similarly covering arcs outside the wall. Sgt White is packing up his kit as his section continues to wake and make themselves some breakfast rations. The day grows warmer as the sun touches their vehicle and the smell of the Afghan National Army and Afghan National Police cooking their food floats around the patrol base. The Afghan National Police regularly take the scraps of their food and dump them at the rear of the Afghan National Army near the gate of the patrol base, the stench growing progressively more potent when it cooks in the midday heat.

Sgts White and Grignon are awake and their troops have finished loading their kit into their vehicles when WO Rouzes and Lt Robb walk over from their LAV to Sgt Grignon's.

Grignon is the first to greet the two. "Good morning, Sir," he says to Lt Robb. "You look like you slept well."

"Yeah, it's always a good sleep out here," the Lt replies sarcastically. Quickly moving on to serious matters as was his custom, he asks the Sergeant to gather both his section and 31 Echo for a brief on the day's work. Cpl Warren Reid, a heavy equipment operator with eight years of experience in the Canadian Forces, is also asked to join the Sappers in the briefing. Though his specialty is cranes, his time with the 1 RCR Battle Group in theatre will see Reid using equipment ranging from backhoes to dozers, barging ahead to clear paths and build combat roads.

Sgt Grignon sends one of his guys over to Echo's LAV and within 10 minutes they are all gathered around the 31 Delta LAV as WO Rouzes takes over for the Lt in explaining what needs to be accomplished.

"I trust everyone had a good night's sleep and is good to go today," the Warrant states to no one in particular. "It has been brought to our attention that the fuel truck is being targeted by enemy mortars as it is both vulnerable and visible to enemy observers," the Warrant says, nodding towards the fuel truck parked behind the Afghan National Army building.

"What we need to do is dig a run-up position for the fuel truck so it is less exposed to fire," the Warrant says. "There is some Hesco over in our engineer stores that you can use to further protect the sides of the truck," he continues pointing to the area of the patrol base where barbed wire, concertina and Hesco are stacked along with other defensive stores. The concertina, or 'razor wire', is a defensive favourite to engineers and infantry alike for fencing and restricting movement across land. Later the perimeter fence around Patrol Base Wilson will be constructed from the abundant concertina in the engineer stores.

WO Rouzes turns his attention back to the gathered troops and continues. "As well, Sgt White, a few of the buildings need their roofs shored up to support the weight of the Observation Posts on top."

"Warrant," Sgt White pipes up acknowledging his task. "We'll get to work in the Afghan National Police building."

"Good, Sgt White," WO Rouzes says. "We have some wood over near our stores that you'll be able to use. Some of it's warped so you'll have to find the best and work with that. Sgt Grignon, keep that in mind when building the 'saw horses' that the medics asked Foulds to build for them."

"So," Lt Robb breaks in. "There are a few tasks to get done today - no need to rush through them but remember to keep hydrated and take breaks when you need to."

The group disperses with 31 Echo walking back to their vehicle and the Warrant and Troop Commander returning to their corner.

Sgt Grignon gathers his section around him and whips out his Field Message Pad, a small ringed booklet of blank grid paper. Before he gets started though, he tasks out Foulds, Boychuck, Oland and McEachren to build the horses for the medics at the Command Post. After drawing some designs on the Field Message Pad, he comes up with a couple of ideas of how to dig in the fuel truck. Taking some advice from his guys, he decides on putting up two layers of Hesco to protect the sides and then digging down to make a ramp. Checking to make sure he has the supplies, he helps in pulling the Hesco over to the area where they will dig their ramp and starts to expand the Hesco cells.

Hesco's purpose is to make fortifications where there were none before. Made of geotextile and bound by wire grids, it ships flattened. It is then unfolded and filled with dirt or gravel as needed to make a solid wall. One by one, the cells open and the 8-foot Hesco unfolds to the long length that will protect the front of the truck. Forming empty, standing squares, Sgt Grignon helps the guys open the cells on the sides and push the lines perpendicular to the wall. With the two lines of Hesco in place, the defensive wall is created using the two lines of Hesco intersecting the third, forming an open box or "U" for the truck to park. With these expanded and in place, Sgt Grignon orders his troops to cross-wire the inside of the Hesco, to prevent the Hesco from bulging outwards under the heavy fill.

With the Hesco in place, Reid is called up to fill each cube with dirt and gravel found in the corner of the patrol base. After several fillings, the Hesco is topped up and Reid backs off so Grignon and his section can start to open five-foot Hesco on top of the filled 8-foot Hesco. Again wiring the inside after they are put into place, Reid fills these Hesco as well and again backs off so Sgt Grignon can lay out the rest of his plan.

Meanwhile, inside the Afghan National Police building, 31 Echo is working hard on shoring up the roof, as the Observation Post built on top by them earlier is causing the roof to slowly buckle. Looking from within, there are noticeable cracks developing on the ceiling and left unbraced, the roof would most likely collapse sooner rather than later.

Having found the most suitable wood to shore up the roof, they then move to measuring the height of the room and start cutting. It'll take about three 8' x 8' beams standing vertical to shore up the roof. After cutting portions of the beams that will stand a little less than the height of the room, they then cut four-foot lengths to be put on their sides and pressed against the ceiling by the beams. Forming a horseshoe on the ceiling the roof is thus strengthened and 31 Echo rests before moving back outside.

During their work the day grows hotter and the troops take cover in the shade to eat their lunch rations. Gulping down bottle after bottle of water - sometimes two or more during lunch alone - they take a short break near their worksites in order to rest before continuing with their work.

Outside near the wood pile at the centre of the patrol base, the four men tasked earlier to build the two saw horses for the medics have finished lunch and are finishing up their project. Having found the least warped wood available they construct the horses with the nails provided and after testing the weight, determine that a troop could be placed across the two sets without them breaking.

With their job complete, they deliver the horses to the Command Post and start walking over to the fuel truck where Reid is digging down in the horseshoe of Hesco with his backhoe so the fuel truck can drive down into even greater protection. With the front and sides of the fuel truck protected by the Hesco, and a ramp down into the ground the vehicle gains some more protection from the rear as well and ensures that the truck will be well under cover.

The troops continue their work and Reid continues digging the run-up for the fuel truck when a medium-sized convoy rolls into Patrol Base Wilson. Zigzagging through the security obstacles at the gate, the convoy circles to the right around the centre of the patrol base before coming to a halt facing the entrance. With creaks and hisses, the LAV ramps drop and fully-kitted troops start to emerge from the backs of each vehicle, looking around at Patrol Base Wilson.

Near the rear of this convoy is the engineer call sign Echo 32 Alpha with the 2 Troop Commander, Lt Behiels. Coming to a halt, he looks around the patrol base and after giving the go-ahead for the guys to relax and kit down, he takes off his headset and crawls out of his hatch in the passenger (commander) side of the turret.

Sgt Grignon is now looking over his finished work on the fuel truck run-up while the convoy is relaxing near their vehicles. Troops take off their kit and try to air out their sweat-soaked armour and combat shirts, which are all dark brown from perspiration.

With his section gathered around him, Grignon decides that with the work complete, it would be good to send his troops to their first showers since their arrival on August 18th. The showers are built as stalls with a large water jug up top. Members are forced to turn on the water, wet themselves, turn it off to lather and then turn it on again to rinse. Since water re-supply can be scarce, troops are conservative when showering, especially when there is a long line waiting.

Since the day is getting on, Sgt Grignon decides to send his Dragoon crew over to the shower as well and then grab one himself. They wait and some troops start eating their dinner while others sit in the back of the LAV or in the shade.

Over at 31 Echo's LAV, the troops are having something to eat while others are into the multiple copies of Maxim and various styles of porn.

The Dragoons finish their showers so Sgt Grignon, MCpl Foulds and Cpl Sugrim walk over with wash kits in hand to the shower area. Since troops are showering at the time, Sgt Grignon lets Sugrim go first while Foulds walks over to the area set up as a wash station. Using a state-of-the-art washboard, he fills a pail with a little water and some soap before bringing out his clothes to start washing. Built beside a wall of the patrol base, the shower, shave and wash stations are granted a degree of protection from outside shrapnel so long as it's not coming from the other side.

At 32 Alpha's vehicle, Lt Behiels is finished laying his armour on the ground and is walking over to 31 Alpha's LAV in the far corner of the patrol base. Seeing Lt Robb at the rear of the vehicle with his kit placed on the ramp, he wants to get some information on the area and what has been going on over the past little while. He suspects that there is a major operation coming. Things are in the works for an offensive but the details of Operation Medusa have not yet been fully released to the troops.

Lt Robb sees Lt Behiels walking over and decides to meet him half way. Smiling, they walk towards each other, happy to meet up outside the wire of Kandahar Airfield. The situation is real now and it is no longer training back at Petawawa or in Wainwright. Leading troops in the field, they are now doing what they have trained so hard to do. They are walking towards each other, away from their LAVs and don't hear the distant "Pop."

Sugrim is out of the shower and is standing in his military-issued green briefs, lathering up to shave when he hears the "Pop." Looking around at the people in the patrol base, he sees that no one has really paid any attention to the sound and all are continuing with their work.

Hearing a whistle, Sugrim drops to the ground. Looking over to their LAV on the other side of the base he sees small amounts of rocks and sand showering down on the opposite side of the wall.

Mortar fire.

Troops now run to their positions and yells of, "Stand – to!" sound around the base. Sgt Grignon, having finished his shave, looks over to Sugrim and yells, "Get under the Bison, *estie!*"

Sugrim drops his shaving kit where it is, grabs his pants and still in his briefs and flip-flops, runs and dives under the Bison parked against the Command Post wall near the showers.

MCpl Foulds faintly hearing the blast but nearly being hit by a piece of shrapnel drops his laundry and with Grignon coming up beside him, dives underneath the Bison as well. Another soldier is walking by the area, talking on a satellite phone when he hears the blast. Looking towards the general vicinity of the explosion, he comes to the realization that they are under attack and seeing Sgt Grignon, Foulds and Sugrim under the Bison, crawls underneath to take cover beside them.

Having not heard the firing of the mortar, both Lt Behiels and Lt Robb are unaware of the ordnance sailing through the air and are walking towards each other. Only when it hits, do they realize that they are under attack and they rapidly change direction and sprint away. With no personal body armour on Lt Robb runs the 10 meters to the back of his LAV while Behiels runs a considerable distance further to get back to where he placed his armour. Running up the ramp of the LAV, he grabs his kit and ducks inside while Cpl Scott runs to his driver's hatch and without climbing up the side of the LAV, dives head-first into his position.

Inside, Spr King has already squeezed through the side of the turret and is closing his gunner's hatch from the inside and preparing in case they have to move. Meanwhile in the back, Lt Behiels sits beside MCpl Matte and WO Perrault who has just finished closing the air sentry hatches as the ramp is raised.

Inside the 31 Alpha LAV, Loder has just finished re-supplying all the rations, water and packing all the kit with the help of Cpl Sit as they had been told by Lt Robb earlier that they would be going on a route recce later that night.

"Oh fuck, here we go," Loder says, standing on top of the LAV when the first mortar round hits. He sees it land about 50 meters in front of 31 Delta LAV and takes it as a cue to rush over to his gunners hatch and jump inside the turret. Leaving the hatch open, he starts putting on his armour and helmet while he waits for orders from Lt Robb.

Lt Robb, having made it to the back of the LAV jumps in the back while telling Cpl Sit to jump in the drivers hatch. Squeezing past WO Rouzes, he tells Loder to not move the turret while he manoeuvres through the side of the turret into the crew commanders' seat. A tricky and dangerous place to squeeze through, the narrow opening inside the vehicle on the passenger's side allows a crew member to squeeze through where the turret rotates in its cage. Were the turret to rotate while a member was climbing through, the result could be fatal as the member could be crushed as if stuck halfway out of an elevator while it starts moving.

Taking his position in the crew commander's seat, Lt Robb hears the vehicle rumble to life as Sit has turned the engine over so they can power the turret and move if necessary.

"WHOMP."

Another round lands outside of the camp wall, not visible to the troops. Lt Robb looks at his watch when he hears the explosion and starts counting off the seconds.

1..2..3..

"Loder," he says, "If you find who's mortaring us, shoot him."

12.. 13.. 14..

"Roger, Sir," Loder replies, looking through his optics, trying hard to find the mortar team.

27.. 28.. 29..

In the other engineer LAVs down the western wall, the troops have taken cover and are manning their stations as well. With ramps raised, they close their hatches just in case that unlucky round comes down on top. With engines on, they scan for targets on the horizon, looking for the culprit who is dropping rounds on the base.

32.. 33.. 34..

Back underneath the Bison, Sugrim, Foulds and Sgt Grignon watch alongside the infantryman as their LAV turret scans the horizon.

42.. 43...

"WHOMP." Another mortar explodes.

Inside the 31 Alpha LAV, Lt Robb stops counting and looks through his optics in the turret, looking at what Loder is pointing at. The mortar crew is not the fastest compared to Canadian standards, but they are quickly readjusting and firing their rounds. Since they have not yet hit their target, which is most likely the fuel truck, they can't fire for effect on the patrol base - a mortar bombardment that would see the maximum amount of mortar rounds fired within a short time-span. Instead, they are 'walking' their rounds in - firing a round, readjusting and firing again until they hit in the vicinity of their target.

Under the Bison on the other side of the camp, the three engineers watch and listen as another mortar falls in the vicinity of the base with a "Whomp." There are no troops out in the open now, all having hastily taken positions of cover as they've been trained. The base is awash in the sounds of LAV engines and radios, the turret crews scanning their arcs for the mortar crew.

Sgt Grignon looks over at his team after the third mortar lands and decides that they should get inside the Command Post in case they are needed. "Alright," he says, "We're gonna make a dash for it to the Command Post, *estie*."

Sugrim, now on his side trying to put on his pants, acknowledges and rushes to finish while Foulds and Sgt Grignon prepare to move. There is a delay now since the last mortar landed outside of the patrol base and the Sergeant wants to move his guys to better cover.

Finally doing up his pants button, Sugrim edges towards the side of the Bison, faced towards the building. On the command of "GO NOW!" from Sgt Grignon, both he and Foulds get up from under the Bison and sprint the 10 meters around the Command Post wall, up the short steps and in the entrance. Sgt Grignon is quick on their heels and follows within seconds.

Inside the Command Post, the troops are greeted with a plethora of action as people bustle about in work. The smell of coffee is strong as a large coffee urn is silently making coffee outside of the command room, brewing around the clock.

Troops are bustling around the anteroom of the Command Post. Foulds starts talking to another soldier about his job while Sugrim makes himself a coffee. Sgt Grignon stares at the windows which are "boarded up" with boxes of bottled water from re-supply convoys. There is plenty of water to go around so these boxes sit, unopened and gathering dust, blocking the sun from entering the Command Post. Looking around, he sees children's drawings on the walls, a relic of the former owners who occupied the house before the current Battle Group.

"WHOMP"

The explosion is loud and sudden, shaking the building and causing dust to fall from the ceiling. To stay out of the way, they take refuge in one of the medical rooms. The building is fairly sturdy and all the windows are protected with several boxes of bottled water cases. Troops are not afraid inside the Command Post, knowing they are protected.

Across the patrol base, Lt Behiels sits in the darkened back of 32 Alpha LAV. He counts the mortars that have come down while Spr King sits in the gunner seat, waiting for any orders. Together, they listen to the muffled explosions of mortars raining in and listen to the conversation over the Alpha Company net.

The troops wait, under cover of armour or building as the mortar rounds continue to impact in and around the base. They are safe, protected by the armour of the LAVs or bricks and the mortar crew is slow and inaccurate. Time ticks away as the troops wait, muffled explosions ringing out, some closer than others.

30 minutes from the first mortar round hitting, there is silence.

Listening to the Company radio network, they wait for another 20 minutes, listening for either another attack or an "all-clear" from higher. Inside the Command Post, an officer walks out of the command room and looking at Sgt Grignon says, "All clear, Sergeant."

Hearing this, Sgt Grignon turns to his two guys and says, "Okay, lets go," and heads for the door which, not too long ago, he was running through to get to cover. They walk back along the side of the building and up to the shower area which is dry now from the persistent heat. Walking up to the shaving area, he gathers his ablutions kit while Foulds grabs his laundry.

The familiar creaking sound of LAV ramps dropping is heard along with the rumbling engines. Troops emerge from the backs of their LAVs and immediately start stripping off their sweat-soaked kit, setting it on the ground near their vehicles.

At the 31 Alpha LAV, Lt Robb pulls himself out through his hatch in the top of the turret and proceeds to climb down the front of the LAV. He knows that later that night they will be on a route recce, looking over the land for a possible future leaguer where troops will halt and stage for future operations. On the ground, he first checks over his sections to make sure they are all good, moving with WO Rouzes down to 31 Delta LAV before walking further towards 31 Echo where Sgt White is stripped down standing at the back of the LAV.

WO Rouzes reiterates that the threat is very real, that the enemy wants to kill Canadians and that they were inaccurate in their attacks. He believes that they may have been inaccurate because they were unable to locate the newly-protected and concealed fuel truck.

With his sections all right, Lt Robb leaves the sergeants alone to continue their section-level maintenance. Moving back to his own LAV, Lt Robb helps with the vehicle prep, loading rations, water and positioning kit in the back. With this completed, he decides that it would be best to run his crew through a crash course on how to hand ammo through the turret if needed. A crucial duty for the member sitting closest to the turret in the rear of the LAV is to be able to find and open a can full of the requisite ammo when the gunner runs low. Pulling the ammo out of the can, the troop then has to feed it through the envelope-slot that connects the troop-carrying area to the turret. In the armoured world this soldier is known as the 'GIB' or 'Guy In Back'.

Over the next 30 minutes, Spr Loder, Lt Robb and the crew in the back practise this skill and by the end of the session, the guys are able to locate and feed the required ammo in minimal time.

At the 31 Delta LAV, Sgt Grignon has since returned from the shower area with his troops and every member of his section has now had the chance to shower and wash up. The day is growing late, and the heat is starting to wane as the sun sets. Sugrim has hung his sweat-soaked clothes on the side of their LAV along with other members of the section and sits to clean off the dust covering his rifle and pistol.

The troops of 32 Alpha are still joking about Cpl Scott's dive into the driver's hatch when they are told by Lt Behiels that they will be moving shortly. The convoy will leave the entrance of the patrol base, turn east onto Hwy 1 towards Kandahar, pass through Ambush Alley, and moving through Kandahar city, it will then turn southwest and head down towards Ma'sum. Ghar on the south bank of the Arghandab, overlooking Pashmul. The objective is to locate a potential leaguer site that the troops will use at a later date before moving further away from Kandahar.

Lt Robb receives this information as well and gathers his troops together and explains both the route that they will take, and that they will be going out for a few hours after dusk only, until they reach the leaguer position. With this information passed on, the troops take out their sleeping kit for later and then go over the vehicle and ensure it is ready to go when the convoy rolls out.

A convoy brief is called for all the drivers and crew commanders so there are no problems if situations and emergencies arise. Lt Robb and Cpl Sit are in attendance along with Lt Behiels and his driver, Cpl Scott. 31 Delta and 31 Echo sections are given the night off as this is primarily a recce for commanders. Though it may only be commanders at the brief, the convoy is considerably long with about 12 vehicles consisting of both LAVs and G-Wagons.

With the convoy brief concluded, Maj Wright, OC of A Company, states that he'll go with the engineers in 31 Alpha's vehicle.

The sky is dark when the convoy musters into its order-of-march. There is an A Company LAV in front of 31 Alpha which is then followed by an ambulance Bison and then 32 Alpha's LAV which is followed by an artillery LAV. The crews are in their positions when the communications check is performed followed by the short wait until it is time to step off.

The engineer sections that will be staying behind are pulling down their sleeping kit as they have been told they won't be going out tonight on the recce.

Cpl Huard from 31 Delta and Spr Jaworski from 31 Echo aren't as lucky. Selected by WO Rouzes, they are now in the back of 31 Alpha LAV with Jaworski taking the driver side air-sentry with his C9 machine gun while Maj Wright stands in WO Rouzes' position as the passenger side air-sentry with his C7A2 rifle. Fixing his headset on under his helmet, he gains comms with the vehicle and the convoy. WO Rouzes sits beside the Major, smoking cigarettes waiting for the convoy commander to order everyone to move out.

The command finally comes to move out, and the convoy rolls forward towards the front of Patrol Base Wilson. Heading down the short road towards Hwy 1, the lead vehicle hits the highway first and makes the left turn while the vehicles at the rear of the convoy are just starting to move. One by one, the vehicles roll onto the highway and pick up speed, heading towards Ambush Alley.

Back at the Patrol Base Wilson, Sugrim is listening to his iPod and finishing up cleaning his pistol. The convoy is now out of the patrol base and from what he can hear, they have all moved down towards the highway. Looking around with his red headlamp, he searches for the cleaning rag that he had set down. When he looks up again, he sees the highway, down near Ambush Alley being lit up with dancing red tracer fire.

"AMBUSH RIGHT!"

The radios squawk with battle chatter as the lead vehicles come under effective enemy fire up the road. The convoy commander had just finished telling the convoy over the radio that they were approaching Ambush Alley when the first rounds started impacting the lead vehicles. Lt Robb is standing in the crew commander position in the turret, looking down the road with his Night Vision Goggles mounted, while Loder, hearing that they were approaching Ambush Alley has closed his hatch and scans the view in the turret. The tracers are bright green flares on Lt Robb's goggles and he watches as they impact the vehicles and ricochet off in different directions.

"Ambush right," he passes on over the vehicles intercom to the guys in the back, giving the heads-up to the air sentries.

They push forward and within seconds, the first rounds impact 31

Alpha LAV and more rounds whiz by over the top. Maj Wright is the air sentry on the ambush side and is looking for targets to shoot. Inside the turret, Loder has already rotated his 25mm cannon to the right and is looking through his thermal sight for insurgents.

"If you see something Loder, take it out!" Robb says over the intercom after flipping up his Night Vision Goggles and sitting down in the turret. Lt Robb tries to look through the thermals but his Night Vision Goggles are giving him a hard time, banging off equipment mounted above the thermal sight.

Explosions erupt throughout the convoy as the vehicles continue down Ambush Alley towards the bridge crossing the Arghandab River. Neither Loder nor Lt Robb is fazed, continuing forward scanning for targets as the rounds impact on the convoy.

Further back in the convoy, behind a Bison Ambulance, Lt Behiels and his men are in the 32 Alpha LAV, racing forward in the convoy. Behind them is the artillery LAV, Golf 23, with the Forward Observation Officer in the back calling in the coordinates of the ambush and for potential impact areas for a bombardment.

32 Alpha continues to race forward amongst the dance of flying lead as round after round of Rocket Propelled Grenade is launched with a *boom* and flies towards its target. Cracking explosions are heard as the Rocket Propelled Grenades impact on the ground to the left of the convoy, missing their marks as they fly over or between the vehicles. The occasional Rocket Propelled Grenade falls short and impacts on the ambush side of the road, while others fly off relatively harmlessly, as the round has not had enough flight time to properly arm itself.

Lt Behiels looks for targets through his Night Vision Goggles while standing in the crew commander hatch of his turret, with his head out just enough to see over the periscopes.

He sees them. Running from the roadside are a number of men who moments earlier were firing on the convoy. Lt Behiels, still standing in the turret, reaches down and grabs the control grip. He aims the turret in the direction of the running insurgents and shouts down to Spr King.

"Get 'em!" he shouts. King doesn't hesitate and, focusing on the running insurgents, he begins to open fire and one by one, the 25mm High Explosive rounds leave the barrel and rip towards their target.

At the same time, further ahead in the convoy in 31 Alpha LAV, Loder and Lt Robb are looking for insurgents. Loder, seeing some targets down range from their vehicle, switches to his co-axial 7.62mm machine gun and depressing the trigger, the gun lets out a *thunk* and dies.

Loder looks up from his thermal sights at the gun and then over to Lt Robb who is standing. "Stoppage!" he yells up to the Lieutenant, reaching over to try and re-cock the weapon.

Lt Robb hears Loder and looks down from the turret hatch. Ducking down with his Night Vision Goggles still mounted on his helmet, he reaches forward and grabs the cocking handle of the co-ax. Giving a tug, he manages to re-cock the machine gun and watches Loder as he gives it another shot.

Thunk The C6 co-ax jams yet again and no shots are fired.

"Switch to HEI-T!" Lt Robb yells down to Loder who is already switching weapons. The C6 co-ax has been giving troops trouble already in the LAVs, jamming for various reasons and forcing gunners to use up their 25mm rounds. Loder has no hesitation and having switched weapons, he looks back through his sights and lets loose with several of the explosive rounds while Lt Robb ducks down in the turret to look for insurgents with Loder through the thermals.

Almost immediately they see another insurgent and through the continuing communications chatter over the radio, Lt Robb gives the quick order. "Go ahead," he says.

Loder, having already brought the target into line, squeezes his trigger and with a metallic clunk, the 25mm is fired. Round after round leave the barrel of the turret and fly supersonic towards their target scoring a direct hit. Through the sights, Loder watches as a round hits the insurgent square in the chest. There is a slight *pop* heard as the arms, head and legs explode in different directions, the torso being blown into tiny fragments across the slightly vegetated area.

Lt Robb stops looking through the thermals and stands up once more and flipping down his Night Vision Goggles, he continues to sight insurgents. Looking closer to the LAV, he searches for insurgents who may be too close for Loder to hit, while he also keeps an eye on the position of the turret. During a battle, it is fairly easy for a gunner to lose track of the position of his or her turret as they concentrate on the targets. In Battle Override mode, the turret can manoeuvre 360 degrees and strike an air-sentry troop standing out of one of the two hatches in the rear.

In the drivers hatch, Cpl Sit is concentrating hard on keeping up with the convoy and keeping the LAV on the road. The vehicles are constantly speeding up and slowing down, the convoy lengthening and shortening up as drivers deal with the threats ahead. Sit sees the brake lights of the LAV in front switch on and slows the 31 Alpha LAV through the ambush.

Loder continues to fire and his thoughts are broken when he catches the last part of something said over the radio. "... We have a casualty! Pri-One!" the voice says over the distinct sound of a G-Wagon engine.

Not stopping, Loder continues to look for targets and opens fire into the field to the right. Back in 32 Alpha LAV behind the Bison ambulance, Lt Behiels and Spr King searching for insurgents as their vehicle slows slightly with the rest of the convoy. They hear the casualty report come over the radio and hearing that it is a G-Wagon, they know how far up the convoy the G-Wagon is driving. Reports continue and Lt Behiels hears that the.50-calibre machine gunner in the G-Wagon's turret was hit in the helmet, but the bullet had ricocheted into his eye taking him out of the fight.

Concentrating on the surrounding area, Lt Behiels and Spr King spot insurgents moving along a wall towards the road up ahead. The LAV continues forward and the two watch, as the insurgents appear to aim Rocket Propelled Grenades at the convoy, specifically at the Bison Ambulance. This vehicle, however, is currently undefended as the crew are all hatches down. The crew commander is not able to man the C6 pintle-mounted machine gun above his hatch and the Bison is less well-armoured than the LAV. King and Behiels process this instantly, and as the Bison continues to roll towards the awaiting ambush, they begin levelling their turret on the group of insurgents and Behiels gives the order to open fire.

The first round fires and the chain gun expels the casing through the ejection port at the front of the turret and a new round is chambered and fired. The rounds hit the insurgents before they can fire. Some rounds strike the wall, and the remaining two insurgents are peppered with hot shrapnel seconds before they are hit themselves. The exploding 25mm rounds send sparks in all directions, lighting up the area with beautiful but deadly sparkles.

Back in Patrol Base Wilson, 31 Delta is gathered behind their vehicle watching the display. Glaring red tracer rounds dance towards the convoy in the distance and some hit their mark and bounce of the armour and fly off in a different direction, floating high into the sky before their red phosphorus is expended and the rounds' trailing red glow fades. Red tracers are exchanged between the vehicles and the insurgents, the large and bright red tracers of the 25mm rounds sailing straight and fast towards their targets, dwarfing the 7.62mm rounds impacting on their hulls.

"That is an amazing amount of rounds," Foulds says to no one in particular as they watch the exchange of fire. Rounds are ricocheting off hulls and sailing in all directions. A few rounds impact on the hulls of the last two vehicles and change their trajectory towards the patrol base, flying high into the sky and disappearing as the tracer burns out.

"All right everyone, into the LAV," Sgt Grignon says, moving close to the ramp. "Those rounds are coming this way and I don't want to take any pointless risks," he continues. The troops of 31 Delta take seats inside the LAV and wait, hearing the distant firefight and the distinct explosions of artillery. The shots are distinct and if close enough to the trajectory, the whistling or whizzing sound is something out of a movie.

Down the road in the ambush at the rear of the convoy, call sign Golf 23, an artillery LAV, is giving coordinates about 300 meters behind their vehicle to fire for effect.

The rounds whistle in and the ground explodes, shredding remaining insurgents to pieces. Few will be able to survive the bombardment that continues behind the convoy and the ambush area to the right being pounded by the 155mm High Explosive rounds.

In 31 Alpha LAV, Loder continues to engage targets while Lt Robb stands in his hatch and monitors the position of the turret while searching for targets close to the convoy. Rounds continue to be fired on the convoy while the occasional boom of a Rocket Propelled Grenade is heard.

Loder finds another insurgent and swings the turret to the right, tracking his target for the shot. The LAV continues to move forward and the computer keeps Loder's aim centred. Up top, Lt Robb watches as the barrel continues to creep closer to Maj Wright who is standing in the right air sentry hatch closest to the ambush.

Over the intercom, Lt Robb clicks in and gives the air sentries the heads up. "Air sentries," he says over the crackling wind, "Let me know if the turret gets too close to you." Clicking out, he continues to monitor the area around him as tracer-fire continues to sail by the vehicles in what seems like another tough ambush area ahead.

Loder waits and continues to track, confirming if the thermal image is indeed an insurgent. The turret continues to move to the right and within seconds now has crept to the point where the muzzle of the 25mm cannon is now beside the Major. Lt Robb, sensing that Loder's' shot is now too close to the Major, goes to tell him to watch his arc but it is too late.

Confirming his target, Loder squeezes the trigger on the control grip and lets out a burst from the 25mm cannon. The blast is muffled inside the turret but at the end of the barrel where the Major's head is barely two feet to the right, the blast is overwhelming. Maj Wright drops within the LAV, not hit by the round but by the concussion and sheer sound of the blast.

Grabbing the Major, WO Rouzes shakes him vigorously and looking into his face, asks him if he is all right. Spr Jaworski, who is watching the rear and left side of the road, is oblivious to Maj Wright's predicament and continues to cover his arcs with his trusty C9. Warrant Rouzes, still dealing with the Major, hits Jaworski in the leg.

"GO!" he yells up to Jaworski who is looking down through the hatch at the Warrant. He nods his head and sweeping his C9 over to the right, covers Maj Wrights' arcs.

Within seconds he has sighted-in on a target and taking his C9 off safe, he pumps round after round into an insurgent who drops lifeless to the ground. Still firing, he shifts arcs and continues to open up at targets, sending a stream of lead towards the enemy while surveying the area.

Coming close to the end of his box of ammunition, he signals below that he needs ammo.

"Huard," the Warrant yells, "C9 ammo!"

Spr Huard reaches into the storage area behind the cargo nets of the LAV and grabs another box of ammo while Jaworski continues to fire, the muzzle flashes lighting up the inside of the LAV.

Meanwhile, Maj Wright, coming to with his senses, realizes that he is no longer standing in the air-sentry hatch and that no one has taken his position – not realizing that Jaworski is now facing right. Moving over on the bench, he moves to stand up and is beginning to stand up in his hatch when the Warrant grabs him and pulls him down. Pointing to the Major's air sentry hatch, he indicates the muzzle flashes that belong to Jaworski's C9. The rounds are flying over the hatch where seconds before the Major was about to put his head.

The convoy continues forward and Jaworski, with a new box of ammo, continues to belch lead at anything suspicious.

Loder is sweeping his arcs for more targets when the radio chatter is again interrupted.

"We have a Pri-one casualty... zap number to follow," the radio continues with, yet again, the familiar sound of a G-Wagons engine in the background.

Loder continues to shoot at suspicious rooftops where insurgents are positioned while back in the 32 Alpha LAV, Lt Behiels and Spr King continue to search for targets.

After what seems like an eternity, there are no more tracers and the fight is over. All that is heard is the sound of artillery impacting in the distance behind the convoy as a fire mission continues at the ambush areas.

At Patrol Base Wilson, Sgt Grignon has let his troops leave the LAV as he sees that the ambush is over and except for the artillery barrage, there are no further shots fired. Getting out their sleeping gear, the members of 31 Delta continue to bed down after the long interruption, knowing that they will be required to pull a gate duty at some point in the night.

The convoy is now over the Arghandab River when it is instructed by Lt Redburn, commander of A Company's 1 Platoon that they will detour to 2 Corps, the Afghan National Army contingent in Kandahar so they can evacuate the casualties and fix the numerous flat tires sustained in the ambush.

Pulling up towards a darkened soccer field, the vehicles move in a large circle and come to a stop taking up an all-around defence to provide 360 degrees of cover. One by one, the ramps drop and the troops step out for some fresh air and to inspect the damage to their vehicles.

Lt Robb is in the 31 Alpha turret and looks over at Loder. There is a silence for a short while as they process what they have just done. "I need you to re-bomb your ammo, submit an ammo cas (a verbal or written statement of how much ammunition has been expended) to me then see if you can't pull all the spent link and brass off the vehicle," Lt Robb says. Loder understands and gets to work while Lt Robb pulls off his headset and pushes himself out of his crew commander's hatch.

Outside, WO Rouzes is over with the medics who are circled around the first casualty who took a ricochet to his eye. Maj Wright asks WO Rouzes to get the vitals on the casualties so he can submit a 9-liner for medical evacuation. The medics, however, ask WO Rouzes to grab bags from the back of their Bison ambulance so they can continue providing first-aid.

WO Rouzes runs from the back of the Bison Ambulance and back to the medics three times before getting the vitals on the first casualty.

Back at 31 Alpha LAV, the crew are re-bombing and throwing the empty ammo tins in the field. Watching the events, Maj Wright is waiting on WO Rouzes to report in with the casualty's vital signs.

WO Rouzes, has moved with the medics over to the second casualty. He is finally able to get his vitals and scribbling them down on his small notepad, he runs back to Maj Wright and delivers the information. Maj Wright, still in communication with the Battle Group Command Post, passes on the information so that a Black Hawk helicopter is soon dispatched.

Cpl Sit has just conducted a driver's inspection on the LAV and is having a cigarette when Lt Robb tells him that he has to raise the ramp on the LAV so they can take their spare tire off the back.

With WO Rouzes beside him, Lt Robb does a quick count of flat tires in the convoy and returns to his LAV. A group of infantry have already taken the spare tire off the back of 31 Alpha LAV and have replaced it with their own flat, happy to be rid of it.

Over twenty more minutes pass until they hear the distant patter of helicopters. Difficult to spot with the naked eye against the dark sky, they come in close and within minutes a Black Hawk is preparing to land in the circle of LAVs while a Dutch AH-64 Apache helicopter circles overhead as outrider.

Within 10 minutes the casualties are loaded onto the Black Hawk and it takes off, the Apache circling one last time before beginning its escort duty back to Kandahar Airfield. The medics grab their bags and move back to their ambulances while the rest of the troops prepare to mount back up in their vehicles. The recce of the potential leaguer is still on despite the one-hour delay at 2 Corps and Lt Redburn has the vehicles pull out to head down towards the Panjwaii District Centre.

The convoy pulls out of 2 Corps without problems, leaving empty ammo tins behind. They head down the main road towards the District Centre without any inconvenience and Loder scans his arcs.

An hour of driving passes and the convoy pulls off the road to the right. Circling around once again, the vehicles form an all-round defence and drop their ramps, the troops exiting into the hot night air to prepare their beds. There would be no further work tonight.

A sentry list is drawn up to take shifts in the turret to keep watch while the rest of the section sleeps. Everyone in 31 Alpha has to pull a shift and everyone is eager to get to sleep.

Lt Robb is getting ready to go to sleep but stops and talks to WO Rouzes about the day. The troops did well, he believes, and they talk about how they reacted to the ambush. Finally, one by one they get some shut-eye. The remainder of their work would be done tomorrow. Lt Robb sleeps well through the night, not having any problems with his sentry shift or waking up tired.

Spr Loder isn't the same. Having fired over sixty rounds of 25mm, he has destroyed numerous targets and watched as he landed direct hits on three insurgents. Still pumped up and believing they would be attacked, his sleep is restless.

Spr Jaworski's life is now permanently different having engaged multiple targets as enemy bullets flew all around him.

Back at Patrol Base Wilson, Cpl Sugrim and Cpl McEachren are on gate duty together. They walk around the area and ensure that no unauthorized vehicles or people approach the gate. Flanked by observation posts they had built earlier in August on top of the Afghan National Police and Afghan National Army buildings, they look off into the distance where the enemy waits.

"My goggles are fucked up," Sugrim says to McEachren, playing with the focus dial, "the thing won't focus." McEachren watches Sugrim try fixing his Night Vision Goggles and then give up. "So, any plans for leave?" Sugrim asks, looking out towards the mountain of Ma'sum Ghar.

"Yeah," replies McEachren. "Gonna go visit someplace nice with my wife. Some place far from here."

"That sounds nice," Sugrim says, looking down at his watch. "Almost time to wake up the next guys."

McEachren looks at his watch and then back out the gate. "I wonder what we're doing tomorrow?"

ATTACK ON FOB MARTELLO

Cpl Austin

"I fought them off with a single bayonet and half a grenade."
— *Sgt Coates*

While fighting continues down in the Panjwaii District, Sgt Coates and three of his soldiers from 32 Echo are up in the mountains at FOB Martello supporting operations with Dutch forces. Coates, a former British soldier from 59 Commando has fought previously, in the Falkland Islands in the spring and summer of 1982. He has been tested in combat and carries the scar of a bullet wound in his right leg as proof. Born in Durham County in northeast England, Coates is known for his English accent and wit. He and his troops now spend their days at Martello improving defensive positions and making life better for the troops by building structures like the tri-station toilets, much to the delight of the Dutch. Three other Canadians are present besides Sgt Coates's engineers, and each has his own role in the camp, from cooking to working the fuel pumps.

The alarm goes off at 6:30 am signalling to the guys it is time to start work. 6:30 am is a normal time to rise for any troop, and today isn't any different. They work until the Sgt tells them to shut it down for the day. They have worked fairly hard recently, completing their three-toilet shitter, nicknamed the 'Drop Zone,' and were moving on to reinforcing the bunkers at the Observation Posts

One by one, each troop starts to stir and then sits up on top of their cots. Sgt Coates is the first up. "Morning, pumpkin," Coates greets his troops, putting on his uniform. Even in the mountains it is very hot. FOB Martello is at a much higher altitude than the Panjwaii district where the bulk of the Canadian troops are so it is arguably harder to breathe, while sharing the same 50-degree heat in the daytime.

Each troop puts on his kit and starts breaking into the morning Individual Meal Packages. Beans and Wieners is a big hit amongst the troops as well as Sausage and Hash Browns. No one really likes the Omelette with

Salsa, with unopened boxes of them seen around all the FOBs.

The group continues on with the morning activities of breakfast, washing and shaving. The group then disperses to some personal tasks like the checking of e-mails or making phone calls back to Canada while Coates goes up to the Command Post to find out the daily news from his higher-ups back at Kandahar Airfield.

Marcus, one of Coates's men finishes checking his email. A 27-year-old with a shaved head, Marcus joined the forces to escape from British Columbia, and especially from his hometown of New Westminster. His father's family came from Holland and his mother's from Canada. The Dutch personality and accent can both be detected at times. Walking back to their tent, he finds Coates has already returned from the Command Post and is clearly shaken.

Looking at his troops Coates says, "Shane's dead." The tent is silent as his words sink in. "He was killed attacking from the south in Panjwaii," he continues.

Everyone remains silent. Sgt Shane Stachnik has been a friend to all of them, Coates having known him for a considerable length of time. Now he is gone.

With the morning routine complete, Sgt Coates takes a look at the tasks that need to be completed for the day and, considering the terrible news he has just passed on, realizes that he has to take control of the shaken troops.

"All right, we're gonna continue work on the bunker we started yesterday," he states to his group. The bunker that they are working on is located directly across from the large modular tent they sleep in, one in a series of three tents close to the command post. Taking a right when leaving their tent takes you down to several rows of tents, reserved mostly for the infantry. Martello is built in what seems like the bottom of a taco, surrounded by mountains much like *Dien Bien Phu,* the French outpost overrun by the Viet Minh in 1956. On his Tactical Reconnaissance a couple of months ago, the Squadron OC, nicknamed the place 'FOB Bob,' borrowing a line from the movie *Platoon* when one of the American sergeants presages ominous times ahead, telling his Platoon Sergeant, "I got a bad feeling about this one, Bob. Come on Bob, you got to get me on a bird out of here."

They grab the equipment needed, already laid out on the ground from the work yesterday. Heading over to the Observation Post, the troops pass the new shitter they have just built, with its burning refuse in the half-cut barrels belching out a long line of black smoke which streams into the air.

"A magnificent shitter," Sgt Coates remarks as they walk past the Drop Zone.

"Magical," Marcus adds, laughing. The men pass the shitters and the washboard stations where clothes can be washed the old-fashioned way. Arriving at the Observation Post, they take a break to have a smoke and look out through the large openings in the bunker. Dutch troops have been busy writing graffiti inside the bunker, down the tables and even on the ceiling. Shifts can be pretty long at an Observation Post and no doubt, the Dutch troops are bored.

Finishing their Colt mini-cigars, the team gets to work with the empty sandbags they have brought over. The bunker is integrated into the two-story Hesco wall that stands over 4 metres tall. Though it is reasonably well constructed, the openings for the troops to observe the mountainside are far too large, increasing the odds that a Rocket Propelled Grenade round could impact inside. It is for this reason that Coates and his troops are now filling over a hundred sandbags.

Taking a few breaks during the work, the sappers finally fill the last sandbag needed and Coates eyes out the positioning. Each sandbag has to be laid in a position interlocking another, adding support to the overall sandbag wall. Deciding on the best plan, they get started and within an hour manage to close the gaps in the bunker.

Sgt Coates stands back from the bunker and takes a look at the finished work. "Looking pretty sexy," he says to the boys who are standing around him.

"Pretty nice," one of them adds. "You'd have to be a moron to rush this."

Thompson laughs, "Well, have you seen some of the Taliban? They're using small arms on LAVs, gunner's just gotta rotate his turret and blow them away."

"Yeah," Marcus quips in, "they're definitely not brilliant."

Coates jumps into the conversation and tells everyone it's time for lunch. They have been working on and off in the heat for the last five hours and it is now approaching noon. Turning, they start their walk back to their tent, carrying the shovels and unused sandbags. On their way, they see to their right that the dog handler was out playing fetch with his black lab search dog. Dog handlers are frequently employed in camps outside of Kandahar Airfield to sniff out explosives and gunpowder. With their powerful sense of smell, they find the faintest bit of residue on an individual and let the handler know.

Back at the tent, they grab some seats from inside, where it has become quite hot, and sit out in front, grabbing some rations to eat for lunch. They relax and talk about the attack that happened a couple of days ago down in Panjwaii, where Op Medusa was taking place. They talk about the fight; the bombing that was happening and the artillery being used. Finally they talk about Sgt Shane Stachnik, their friend who was now gone.

With lunch over, Coates tells them that they are taking the rest of the day off for administration, a joke from back on base when troops are let off early to "sort out personal admin." They all relax with some of them reading and smoking Colts.

A few hours pass and the sun now starts to crest the mountain and cast a growing shadow on Martello. With the shadow comes a welcome change in temperature, giving relief to the sweating troops in the camp. Marcus is over talking to the Dutch troops about the A-10 attack on the Canadian troops. They tell him that during the earlier stages of the current war in Iraq, stuff like that happened almost daily.

"How the hell does that happen?" he asks the three Dutch troops in front of the tent.

"Sometimes pilots make mistakes," one replies.

Marcus walks back to the tent and relaxes with the others out front when a Dutch padre comes up to them. "Hey guys," he says, "how are you all doing?" The Dutch padre had been asked by the Canadian command in Kandahar Airfield to talk to Coates and his men, as they knew Stachnik was a good friend to them.

"Hey Padre, we're doing all right," replies Coates.

The Padre takes a seat with the group and starts talking about Stachnik. He asks how well the troops knew him and goes on to talk about death and life, a discussion to help the grief. The group is discussing this topic and how great a guy he was when their conversation is cut short by an odd sound.

Snap

They look around wondering what it is, hearing it come from the Hesco behind their tent.

*Snap*Snap*

"What the fuck is that?" Coates asks the guys. The Padre has stopped mid-sentence and looks at the Hesco as well. Five metres in front of where the troops were sitting there is an impact in the sand, sending up a small plume of dust.

"Oh shit!" Thompson yells, grabbing Coates by the shoulder and pointing to far ridge of the mountain across from the front of their tent. There on the ridge beside the lone tree named "Joshua Tree," are small white flashes coming from a number of places, followed by the occasional *snap* in the Hesco behind their tent.

"Get to cover!" Coates yells as the troops get up and go to run inside.

Snap

Dutch troops are yelling all around the camp and running to positions as more rifle fire comes from the ridge. Up at the Observation Post closest to where the firebase has opened up on the camp, the Dutch troops have run to their posts to return fire against the insurgents.

As Coates and his men run into their tent, behind them up at the Observation Post they can hear the battle start. The Dutch machine guns start opening up on the ridge with an intermixed "ta-ta-ta." The insurgents are still firing into the camp, trying to hit the command post which is located behind the Hesco which they hit instead, when the Dutch fire on them. Coming under attack, they change their target to the Observation Post and a fierce exchange of bullets begins.

Inside the tent, Coates and his men run for their cots where their kit is placed. Grabbing their armour and vests, they drop to the ground as the gunfire outside is picking up.

"Stay on the ground and put on your shit!" Coates yells at his troops from his cot. "Get out through the back and take cover behind the gennies!" The "gennies" or generators were trailer-mounted and towed to where they were needed. Operating on diesel, they were not extraordinarily loud but did need refuelling regularly. In Martello, they sat behind Coates's tent, powering most of the camp.

Coates is kneeling down beside his cot, putting on his armour when Thompson runs out the back of the tent. He grabs his helmet and tactical vest and runs after Thompson when he hears a "humph" from behind. Stopping to look back he sees Marcus trip and drop to the ground. Hitting the floor, Marcus then rolls under a cot to take cover.

"Marcus!" Coates yells back to him. "Unless that cot's bullet-proof, get your ass outside!" Marcus jumps to his feet with his kit on and continues out the rear.

Outside, the insurgents have started taking aim with their Rocket Propelled Grenades. With a loud "boom," a one misses the Observation Post and, curving to the right impacts at the front gate, sending a plume of sand through the air.

Marcus runs outside to take shelter behind the genny. Dutch mortar men who had been working out in the gym join them from where they watch the attack. The leader of the group yells out to Coates that they need to get over to their mortars. Coates understands and tries to figure out how they can get across. Looking around, his eyes come to rest on their G-Wagon parked beside their tent and he moves closer to Thompson who is crouched beside him. Thompson, meanwhile, is scouring the ground.

"What are you looking for?" Coates yells at Thompson who then looks up at Coates.

"My cigar!" he replies, upset.

From the enemy position, an insurgent takes aim again with a Rocket Propelled Grenade and pulls the trigger, letting off another one at the Observation Post. It smashes low into the dirt just in front, spraying rocks and dirt.

"Thompson," Coates shouts, "you need to take the G-Wagon and get these men to their tubes over at the artillery tent."

Thompson understands what is needed and looks over at the G-Wagon, the not-too-distant artillery tent and then at the four mortar men huddling behind the two gennies. "Alright," he says and looks up at the battle raging on over at the ridgeline.

For a second, everyone at the gennies stop, watch and listen as another "boom" is heard as a Rocket Propelled Grenade sails down to the Observation Post. It shifts right and flies at the front gate again, exploding in a black cloud of smoke and sand. Returning tracer fire leaves the Observation Post, coming from the machine gun positioned there. With every few tracers firing out, a few fly back in reply.

Their attention switches to the South African dog handler who runs out of his tent and around the side to a parked RG-31 vehicle with his dog in tow. He stops, throws open the back door with a large heave and then grabs his labrador whose tail is wagging excitedly. Lifting his dog up, he pushes it in the back and then jumps inside, closing and locking the door behind him.

"Ok," shouts Thompson for everyone to hear, "I'm gonna take you four guys across to your mortars. Get in that truck!" Thompson points at the G-Wagon. Not moving, the mortar men just look at each other.

Finally one speaks up, "I'm not getting in that... it doesn't have armour!"

Thompson is already standing, getting ready to go when he turns back to reassure them, "Yes it does. It has armour - trust me."

"I don't know," another hesitates, "it doesn't look armoured."

Thompson is getting upset when Coates takes control of the situation. "Listen," Coates jumps in, "You can sit around here or you can get a lift and go kill some Taliban."

The Dutch soldiers think about it for a second and then run to the G-Wagon with Thompson. Thompson opens the driver door and the four pile into the back, squishing together on the two seats. Thompson guns the engine and the G-Wagon flies across the open space to the artillery tent. Arriving, they jump out and run over to their tubes, then just as quickly take cover, realizing their mortars are exposed to enemy fire.

Thompson throws the G-Wagon into reverse and guns it back across the open area to park back beside their tent. Shutting off the engine, he throws open the door and runs back behind the genny alongside Coates.

"Their mortars are exposed to the enemy," Thompson says to Coates over the rumble of the genny and the constant gunfire.

"Well," Coates replies, "I guess they won't be firing much for now."

Up on the ridge behind Coates's tent, three Dutch armoured vehicles rotate their 30mm turrets around to face the opposite ridgeline. Sighting in the insurgents through the crosshairs, they join the firefight with a loud "pom-pom-pom," firing 30mm exploding rounds, which chew up the ridge and smashing rocks. The insurgents terrorized by this powerful gunfire stop shooting and take cover.

Seizing the chance, the mortar men run over to their tubes and start positioning them to fire on the ridge. Raising their elevation, they set them to bear down on the ridgeline and under the order of "Fire!" they start dropping mortar rounds into their tubes. With a "toonk," the projectiles shoot out into the air, visible to anyone watching them leave. They fly high and close, hitting their max altitude and then begin to fall towards the ridgeline.

Finally with a "crack," they explode with a small flash consumed by black smoke.

On the ridge behind Coates, the 30mm cannons roar across the mountains. The vehicles start to move, taking better firing positions as they continue to pin down the insurgents.

Coates's men realize that something is happening at the back gate when a machine gun in the rear Observation Post starts opening up. Outside of the rear gate are the ranges for troops to hone their gun-fighting skills. Unknown to the camp's defenders, the insurgents had managed to sneak through these ranges and had now initiated an attack on the back gate.

"Fuck, we're getting attacked from two sides," Thompson says to no one in particular. His attention on the rear gate is redirected where there is an explosion to the right of the Observation Post closest to the ridge.

"Did they fall short on that one?" Thompson asks, wondering if their friends at the mortar tubes had misjudged. There is another explosion to the right of the same Observation Post, except this time closer to the large Hesco perimeter of the camp. The guys look at the mortar tubes and at the explosions and notice that the timing had been considerably off. A third explosion erupts, even closer to the perimeter than the last two. The insurgents must have a mortar tube of their own somewhere nearby. As well, there had to be an observer who was helping the insurgent mortar crew walk the rounds into the camp.

Coates looks at the black smoke and dust as it starts to blow away. "They're not close at all," he says. "They're wasting rounds."

At the rear gate, the insurgents have started their attack on the Observation Post, clearly underestimating the effectiveness of the machine gun housed inside.

"It sounds like one hell of a battle is happening at the back gate," Coates exclaims.

"Yeah," Thompson adds, "and look there," pointing up at the corner of the camp up on the ridge behind their tent.

Hidden away on the hill behind and to the right of Coates's tent, tucked into the corner of the camp was a Dutch Armoured Personnel Carrier with a .50-calibre turret-mounted machine gun on top (known as a 50-Cal or a Fifty). Having heard the firefight start up, a gunner immediately poked up through the gunner's hatch and was now grasping the 50-Cal by its two handles at the rear and rotating the turret with his foot pedals. The vehicle starts to move backward, as it was facing outward, and starts to pull away from the run-up position in which it had been sitting. It turns around to take a better firing position at the distant ridgeline, the turret gunner opens fire. The Armoured Personnel Carrier then rolls down the hill and takes up a firing position behind the back gate, engaging the dozen insurgents left in the open.

Coates, seeing that the Observation Posts are being attacked, decides that the Dutch may need more men to man the positions. Looking over to Thompson, he says, "I'm going up to the Command Post, I'll be right back!" Thompson nods and then holds up his hand signalling "stop" to the other troops who watch as Coates gets up and starts running along the side of the Hesco protecting the Command Post, and up the hill. The rear gate still rings with 50-Cal fire as the Dutch continue to mop up the situation and the 30mm cannons and mortars pound the ridge.

Running up the hill in full kit, Coates turns into the Command Post compound. Racing around to the front, he enters and is greeted with multiple radios blaring with sitreps and information from higher. Men are working on computers and some are operating the radios while the commander stands looking at a large map of the FOB.

"Sir," Coates says to the commander.

The commander looks at Coates and replies. "Sgt Coates, what's up?"

"Sir," Coates replies, "my engineers are down behind our tents and we can help man an Observation Post if you need it."

The Dutch commander is thankful for the offer, but thinks the situation is under control. "Thanks for the offer, Sgt Coates," he says, "you can bring your troops up here in case we need you."

"Yes Sir," Coates responds, turning to leave. He leaves and starts the run back down behind the generators. Turning the corner and sees that his troops are still crouched down watching the firefights.

"What's up?" Thompson asks Coates who is slightly winded.

Coates looks over the scene and then at Thompson. "We're moving up to the Command Post," he informs them. The four troops get up and, with Coates leading, make the dash up the hill to the Command Post behind the thick Hesco. Arriving inside they take a position against the Hesco wall and sit down. Coates runs into the Command Post and lets the commander know they are in his position and then returns back to his troops who are relaxing, listening to the firefight in the distance.

Coates walks over to the troops and starts taking off his tac-vest. "Alright guys," Coates says, "you can kit-down to your armour." The troops respond and lay their rifles against the Hesco. It is much cooler as the sun has set. The troops are no longer sweating but their kit is still wet, making for a cold chill.

"Well," someone pipes up, "this has been an exciting day so far."

"It's not done yet," Thompson replies, looking back at the Dutch vehicles. They continue to sit and wait until a fighter plane buzzes low over the FOB and ridge, looping up high into the air.

The Dutch Sergeant-Major comes out of his tent just in time to see the plane fly over into the distance.

"Our planes are here now and say we have scared off all the insurgents," he says. "They left a lot of their equipment behind so they will shoot at their kit." Marcus finds this funny and starts laughing as the Sergeant-Major goes back inside the Command Post just as a distant "boom" is heard.

The shots have begun to die off, and there is no more movement of vehicles on the ridge as the mortar tubes are now silent. Sitting against the Hesco, the troops' attention is brought back to the fight when the South African dog handler runs around the side of Hesco clearly out of shape and breath.

"Hey chief," Coates says, greeting him as he comes close, "we saw you shot-put your dog into the RG... where's the pup?"

"Fuck this shit... fuck this shit," he says, clearly distraught and out of breath. He bends over with his hands on his knees, "I didn't sign up for this shit."

"Little fuzzy today, wasn't it?" Coates says to him, offering him a bottle of water, which he takes. The handler looks down at the ground bent over, "I've spent a year in Iraq... I didn't sign up for this shit." His dog is still in the RG-31 down below, protected by it's thick armour while the handler takes a seat beside the soldiers.

Night falls and the sun dies behind the mountains. The stars are becoming visible and are bright pricks of light. Everything is pitch dark though, until the moon appears. Coates looks at his watch, then over at the silent Dutch vehicles. Their guns have been quiet now for over an hour but their turrets still sway left to right, right to left, surveying and keeping watch over the ridge. A couple of the vehicles have made their way back up to their run-up positions to keep sentry on the other side of the FOB just in case the insurgents might try another offensive.

"Okay guys," Coates says, getting their attention. "In pairs, go down to the tent and grab any kit you need. We'll be sleeping up here tonight."

Marcus is the first to go, followed by Coates and Thompson. Grabbing sleeping bags to act as makeshift mattresses, they start to bed down up at the Command Post. Marcus has his air mattress and is letting it auto-inflate when he looks over to Coates.

"Hey Sarge," he offers, "I'll share my air-mattress with you if you want."

Coates sees him smiling through the darkness, "No, Marcus, but thanks."

"You can kit-down including armour," Coates adds once they are all together at the Command Post, "but keep your armour and kit close by."

Spreading out their sleeping bags and taking off their kit, they all look up when Thompson is finished laying down his sleeping bag. "Aww shit," Thompson exclaims.

"What's wrong?" Coates questions, leaning over to look at what Thompson is staring at.

"Well," Thompson says, "at least I found my cigar." Holding up his cigar, he points to his sleeping bag and indicates where his cigar must have landed when he ran through the tent. It has burned a hole through the top layer and a bit of the insulation, leaving a burnt plastic ring.

As the moon slowly begins to rise over the mountains, the dog handler starts to bed down beside the engineers. The day had been long and eventful, the air filled with both tension and bullets. One by one they fall asleep. Time moves on and the moon rises high in the sky. Where it had been pitch black only a few hours earlier, the ground is bathed in soft light and the temperature has dropped to a strange cold. Time ticks away, and with it yesterday's incident, as the ground surrenders its heat to the sky.

At around 3:00 am, Coates and Marcus are awoken for sentry shift. For about an hour, nothing is seen and once 4:00 am approaches they are relieved and both bed down again for the remaining hours.

Slowly, the sun fights the moon, and on the horizon the yellow hues of another random day begin to rise.

Sgt Coates is the first up and lights a Colt cigar. It wasn't the best sleep, but it felt good to get some rest. Today they are going to be heading back to Kandahar Airfield and he is a little excited that they will be joining the rest of the engineers fighting on Op Medusa. Coates looks at his troops and lets them sleep in; their first timing isn't till much later in the day. As the men sleep, the sun starts to peak past the mountains, flooding the FOB with light. The men start to stir and then rustle around, beginning to wake. It isn't abnormal for one soldier to begin waking many others simply by shifting around in or on his/her sleeping bag. The effect is almost subconscious; simply turning over in your sleep results in many troops turning over and so forth.

Today they wake somewhat stressed but excited about going back to camp. More Dutch are scheduled to arrive at the FOB and they are expected to convoy out. After eating breakfast, they start packing their kit, ready just in case they need to leave on short notice. They sit and wait, sleep and read, smoke cigars and joke. The Dutch are on a 50% stand-to, meaning that half of the camp's firepower is manned at all times.

At around 10:00 am, the troops stop reading and look to the sky where they are hearing a familiar sound. Looking up, they see three dots on the horizon, one larger than the two others, coming towards the FOB.

"Chinook," Coates says to his troops, recognizing the largest of the dots. A Chinook or "flying school bus" is a dual-rotor transport helicopter capable of lifting over a platoon of troops to a distant area. As well, they can be used to drop off supplies loaded on skids or light vehicles, which could be driven inside.

Two of the helicopters, a Chinook and a Black Hawk, start their approach as the third, a Dutch AH-64 Apache gunship, breaks formation and starts to circle the FOB, keeping a lookout for any insurgents. Sweeping in, the two helicopters position themselves to land a short distance outside the FOB but still within the wired defence. Signalled by the blowing smoke from a smoke grenade, they kick up a storm of dust and sand as they descend the final few metres to touch down. Watching the great plume of dust settle, Coates and his troops remain sitting while a platoon of Dutch reinforcements marches into the FOB.

"Should help this FOB," Thompson comments, watching the long line of troops march past the fuel area.

With the troops unloaded, some Dutch troops and equipment are loaded onto the Chinook and Black Hawk, destined back to Kandahar Airfield. Many of the departing troops had seen combat, firing and being fired upon for what must have felt like an eternity. With another great plume of dust and sand, both helicopters begin their accent into the sky and arching forward, they start their trip back to camp. Flying back to camp on the Black Hawk is the black lab and his handler, who earlier had phoned his boss and quit.

As the sun continues its ascent, the day grows hotter and lunch rations are dished out. No sooner have they eaten than more Dutch arrive at the FOB, this time in a long convoy of armoured vehicles, all mustered into the camp. Arriving to drop off more armour to reinforce the FOB, the convoy will also act as security for Coates's convoy on its way back to camp.

Seeing the vehicles, Coates walks back to the troops at the Command Post. "Alright guys, convoy's here so get ready to go," he instructs his soldiers. Their G-Wagon is packed and ready to go with the convoy. It is now inside the camp with some vehicles pulling out to man the wall. After Coates has checked with the convoy commander, the troops cram themselves into the tight confines of their G-Wagon and pull into their order of march in the convoy.

They remain in their vehicle until informed that a threat warning had been issued. Apparently there are Taliban in the area who are planning to attack the convoy, leading the commander to delay the convoy's departure time.

Once ready to move, the convoy roars to life just in time for the order to come down that there is another threat warning against the convoy. They repeat this one more time until a Dutch Apache comes on scene flying over the area scanning for threats. Two hours later, near dinnertime, everything is good to go from above, and they load back up in the tightly packed G-Wagon and start the two-and-a-half hour drive back to Kandahar Airfield. The sun is close to the horizon when they leave FOB Martello and after winding through the many villages, crossing the mountains and over the rivers, it is setting when they pass through Kandahar City. Some shops have lights out in front of their buildings while others remain dark with the people living near their shops using wood fires to provide light and heat.

Heading down past the Golden Arches, Coates and his men traverse the last strip of highway before making their right turn off Highway 4 into Kandahar Airfield, greeted at the gate by the Afghan MiG. After filling their vehicle with diesel at the pumps, they finally arrive at the Squadron Quartermaster stores.

"Ok, guys," Coates says to his team as they dismount, "take your kit to the shacks. Do what you need to do for the night."

The men understand, and the G-Wagon takes off as Coates carries his rifle with him to the Squadron Quartermaster. The boys are already pulling the kit from the back and van Santen leaves to grab one of the six-wheeled Gators to ferry their kit over to their rooms.

Safe again behind the well-guarded fences of Kandahar Airfield, Coates walks over to the Squadron Quartermaster and opens the door. Inside he finds the building lit as it always is, the lights hardly ever being shut off. The Squadron Second-in-Command, Captain Busbridge, is hard at work in his office, looking up only to return the greeting when Coates says hi to him. Coates is quick and like his troops he wants to catch some sleep on his bed. Grabbing the mail and looking over the parcels in the 2 Troop office, he starts his walk over to the shacks. He passes the north mess and continues past the Command Post until he finally reaches the building he calls home. His troops were good to him and have taken his kit directly to his door, and opening up his room he is greeted by the cold draught from his air-conditioner. Setting the mail down on his top bunk, he then moves his kit inside the room and strips down for a warm shower to wash the dirt away.

Later, reports come back to the Command Post that on September 5th, 2006, close to 100 Taliban fighters, in a joint attack using two advances and supported by mortars, had attempted to take FOB Martello. Besides suffering serious losses on the ridgeline, at least ten Taliban were killed during their foolhardy rush at the rear gate. Further numbers can't be reported as wounded and dead Taliban are always removed by their own for treatment or burial.

THE KING OF COSTALL

Cpl Matt Austin

One hundred kilometres south-east of Kandahar at the end of Highway 4 lies what is known as FOB Costall. Positioned less than 10 kilometre from the western Pakistani border, it is a stopping point for coalition and Afghan troops on patrolling and provincial reconstruction missions alike.

Named after Pte Robert Costall of the 1st Battalion, Princess Patricia's Canadian Light Infantry (1 PPCLI) Battle Group, who fell in a fierce fire-fight with Taliban forces in March, 2006, it is home to soldiers of many nations. Though troops were still calling it FOB Costall when 23 Field Squadron arrived in theatre, by the end of August it was formally known as "FOB Spin Boldak."

It was during the changeover from the 1 PPCLI Battle Group to the 1 RCR Battle Group that MCpl Thomas was slated to head down from Kandahar Airfield to FOB Spin Boldak. Sappers were being sent down to the area to support local operations and the FOB, and to be on call to support any engineer requirement. The stay for MCpl Thomas, however, would be lengthy.

August 18th began like any normal day in the desert. Having arrived in Spin Boldak the previous day, MCpl Thomas had hooked up with Charles Company and some American troops in the camp. The duties for him and Spr Flikweert, a 19 year-old reservist from Waterloo, would be to help re-construct the camp and improve defences where he saw fit. Divided into several areas, Spin Boldak was home to American, Canadian and the Afghan troops, all staying in their own areas of the camp and sometimes inviting each other for a meal or, in the case of the Afghans, tea. In terms of the multicultural mix of the camp, it was little different from FOB Martello and later FOB Spervan Ghar.

After a few days, Thomas and Flikweert had already moved on to their first few jobs, reconstructing bunkers and fortifying mortar pits. As well, there was a need to raise 10B Hesco (10 feet tall with considerable weight) at the front gate, which was done with the backhoe.

It wasn't long before the camp started to thin out. After only a couple of days, Charles Company, minus their Company Sergeant-Major, departed for the Panjwaii having been replaced by call signs from Recce Troop. Leaving with them were all the Afghan National Army in the camp except for 15 of their soldiers. Thus, MCpl Thomas was left with a handful of contracted guards armed with AK-47s, the American security contractors, a Canadian cook and Flikweert.

As August dragged on, Thomas and Flikweert continued their engineer tasks and reconstructed a bit of road at a time by filling the growing potholes. At night they drew sentry shifts and found themselves staring at the desert for hours at a time, walking around the camp in search of an enemy that did not appear. Up north, in Panjwaii, Canadian troops were being attacked rolling through Ambush Alley and Operation Medusa was being planned for September, while down in Spin Boldak, Thomas and Flikweert continued to labour in isolation.

Cpl Nason and Spr Kendall arrived in a G-Wagon with a convoy from Kandahar Airfield on the afternoon of the 24th and joined the two in order to assist with engineer support to the Recce troops. The other half of 32 Echo, however, was located at FOB Martello, building "the finest toilet ever built" for the Dutch.

The 28th of August approached and Recce Troop also pulled out, being relocated to another area of operations. When the convoy arrived with their replacements, Thomas was amazed to see that the troops were all soldiers from the 2nd Royal Air Force Regiment. They were friendly and helped in upgrading the bunkers and the FOB, lending a hand whenever they could. With 38 British soldiers now occupying the camp, they decided that the engineers should no longer have to pull sentry at night.

Days wore on and the troops in Kandahar Airfield were getting antsy preparing for Op Medusa. Most of the troops don't know the exact date or specifics but rumours started trickling down to Spin Boldak.

On August 31st, Thomas was told by Squadron Headquarters to send Nason and Flikweert back to Kandahar Airfield, most likely to prepare for the upcoming operation. By the end of the first day of September, however, Nason and Flikweert were still in Spin Boldak, as no convoy had been sent to re-supply the FOB.

Operation Medusa began in Panjwaii on September 2nd with the bombardment of the area around the "White School" in Pashmul. Battle Group soldiers watched as seemingly endless artillery rounds and bombs from close air support created a continual iron rain on the enemy positions.

In Spin Boldak, Thomas and his three sappers went on filling in pot holes in the camp's road. They worked for several hours, rested and then continued their work, talking every once in a while with the British troops. The sun set after a day of labour and though Thomas heard reports on the preliminary bombardment, he was not troubled with the news, focusing instead on the camp and its improvements.

The following day, around noon, Thomas was disheartened by the account of the ground attack across the Arghandab River and the death of Sgt Shane Stachnik. From his arrival for work-up training with 2 Combat Engineer Regiment, Thomas had liked Stachnik. Now he was gone. Thomas passed the news on and a sombre mood descended over the small Canadian Engineer contingent. Everyone had known Shane and felt the keen loss of one of their own.

By 6:00 am on September 4th, 2006, over 35 Canadian troops were wounded by the accidental strafing of their position by an American A-10 fighter plane. Based on the number and severity of the casualties, the Spin Boldak Camp Sergeant-Major was told that he would be leaving to head north to replace one of the wounded. He handed over care of Spin Boldak to MCpl Thomas who would be the highest-ranking Canadian on the ground. Thomas was now responsible for the running of the camp, including paying the guards and re-supply. After the brief chat, the Sergeant-Major introduced Thomas to the contracted guard commander and the Afghan National Army commander, both of whom acknowledged their new boss.

By the end of the day, MCpl Thomas was the new Canadian Camp Sergeant-Major, earning him the moniker "The King of Costall." Far to the north, at FOB Martello, the mood was filled with excitement as the other half of the section was under fire from a considerable Taliban force attacking the camp. The firefight continued for a good portion of the day, dying off as the sun set.

Meanwhile, in Spin Boldak, the RAF troops continued to help with security and left Thomas to command the local guards. Sea cans arrived on the backs of heavy logistic trucks, bringing equipment, ammo and rations. The soldiers always welcomed these deliveries, with their morale-boosting delights of Spunkmeyer muffins, Pop-Tarts and Pepsi. The truck drivers were a special breed of soldier, as they drove constantly through Ambush Alley and suspected roadside bomb areas. With trucks their size, they were bullet magnets and easy targets for the insurgents. Over the length of the tour, these trucks would increasingly arrive with more shrapnel or bullet holes down their sides as the drivers continually ran the gauntlet to support the troops.

Once the re-supply convoy finished rolling in, Thomas ordered the sea cans unloaded and replaced with empty ones. Before the convoys left, Thomas extracted as much information as possible from the crews on what was happening in the Panjwaii. With no real or apparent hostile threats in his area, the contracted guards and the sappers were becoming a little bored.

Every once in a while, members of the Canadian Kandahar Provincial Reconstruction Team arrived at Spin Boldak on their way to the Pakistani border. Stopping to check in with Thomas for intelligence on the area, they would leave shortly thereafter, continuing on their way to the Pakistan.

The 14th of September arrived and with it a Dutch helicopter descending from the sky. Sent from Kandahar Airfield, the helicopter carried a paymaster for the contract guards who were helping to defend the camp. Squadron Headquarters had reconfirmed that Thomas was to load up Nason and Flikweert on the helicopter back to Kandahar Airfield to join the remaining members of 32 Echo left behind after Sgt Coates and Marcus joined 32 Delta.

At this point, the Canadian contingent comprised Thomas, Kendal and a cook. On September 17th, LCol Irwin, the Chief of Staff of the Canadian National Command Element and former Commanding Officer of 2 Combat Engineer Regiment, arrived at Spin Boldak. He stopped only long enough to talk briefly with Thomas and Kendall, inquiring about their time at the FOB and any enemy movements in the area.

A few days later, Kendall and Thomas were alerted by yelling and the intermittent sounds of gunfire near the Afghan National Army side of the camp. Running to see what was occuring, the two sappers were shocked to find that the cabins that the Afghan National Army had built were ablaze. The fire rose high into the sky. From within the conflagration there came the *pop* *pop*pop* of gunshots and in an instant, Thomas realized that the ammunition left inside the cabins was now cooking off. Afghan troops crowded around the cabins holding buckets of water but Thomas shouted at them to back off, as the trajectory of the rounds couldn't be trusted. For a short while, troops from all the nations inside the camp watched as the blaze consumed the building, waiting until the rounds stopped firing before they attempted to put out the fire.

As the second cabin ignited, Thomas noticed how close the flames and the sea container holding ammunition were to one another. Reacting quickly, Thomas told Kendall to use the backhoe to remove the sea can as quickly as possible from the vicinity of the blaze. Kendall, noting for himself how quickly the fire was growing, ran to the back hoe and despite the intense heat, dragged the container to safety.

Down the line near the first shack, a pile of wood about 20 metres away started smouldering and then burst into flames, fire casting upwards into the sky with the crackling of wood mixing with the sounds of gunshots from the cabin line.

After a short while, the ammunition was expended and the area was somewhat safe. Thomas yelled at the Afghan National Army to extinguish the burning remnants of their cabins. They did so and brought the blaze under control. They then moved to the woodpile, dousing it with their remaining water. In the end only one cabin remained while the other five smouldered, reduced to heaps of charred wood and ash.

Three days later the ruins that were once their homes finally stopped smouldering and were finally out. The cause was eventually determined to have been an Afghan soldier who was smoking in one of the cabins. Nothing else was ever said of him.

On September 27th, Thomas was informed that he would be leaving with Kendall on a re-supply convoy on the 30th. Both were greatly relieved, having spent almost all of the tour to date in Spin Boldak.

A troop convoy arrived on the 29th comprising 8 and 9 Platoons from Charles Company along with a contingent of American and Afghan forces. With their arrival, the British RAF Regiment soldiers departed.

In the afternoon of the 30th the re-supply convoy finally arrived. In a G-Wagon, Kendall and Thomas travelled back to the Airfield as planned. After an uneventful trip, they cleared their weapons at the berm and passed through the several levels of security before entering Kandahar Airfield. They emptied their vehicle at the shacks and stowed away their kit, and Thomas dismissed Kendall for the day and headed over to the Boardwalk for a taste of civilization. Sitting down with his personal pan pizza from *Pizza Hut*, he looked at the beehive of activity as people from the many nations rolled past. He then proceeded to get a long-overdue haircut. Everyday that he was down in Spin Boldak, MCpl Thomas asked the Squadron Headquarters to send him some hair clippers on the resupply run. Since none ever managed to arrive, upon his return he was sporting a full Afro. From Maj G on down, we were very proud of our non-standard haircuts in the Squadron.

MCpl Thomas had been away from Kandahar Airfield for about 45 days, improving Spin Boldak for all the nations who used the FOB. Thomas and Kendall received orders to relax the following day, before the remainder of the section, who were now working on Route Summit, returned from the Panjwaii. Three days later, the section together again at last, they were back in the field and the King of Costall was back to work.

MINEFIELD EXTRACTION

Maj Rich Busbridge

As the only EOD qualified officer in 23 Field Squadron, I was responsible for the EOD teams on behalf of the OC. At times, when the number of EOD operators in the Squadron dropped below six, because of mid-tour leave, injuries or other tasks, I would be required to backfill as the second-in-command for the airmobile EOD team based out of Kandahar Airfield. The week of November 20th – 26th, 2006 was one of these periods where we had three EOD operators on leave and I was on stand-by for EOD tasks. PO2 Jim Leith was the Number One for the airmobile EOD team and we operated under the Callsign 'EOD 2.'

At this point in the Operation, the Tank Squadron (B Squadron or Call-sign 'Tango 2') had wrapped up initial maintenance on the Leopard C2 tanks, which had only recently arrived in Afghanistan, and was preparing to deploy *en masse* for the first time in order to join the fight in the Panjwaii. Their plan was to exit Kandahar Airfield to the south and travel cross-country due west, thus avoiding the major urban centre of Kandahar City (as well as any of the often-used routes). During their battle procedure they consulted the Engineer Support Coordination Centre so as to identify and avoid any known mine and IED threat areas along their selected movement corridor. We did not have any indication of a mine threat in the area where the mine strike eventually occurred.

Tango 2 deployed at first light on the morning of November 22nd, 2006. Just to the south of the Kandahar Airfield's perimeter fence, while shaking out into the "box" formation they would use to move across the countryside, one of the tanks struck a mine and was immobilized. They immediately stopped all movement and requested engineer support.

For any explosive incidents, we would initially assume them to be IED attacks and use EOD teams as primary responders. Because of the proximity to Kandahar Airfield, EOD 2 was tasked to respond. I received a call to report to the Battle Group Command Post at about 7:00 am that morning.

I arrived at the Command Post at the same time as PO2 Leith and we were quickly briefed on the situation. Given the fact that the incident had occurred in an area not previously used by coalition forces, it seemed very unlikely that it was a result of insurgent activity because it was doubtful that they would be able to predict where our forces would be and put something out there to target us. Mine strikes are normally dealt with by Field Engineers, but since all of the engineer field sections were deployed in Zhari and Panjwaii Districts, and there was still a possibility that it could have been an IED, we decided to continue to use EOD 2 in response.

Since there was a possibility that an IED was involved, we were going to be joined by WO Bryan Waters, a Canadian Ammunition Technician working for a higher-level organization that exploits IED incidents to gather tactical and technical information in order to determine who is responsible and how they are targeting us.

Normally, the airmobile EOD team would be transported to an incident location via helicopter, but because of the incident's proximity to Kandahar Airfield it was decided that we would drive out to the incident location using the team's G-Wagon. This vehicle was normally only used inside the confines of Kandahar Airfield in order to transport the team members and equipment to the helicopters when flying out on a call. We were going to be escorted by Kandahar Airfield's Quick Reaction Force manned by the UK's 2nd Royal Air Force Regiment. Our next stop after picking up WO Waters was at the Kandahar Airfield Command Post for the purpose of linking up with the Quick Reaction Force. While we were there we were able to see video imagery of Tango 2 using cameras set up as a part of Kandahar Airfield's defences. Unfortunately the cameras had not captured the event when it occurred.

It was a quick trip out to the rendezvous location where we were met by Tango 2's Squadron Sergeant-Major. At this point the Quick Reaction Force returned to Kandahar Airfield as Tango 2 had no shortage of firepower and could thus provide their own force protection during the extraction operation. He then guided us forward to where the Squadron was located.

As we approached we could see two troops, of 4 tanks each, and the Squadron's echelon waiting to go through a crossing point over a *kharez*. A *kharez* is an underground irrigation system characterized by a line of large vertical shafts cut across the countryside. This one ran roughly east-west, about 500 metres south of Kandahar Airfield. We were led across the *kharez*, and then oriented to the small grouping of tanks about 50 metres away where we would be briefed by the Squadron's Battle Captain – Mark Lubiniecki. We could see another troop of tanks 200 metres further to the north, which is where we assumed the strike had occurred. We pulled up behind Lubiniecki 's tank and climbed up onto his back deck to get the details on the situation. He pointed to Maj Cadieu's disabled tank, located 15 metres to our front.

We were told that the Squadron had been moving tactically and that the tank troop 200 metres to the front (Tango 21) had crossed at the *kharez* and moved to their current position without any incident. There was a second tank troop (Tango 22) that had also crossed the *kharez* and had moved to the west about 300 metres before going firm, again without incident. It was when the Headquarters element was moving to take position on the north side of the *kharez* that the explosion occurred, causing that tank to throw a track. There were no physical injuries.

As the team leader, PO2 Leith, proceeded to clear his way forward to the damaged tank in order to assess the cause of the explosion, I used the height of the tank I was on to get a better view of the terrain in order to help assess the situation. The *kharez* to our south was the most prominent terrain feature in the area and seemed to be a logical southern boundary if we were in a mined area. Many of the tank crews were reporting in that they could see possible mine indicators around them. The ones that were pointed out to me were roughly circular depressions, protrusions and discolorations on the ground. None of them provided any positive indications of mines, nor did they seem to occur in any sort of pattern.

When PO2 Leith returned he reported that the explosion had taken place under the right track of Maj Cadieu's tank, near the front of the vehicle. The tank's momentum had caused it to roll forward to the point where the blast seat was now at the rear of the right track. When he cleared his way around the tank he found a live TM-57 (Soviet-era anti-tank mine) situated at the front edge of the tank, a few feet to the left of where the track was laying.

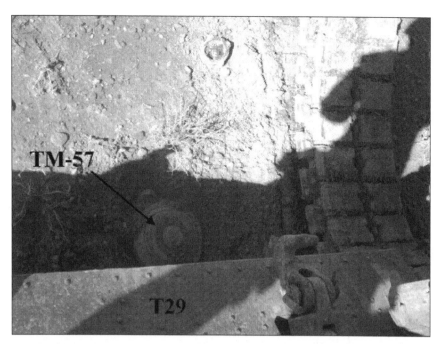

At this point we assessed that we were in fact in a minefield remnant from a previous conflict and deemed the safe area to which we would extract everyone would be the south side of the *kharez*. Since extracting personnel from a minefield is an engineer task rather than an EOD task, I assumed the lead for the operation from PO2 Leith.

I briefed Maj Cadieu, my boss (Maj G) and the acting Battle Group CO (Maj Marty Lipcsey) on the situation over the radio and presented a few options. We could pull engineers back from the Panjwaii District and conduct a deliberate safe lane clearance operation, which would be time- and resource-intensive, or we could employ the tank ploughs resident within the Tank Squadron to clear lanes to and around each grouping of tanks, then use mine detectors to check the spoil[25] for mines in order to confirm the lanes safe for use. There was a little bit more risk associated with the second option, but Maj Cadieu was confident in the effectiveness of his tank ploughs and recommended we go with it. Everyone else concurred. Maj G indicated that he would put together an *ad hoc* section of engineers working in Kandahar Airfield and send them out in his LAV to assist.

In the meantime we proceeded to extract the first grouping of tanks. A plough tank was brought forward from the rear troop and, with everyone under armour, it ploughed a lane up to the rear of Maj Cadieu's tank. We checked the north half of that ploughed lane in order to allow the plough tank to back up a distance and begin ploughing a secondary lane out to Tango 21.

At this point Maj G's LAV arrived with a handful of engineers and one signaller. MWO Brad Montgomery led the ad-hoc crew, which included Cpl Randy Duggan, Cpl Jay Tisdale, Cpl Tarek Foley, his gunner and Cpl Jeff Vomastic. When we met face-to-face, Montgomery greeted me as "Lieutenant Busbridge" and introduced himself as "Sergeant Montgomery," humorous commentary based on the fact that two of the Squadron's senior personnel were conducting tasks normally performed by troop and section commanders. Once I had briefed him on the situation he led his crew in checking the remaining half of the initially ploughed lane and guiding the mobile vehicles back to the safe area.

Meanwhile, PO2 Leith and I looked after the recovery of Maj Cadieu's tank. Before we could bring the Armoured Recovery Vehicle forward we needed to confirm that the area immediately behind the disabled tank was free from hazards as the tank plough would not have been able to move those hazards out of the lane. Nothing was found immediately behind that tank, but as we were heading back to the MWO Montgomery's location I

noticed an item lying on the ground a few feet to the east of the ploughed lane. A closer look suggested that it was a shipping cap for a landmine and it wasn't long before I was able to make out the top of a TM-57 mine peeking through the surface beside it. I marked it and then noticed that the location of that mine, the blast-seat and the mine found at the front of the tank seemed to follow a straight line with an even spacing of about 10 metres. Following that pattern, I was able to visually locate, again by finding the shipping cap first, the next mine to the east in the line and could see that the one after that might fall at or near the left edge of the secondary lane that was ploughed towards the tank troop to the north.

We did not want to bring the Armoured Recovery Vehicle forward until all of the mobile vehicles had been extracted to the safe area, so PO2 Leith and I began checking the secondary lane. It did not come as too much of a surprise when I detected something in the left hand spoil a short distance into the secondary lane. I knelt down and excavated with my hands and uncovered another live TM-57 mine. We marked this one and determined that we would need to destroy it before extracting the tank troop to the north, as it was too close to the safe lane.

At this point the other vehicles had been safely recovered and the Armoured Recovery Vehicle was brought forward to recover Maj Cadieu's tank. The recovery had to be done carefully as there was still a live mine at the front of it. If the tank turned at all when it was initially moved there was potential that it could set the mine off. The recovery occurred without incident. Before carrying on with the extraction of the remaining two tank troops, PO2 Leith and I proceeded to blow-in-place the TM-57 mine I had uncovered on the edge of the secondary lane. We then shifted our focus to the two tank troops that were north and west.

Each troop had stopped in an all-around defence, with each tank facing outwards in a different direction. Tango 22 in the west had stopped near the main road known to be free of mines. So, rather than plough a lane to them from our current location, which was known to contain mines, MWO Montgomery headed back to the safe area with his crew, less Cpl Duggan, and used the road to get close to the troop to the west. From there he directed their plough tank to plough a circular lane passing the rear of each of his troop's tanks and down to the road. Once that was done they checked the ploughed lane as well as the areas immediately behind each tank, which enabled them to guide the tanks onto the ploughed lane and to safety. This was all done without incident and no mines were found around Tango 22.

Tango 21's plough tank cut a circular route from its original position, passing as close as it could to the back of each of the tanks in his troop and connected with the path north. The shape of these two lanes resembled that of a shepherd's crook.

I now had Cpl Duggan, as well as PO2 Leith and WO Waters to assist with extracting Tango 21. I paired up with Cpl Duggan to check the left side of the lane and the other two checked the right side. We cleared the straight section without any incident and without finding any evidence of more mines. As we started to check the curved section we began to hear gunfire to the northeast. We quickly realized that the gunfire was coming from Kandahar Airfield's 25-metre rifle range and that we were likely in the range's danger area. A quick call higher confirmed our suspicions and the range was soon shut down. The rest of the lane was checked and nothing further was found.

While we were checking the area behind one of the tanks, the Crew Commander indicated that he was concerned about an area of rubble 50 metres to his front which appeared to have aiming markers like you might find at a rocket launch site. I could see what he was indicating but couldn't conclusively determine that it was not a threat, even though it seemed too close to Kandahar Airfield to be a launch position. Cpl Duggan and I cleared a footpath for ourselves to the rubble pile to investigate further. As it turned out, the pile of rubble was not a pile at all, but a small trench system. Everything suddenly became clear as I realized that the trenches and the mines were part of the defensive perimeter for Kandahar Airfield, left over from when the Soviets had occupied the airfield.

When we returned to the ploughed lane, PO2 Leith and WO Waters had completed checking the rest of the lane, as well as the spaces behind each tank. We then proceeded to guide each tank onto the path and off to the safe area. I rode on top of the last tank as it made its way down the lane to the safe area, crossing at 5:30 pm. As I commanded Maj G's LAV back to Kandahar Airfield in the middle of an armoured column I felt a tremendous feeling of accomplishment that I had been able to use my combat engineer training to extract a tank squadron from a live minefield without incident.

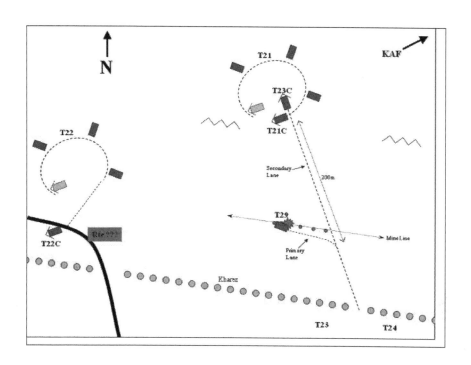

1 TROOP

Capt Anthony Robb

DEPLOYMENT

1 Troop's deployment to Afghanistan as part of 23 Field Squadron was indeed fast and furious. Given the intense pace of operations and the need to provide combat engineer support quickly, Maj Gasparotto had decided to deploy 1 Troop complete (less a few soldiers who remained behind to get qualified on the RG-31) on the earliest chalks going to Kandahar. Essentially, this enabled a full field troop to be declared Operationally Ready and able to support operations for both the outgoing 1 PPCLI Battle Group and incoming 1 RCR Battle Group. It was an extremely hectic time, and we hurried to get all vehicles, equipment and nerves ready ASAP.

In order to get an early start on the Relief-in-Place with 1 Troop, 11 Field Squadron, WO Rouzes, Cpl Pleasance and I deployed to Afghanistan a few days prior to the rest of the troop. Immediately after finishing the three days of indoctrination training that everyone undergoes, we were scheduled to do a recce of the Zhari and Panjwaii districts. Little did we know that this would more or less become our Area of Operations for the major part of our tour. Therefore, on August 5th, WO Rouzes and I joined up with Capt Jerome Patry, the Troop Commander of 1 Troop, 11 Field Squadron, and set out for Patrol Base Wilson. Due to the fact that the Squadron Headquarters was short a LAV driver, Cpl Pleasance was not able to join us. Aside from almost getting shot in the head from a 25mm misfire, he made out just fine. WO Rouzes and I were both excited and anxious to get out and see Kandahar City and the areas where we would be working for the next 6 months. Driving through the city for the first time was without question a surreal experience. People housed in sea cans beside neighbours living in new concrete and glass buildings were a backdrop to seas of white and yellow Toyota Corollas, animals being slaughtered on the street... the list goes on. Upon exiting the city we came up to a 15-kilometre stretch of road known as "Ambush Alley." In order to avoid this area, because of the likelihood of an ambush, our convoy commander decided to take the *Baja* route through the desert. Two hours and 20 kilometres later we arrived at Patrol Base Wilson, covered in dust.

With no disrespect to Private Wilson, my initial thoughts were that the Patrol Base that bears his name was one of the most decrepit places in which I have ever had the displeasure of staying. Upon arrival, both WO Rouzes and I could see that this was not going to be a spot that we would particularly enjoy. This Patrol Base, aptly nicknamed "Impact Area Wilson" or "Permanent Danger Area Wilson," was prone to enemy rocket and mortar attacks. To make matters worse, there had been little or no construction of protective works and what was in place was of the poorest quality. Observation Posts were on the verge of collapse, the fuel bowser was completely exposed and diesel + rocket attacks = disaster. The canvas modular tents were being used as protective bunkers and this did not work well as the Afghan National Army later found out during one particular mortar attack. Upon sharing this information with Maj Gasparotto, he indicated that my troop's first responsibility was going to be to get Patrol Base Wilson "up to code."

Two days later, WO Rouzes and I accompanied Sgt Booker, the Recce Sergeant from 1 Troop, 11 Field Squadron, up to FOB Martello. This FOB, sited in the bottom of a giant bowl, was built in order to interdict Taliban movement between Kandahar and Zabul Provinces. Given the siting constraints issued to Sgt Booker, I must admit that he did an excellent job making the location as defensible as possible. Upon completion of the recce we made the lengthy drive back to Kandahar Airfield. The trip was made longer as a result of having to tow a LAV for most of the way. During the move up to Martello, one of the LAV's rear axles fell off and, unable to conduct repairs, its crew and two force protection vehicles and a Mobile Recovery Team were required to spend the next five hours rigging the vehicle for towing while the rest of us continued to Martello. On our way back to Kandahar Airfield, we linked back up with the broken vehicle and slowly continued our return trip. After a few more recces and briefs, my troop was finally ready to deploy en masse. 31 Charlie stayed behind as they were still waiting for their RG-31 personnel to arrive from Canada. Teaming up with A Company, we departed for Patrol Base Wilson. Despite a minor contact, in the form of small arms fire, while in Ambush Alley, we arrived unscathed and ready to work. What happened over the next few weeks was basically a combat engineer version of "Holmes on Homes."

We inspected all the Observation Posts and decided that all of them needed to be torn down and rebuilt due to a severe lack of structural integrity and poor quality. We put a rush order on dozens of sets of Texas Bunkers and immediately made use of our one piece of heavy equipment, the backhoe, in order to get the bowser as deep into the ground as possible. For the next two weeks we worked non-stop to transform Patrol Base Wilson into a defensible location. In effect, we "made it right." Sgt White and Sgt Grignon redesigned the various rooftop Observation Posts including the reinforcement of the buildings' structural integrity in order to support their weight. It is worth noting that the lumber they used, as is the case with most of the lumber in Afghanistan, was extremely warped and of poor quality. As such, they were often forced to laminate all beams and joists, further complicating the Observation Posts' design. While completing these defensive tasks, we also provided full-spectrum combat engineer support to A Company.

We conducted several overnight patrols in and around the districts of Zhari and Panjwaii and Kandahar City. On one particular patrol, 31 Delta had their first major contact when they were ambushed by Rocket Propelled Grenade and small arms fire. The very next night, while on a patrol with the A Company, we came under fire four times over the 20 kilometre stretch of road that makes up "Ambush Alley." Upon entering, we were immediately attacked from the left with small arms, recoilless rifles and Rocket Propelled Grenades. Completely forgetting most of my LAV crew commander drills I simply told my gunner, Spr Loder, that he could shoot anything that moved. Meanwhile, I manned my pintle mount machine gun by my turret hatch and scanned for targets using my night vision gear. Given the proximity of most of the targets, I had to engage the battle override so that the gun could depress low enough. Maj Wright, the OC of A Company, who was in the back of my vehicle because his was in need of repair, was commanding the combat team through the fight. Engrossed by action, he was unaware that my turret was about one foot from his head. Luckily, WO Rouzes spotted this and yanked Maj Wright down just prior to the cannon being fired. Cpl Jaworski, who was my rear gunner at the time, remained busy engaging targets. This happened three more times until finally we made it into Kandahar City.

Upon consolidation at 2 Corps, an Afghan National Army base in Kandahar City, we started to provide first aid to the two injured personnel, changed tires and reloaded ammo. Meanwhile however, Maj Wright was fully occupied excoriating one of the interpreters. Apparently, this interpreter knew of the intended ambush and was vocal about not wanting to be a part of this patrol. As soon as my ramp went down, Maj Wright grabbed the interpreter by the scruff of the neck, gave him a verbal lashing and then handed him over to the authorities. Once we were good to go, we established a leaguer in the desert five kilometres east of Ma'sum Ghar. The adrenaline rush from these engagements and our successful counterattack left me feeling pretty elated

Despite my initial impressions, the quality of life at Patrol Base Wilson was not bad, except for a few minor inconveniences. The frequent rocket and mortar attacks certainly had a negative effect on overall morale. In addition, given the increase in violence during the month of August, the sanitation truck driver decided that he no longer felt safe coming to Patrol Base Wilson to empty the blue rockets. Throughout our time at Patrol Base Wilson there was always talk of it only being a temporary location and that it was set to shut down "soon." However, after the events of August 19th, A Company's immense battle with insurgents at Ma'sum Ghar and the subsequent planning and staging for Op Medusa, it became quite clear that Patrol Base Wilson was there to stay for the foreseeable future. As it turned out, virtually the entire 1 RCR Battle Group staged out of there. In fact, space was so limited within its confines that all engineers moved outside its brick-walled perimeter. This really didn't faze us as these walls only provided a false sense of protection. So, with Patrol Base Wilson now at an acceptable living standard and with Op Medusa orders issued, 1 Troop redeployed back to Kandahar Airfield during the last week of August in order to start our battle procedure. Ten to fifteen minutes after our departing Patrol Base Wilson, it came under a particularly accurate mortar fire. Recall that several soldiers had been sleeping in modular tentage up to that point. The night prior, however, WO Rouzes advised the A Company Sergeant-Major that he could now move his soldiers behind our new Hesco walls. In the end there were only a few minor Canadian and Afghan National Army casualties - our protective works very likely saved many lives that day.

OP MEDUSA

Op Medusa certainly did not come as a surprise to most of us. Given all of the intelligence reports regarding insurgent locations, the frequent attacks and the particularly large battle that took place on August 19th, 2006, it was no secret that the enemy was massing in the Zhari and Panjwaii Districts and that the Taliban had designs on Kandahar City itself.

Upon 1 Troop's return to Kandahar Airfield from Patrol Base Wilson we immediately commenced our preparations for the operation. First, I attended the Battle Group orders as an observer. I believe firmly that engineer troop commanders need to attend these orders, in order to give us the requisite situational awareness necessary to advise the sub-units that we are supporting. Next, I spent some time planning the operation with Maj Geoff Abthorpe, OC Bravo Company, since I was going to be supporting his rifle company for the operation.

As for 1 Troop and the Bravo Company Combat Team, our job was to advance south, parallel to a series of north/south routes, which was our axis of advance, using Patrol Base Wilson and Highway 1 as our Line of Departure. There was a series of east/west control lines between our combat team and the final objective, Objective Rugby, which was essentially Pashmul on the north bank of the Arghandab River. Our plan was to successively move forward to each of these control lines with movement based on the success and conditions of the other Battle Group combat teams. These control lines coincided with the east/west wadi systems that sliced through our axis of advance.

Finally, our combat team would link-up with the Charles Company Combat Team, which was conducting a similar operation, except that they were moving from the south to the north using the Arghandab River as their line of departure.

It was reiterated that Op Medusa was condition-based, therefore very few concrete times were given. Each successive phase was based on certain conditions being met or, as we would soon find out, not met. Consequently, knowing the overall plan and the tasks that needed to be done, I was able to begin planning how 1 Troop could best support the Bravo Company Combat Team. At this point I had not yet received orders from Maj Gasparotto and for this reason I did not yet know what additional resources I would have.

As it turned out we would have very few to begin with. WO Rouzes, Sgt Houde, Sgt Proulx, Sgt Grignon, Sgt White, Cpl Pleasance and I began going through our estimate process in order to figure out how we were to overcome some of the difficulties we knew we would be facing. We understood that our biggest role throughout would be to provide mobility support to the combat team so that they would be able to manoeuvre, mounted and dismounted, along the axis of advance. Based on the aerial photos we estimated the wadis to be one to two metres across by one to two metres deep. This posed a significant problem for us to overcome. In addition, intelligence indicated that the roads in that area were completely laced with IEDs and anti-tank mines and in this instance the intelligence was completely accurate. We also deduced that IED breach, mine detection, search and urban breach were some of our implied tasks.

Based on the advice that I received from my staff, I wrote up my concept of operations for Op Medusa. My intent was to provide a mixture of centralized and decentralized full-spectrum engineer support to the Bravo Company Combat Team. My scheme of manoeuvre was broken down into phases so that they matched the Battle Group and Combat Team phases of the operation. During Phase One, the aerial bombardment and condition setting phase slated to run from September 2nd to about September 4th or 5th, we would simply deploy with the Bravo Company Combat Team and wait in our assembly area until the intended criteria were set for the actual advance.

During all stages of Phase Two we would provide the requisite mobility support to the combat team. This would be accomplished this by tackling our axis of advance in bite-sized chunks, securing a portion at a time. The plan was to first bombard our intermediate objectives with Close Air Support, artillery and LAV fire. Next, we would send dismounts forward of the main body, secure the east and west sides of our axis of advance, move the Route Clearance Package down that particular section of road, establish a tactical waiting area and then repeat as needed. As for crossing the wadis, we developed a few options: fill them with "tree fascines[26]", employ our backhoe to fill them in with dirt or utilize the bridges that were already in place. Quite frankly, all of these choices were inadequate. We found the trees too thin to use as expedient bridging, however despite their small diameter too tough to be cut down by a regular chainsaw. It is worth noting that our troop lumberjack, Cpl Veinot, was able to fell them using his own personal tree-cutting technique. The backhoe, which was not armoured, was incapable of dozing over a large wadi in a timely manner and the bridges were classic choke points with "IED" and "ambush" written all over them.

During Phase Three, the expansion west, we would simply employ the same tactics outlined in Phase Two. Finally, Phase Four would see us go hard in the vicinity of Objective Rugby and start work on a more permanent coalition defendable area. At the time, I understood this establishment to be the eventual replacement of Patrol Base Wilson. My main effort was always the mobility of the combat team, as everything hinged on our ability to advance and take ground. My end-state was the establishment of a trafficable route linking the Arghandab River and Highway 1 with 1 Troop ready to conduct future offensive and defensive operations in the Pashmul area of the Zhari District.

On the evening of August 30th, 2006 I presented this plan, along with the rest of the orders, to 1 Troop complete at Kandahar Airfield. Showing no regard for the one-third/two thirds rule,[27] 31 Echo departed three hours after the Orders Group. Given that we still had not completely finished all of the defensive works at Patrol Base Wilson, I needed to redeploy them back to the field as soon as possible.

On August 31st, 2006, 1 Troop, along with the Bravo Company Combat Team deployed back to Patrol Base Wilson in order to stage for Op Medusa. In accordance with Squadron orders, Sgt Grignon's 31 Delta had been detached to Squadron Headquarters as part of the engineer reserve. In this capacity, they deployed south of the Arghandab River along with the rest of the squadron. Given that the push from the south was the Battle Group's main effort, 2 Troop initially received the lion's share of the squadron resources. As a start state, 1 Troop consisted of a Troop Headquarters, 31 Charlie led by Sgt Proulx, 31 Echo led by Sgt White, a backhoe (commonly referred to as the "backwhore" after a typo in the squadron orders) and an American Route Clearance Package. It is worth noting that the backhoe, operated by Cpl Reid, was in pretty rough shape and only had half the normal number of teeth on its bucket. However, the "backwhore with no teeth" was the only digging asset that we had.

Immediately upon arriving at Patrol Base Wilson I could see the progress made by 31 Echo. The Texas bunkers had finally arrived and they had managed to set up some bomb shelters and protective accommodations. This more or less completed the defensive works that we had planned for Patrol Base Wilson and I firmly believe that our work greatly increased the morale of those lucky enough to live there. As it would turn out, Patrol Base Wilson, with its jerry can showers, was a shining oasis, which soldiers would look forward to coming to for rest and relaxation in between combat operations. Simply stated - comfort is relative.

After some additional coordination, the Bravo Company Combat Team left Patrol Base Wilson and established an overnight leaguer a few kilometres north of Highway 1. Early the next morning on September 3rd, we set out for the Line of Departure, which ended up as our first firing line. At H-Hour, our primary task was to destroy any enemy residing in and around the "Yellow School," an insurgent stronghold on the north side of our initial control line. Intelligence had told us that the majority of the Taliban who had been hitting us in Ambush Alley, and who had been rocketing and mortaring Patrol Base Wilson were residing in this Yellow School, referred to by WO Rouzes as "Hard Target #1."

Earlier in August, there was a joint operation involving the 1 RCR Battle Group and other Coalition Forces aimed at striking this objective. However, a set of dragon's teeth[28] fell off the lead vehicle in the convoy and several of the following vehicles ran them over with detrimental results. With these vehicles thus rendered immobile, the mission was aborted while *en route*. Operations at any level can go badly wrong for the most banal of reasons, and this one was thenceforth known as Op Dragon's Teeth.

Since I had spent the previous month at Patrol Base Wilson and knew exactly where the objective was, it was my job to lead the combat team over to the firing line. At H-Hour we moved into position and opened fire on the Yellow School. After about 10 minutes of continuous 25mm fire and a 500-lb bomb, Maj Abthorpe decided that the objective was adequately destroyed. Amazingly enough, Spr Loder, my gunner, deftly managed to squeeze off 12-15 rounds before any of the other LAVs even started shooting.

We were then put in a holding pattern while we waited to hear on the progress from the southern offensive. For this reason my next three days were spent rotating 1 Troop on and off the firing line. Our task was simply to provide observation on the report line *Cracked Roof* and destroy any enemy that surfaced. Given that the Taliban had driven all the residents out of their homes, and that the rest had been told to leave by a NATO leaflet drop, our Rules of Engagement were that any person south of our position was considered enemy.

Meanwhile, I tracked the situation of the troops in the southern offensive. I recall listening to Sgt Clucas relaying the events of September 3rd over the Squadron net. I will never forget his ability to remain calm and decisive during the rather chaotic day. I broke the news of Sgt Shane Stachnik's death to my section commanders. I then went to receive orders for what would happen next given that the southern offensive had been stymied. At first, I was told to get ready to move 1 Troop to the south. This, I imagine, coincided with the initial decision to re-attempt the southern offensive. Shortly after, though, I was told to remain in place as the majority of engineer resources were likely going to be moved up to the north to support the Battle Group's new main effort. After the friendly fire incident of September 4th, it became clear that some of the forces in the south were no longer combat effective.

Meanwhile, 1 Troop was still maintaining overwatch on the Yellow School and Cracked Roof. Over the three days that we were there, we slowly crept closer and closer to the control line. Maj Abthorpe had been given specific orders not to take Cracked Roof but over time we found ourselves just metres away. During the third night we were asked to support a dismounted recce patrol behind enemy lines in order to check the suitability of trafficable routes. In an effort to draw enemy attention away from our patrol, I was asked if I could create a diversion.

At that point I recalled a discussion that I had with Lt Justin Behiels regarding the "houseguest." Essentially, the "houseguest" is a block of C4 plastic explosive strapped to a propane tank. This was allegedly used in Iraq to clear compounds. Anxious to try this novel device before Justin, I told Sgt White and MCpl Pittman to give it a shot. Given the lack of propane tanks on hand, we settled for a block of C4 strapped to a full jerry can of diesel. I believe that the loud explosion and extremely bright fireball created the desired diversion.

At my level, the overall plan for the operation did not change much, despite significant Battle Group level changes. It simply meant more work, more objectives and more combat teams to support for 1 Troop. Essentially, the plan was for three combat teams, based on A, Bravo and Mohawk (from the US 10th Mountain Division) Companies to take objectives one at a time, while setting the conditions for a Forward Passage of Lines so that one of the other combat teams could move forward and take the next objective. This leapfrog manoeuvre was to occur all the way from Highway 1 right down to the Arghandab River and Objective Rugby. With Cracked Roof close to being secured by Bravo Company, 1 Troop was tasked to support Mohawk Company as they moved through Bravo Company lines to the next objective.

In order to assist in the planning cycle, I hitch-hiked my way back to Kandahar Airfield to meet OC Mohawk Company. I decided to leave my vehicle and crew in the field so that there would be a mobile troop Headquarters supporting Bravo Company. I remained in Kandahar Airfield for about 12 hours total during which time I met the OC and his platoon commanders giving them all I knew about the Area of Operations. I was also told that I was to receive a healthy portion of Squadron resources, including an EOD team, D7 and D8 dozers. We planned to depart back to Patrol Base Wilson early the next morning.

Not having a vehicle, I jumped in one of their Humvees for the ride (I will take a LAV over a Humvee any day). After linking up with my troop, we conducted the Forward Passage of Lines with Bravo Company. While I was away at Kandahar Airfield, Capt Max Michaud-Shields, 2IC of Bravo Company, had issued the final orders to secure Cracked Roof. WO Rouzes led the troop through the searches of several of the compounds along the control line. When I returned to the front, with Mohawk Company in tow, I recall Mohawk 6 stating, "Well, that's a lot of my work already done." We subsequently moved forward about 1 km south to the vicinity of *Broken Bridge*.

In an effort to burn away the copious amounts of marijuana plants, Mohawk Company fired large amounts of white phosphorus mortar rounds into the pot fields. The overall result was completely ineffective and there was a low haze of pot smoke hovering over the area. I think that if Cheech and Chong were soldiers, this is how they would clear fields of fire.

While en route to *Broken Bridge* I sent two sections forward and kept one section in reserve. One section cleared east of Route Comox while another cleared west. Once the flanks were deemed clear, I sent my two dozers to make new routes on either side of Comox. Once they had reached our lead elements, they then dozed a new firing line that enabled our vehicles to adopt positions as far forward as possible. Finally, I deployed the Route Clearance Package down Comox up to our lead elements, thus opening up a Main Supply Route. At this point we dug in for the night.

Throughout the night, there were numerous sporadic contacts, usually nothing more than two- to three-man enemy detachments with small arms. I recall walking the front line with Cpl Pleasance and seeing nothing but red tracer rounds and friendly mortars firing at enemy both east and west of us. With enemy to our east and west, it kind of made me feel like we were slicing right through the Taliban force, which was exactly what we were doing. We would later find out that 31 Echo had been parked on top of a command wire IED for most of the night. Fortunately, the firing party must have been killed or disrupted, as the device never functioned. The reason that this command wire IED remained undiscovered was likely because upon rolling into position, Cpl Corbierre (gunner for 31 Echo) immediately engaged three Taliban armed with an 82-millimetre recoilless rifle. With the contacts seldom ceasing, five- and 20-metre checks were likely forgotten. In fact, the IED was not discovered until Sgt Coates rolled through a few weeks later. We spent the next three nights on this position, shoring up defences, improving our new dozed routes and waiting for new orders. Given that we had the biggest vehicles in the combat team, the Company Sergeant-Major for Mohawk Company asked WO Rouzes if we could conduct all the re-supply for his company. Not giving WO Rouzes any numbers, he simply requested, "as much stuff as you can fit in your vehicles." So, in addition to providing full-spectrum combat engineering support to Mohawk Company, we also handled their Combat Service Support needs.

In order to maintain the momentum of our offensive, 1 Troop was subsequently attached back to Maj Abthorpe and Bravo Company. Cpl Vienot, however, was sent to Recce Platoon in order to assist them with their nightly patrols deep in enemy territory. We moved forward to the next control line, using the exact same plan as before, and seized Objective Templar. We dozed two new routes up to and around the entire objective, allowing the combat team to completely secure it.

That evening we were attached back to Maj Wright and A Company in order to take the next control line. By now, it was getting pretty easy for me to give orders as our "dismount, doze and drive" plan had been working exceedingly well. In an effort to get a good view of our Area of Operations, Maj Wright, Cpl Pleasance and I joined the artillery Forward Observation Officer atop one of the large compounds. At the time, he was calling in 155-millimetre high explosive on a danger-close objective. Noticing that he was standing straight up observing his target, we all followed suit. I never really thought much of the term "danger close," which means that friendly forces are within 600 metres of the impact area, and never really appreciated the peril of danger close artillery. However, that all changed radically when a golf ball-sized chunk of 155-millimetre came screeching down in between Cpl Pleasance and me. We all stood there looking at each other until I suggested that perhaps we should try and find some cover. Nobody argued. After the successful Forward Passage of Lines with Bravo Company, we decided to conduct a carbon copy of the operation of the previous day. We remained with A Company for the next three days and cleared south all the way to Objective Rugby and the Arghandab River. We then searched and cleared the western portion of Objective Rugby while 2 Troop cleared the centre.

We were then attached back to Mohawk Company and ordered to clear the western portion of objective Rugby. Our task was to clear west, along Route Corner Brook, perpendicular to our previous axis of advance all the way to Route Abbotsford. During a tactical pause, MCpl Foulds approached my vehicle and told me that he thought he saw something suspicious in a grape hut window, after our dozer had clipped the edge of that hut. Keeping in mind that there are several hundred windows on any one grape hut, I was a little sceptical but I told him to investigate. To his credit, he had discovered six cans of Russian 25mm Anti-Armour rounds and an "IED go bag" consisting of a mortar round, detonation cord, detonator, wiring and a battery. One simply had to hook it up and drop it on any nearby road. Further exploitation by MCpl Valois and his EOD team led to the discovery of passports and other significant documentation.

During the clearance to Abbotsford, we came dangerously close to losing the D8 dozer. While we were dozing our new combat roads, the dozer approached a large wall. Not wanting to slow down the momentum, Cpl Reid dozed right through the wall. What he didn't know was that on the other side of this wall lay a 10 metre deep well with a five metre diameter. Once he broke through the wall 75% of the dozer went right into the hole. In fact, the only thing that remained on level ground was one of tracks, which was hanging on for dear life. Given that no Battle Group resources would ever be able to recover this 37-tonne dozer from its predicament, I found myself in a real conundrum. I sent a sitrep to Maj Gasparotto and asked him if he could loan me the D7 so that I could attempt to fill the hole up with surrounding earth, such that the dozer could then claw its way out. Luckily, this plan worked and the D7 dozer saved the day. The parade, however, was short-lived as a week later the D7 dozer struck a triple-stacked anti-tank mine and was more or less abandoned for the next five months.

Upon arrival back at the Arghandab River, we were ordered to link up with Task Force Grizzly, which had established a leaguer on the north side of the river. I must say that this was probably the most unfortunately sited position (Martello excluded because we had inherited it) that I have ever occupied, but then again you do not always get the best ground to work with. Fields of view were about 10 metres in every direction. I was given the warning that this was likely going to be the spot of a platoon or company sized FOB and that I should start planning on how to construct it.

WO Rouzes and I put a plan together that involved a whole lot of compound destruction but strongly encouraged all parties involved to take note that the giant mountain across the river. Ma'sum Ghar, which offered natural protection and unlimited fields of view, was a much better location for this FOB.

I always assumed that Ma'sum Ghar would end up being chosen, so we picked up and moved all of our stuff there and assumed all would work out in our favour. We returned to Patrol Base Wilson in order to grab all of our engineer stores and equipment for use at Ma'sum Ghar. We had two ATVs that we needed to move as well, however we had no lift capability. With limited options, I decided to let Sgt Proulx and Cpl Pleasance drive them down. In hindsight, that was not the smartest decision I had ever made, but it certainly was a sight, to see two ATVs mixed in with our LAVs and RG-31s. As we would see in October, this series of routes in our Area of Operations, including Comox, St John's, Desperado, Vancouver and all our dozed routes, became an IED playground with strikes occurring almost on a daily basis. At one point I tasked 31 Delta with the clearance of the entire six-kilometre stretch of route. Unfortunately, the Afghan National Police, who were supposed to provide strong points along the route once it was cleared, never showed up. This more or less negated all of 31 Delta's efforts as a route is only considered cleared as long as one has observation on it. Consequently, the IED strikes continued after we were done.

Operation Medusa definitely forced us to employ almost all of our engineer skills. Mobility support, Non-Standard Bridging construction, search, Conventional Munitions Disposal, Explosive Ordnance Disposal, fighting as infantry and demolitions were just some of the operations conducted. During our searches we uncovered hundreds of Taliban weapons and ordnance, IED components and intelligence. However, nearly 10 days of dismounted patrolling through two-metre-high grape fields certainly took its toll on 1 Troop. We were exhausted and so were awarded 48 hours of refit and rest at Kandahar Airfield. It is worth noting that to us, 48 hours at

Kandahar Airfield was the equivalent of a week at an all-inclusive resort. Removed from the fray, we all enjoyed the fresh food, comfortable sleep and Kyrgyzstanian masseuses, who insisted on calling Sgt Proulx "Lewis."

MA'SUM GHAR AND ROUTE SUMMIT

We had learned many lessons during Op Medusa, one of which was that once you successfully take ground, you have to keep soldiers there to hold it. As such, the Battle Group decided to establish a company-sized FOB in Pashmul so that we had a solid foot on the ground and could quickly surge throughout the Zhari district. Pashmul, however, was situated in extremely low ground, littered with legacy IEDs and unexploded ordnance and generally not the best place to build a FOB. The best possible location in Pashmul (aptly named the "Old Grizzly Leaguer" due to the fact that this is where Task Force Grizzly had remained during Op Medusa) had the Arghandab River to the south, an area known as the "IED playground" to the west, and dense shrubbery and trees to the north and east. Poor fields of fire, poor observation, and poor ingress and egress routes all added up to a poor location for a FOB. Despite these compelling arguments, and my saying that this was a bad idea, 1 Troop was ordered to design and start construction of a FOB in Pashmul. It seemed to me that the strategic importance of having a military presence in Pashmul was outweighing the tactical importance of siting a FOB in a location where it could actually influence the battle.

At the time when all of this was being decided, 1 Troop was working for Charles Company, who was operating with Task Force Grizzly. WO Rouzes and I walked the ground of this potential FOB location with Capt Trevor Norton, Second-in-Command of Charles Company, and he fully agreed with our assessment. However, we were still ordered to continue planning for a FOB there. After drafting the plan, WO Rouzes and I discovered that this FOB was going to involve a whole lot of senseless destruction and added work.

Ma'sum Ghar is the Pashto translation of "Beautiful Mountain." It is located on the south side of the Arghandab River, directly across from the town of Pashmul. Its peaks offered a virtually endless view in all directions and dominated both the Zhari and Panjwaii districts. The eastern edge of the mountain ridge split into two distinct ridges, thus forming a 100-metre by 500-metre valley, completely protected by the towering ridges. Given these characteristics, I was extremely keen on building a FOB in this location instead of one at the Old Grizzly Leaguer.

When Maj Gasparotto and Maj Wright arrived on the scene, they immediately agreed with my assessment. They were both intimately familiar with Ma'sum Ghar and thus were aware of its inherent advantages. They understood all of my reservations and vowed to convince the CO that Ma'sum Ghar was a far better location. So, not one hour after Maj Wright inherited the Area of Operations from Charles Company, we moved all of our resources to Ma'sum Ghar and began the designs for a FOB there. At this time, the direction to build a FOB in Pashmul was still extant; however, my cunning plan was to start building the FOB at Ma'sum Ghar under the pretext that we were simply working on force protection for our present location. My hope was that as more people were exposed to the tactical advantage and the possibilities offered by Ma'sum Ghar, the decision would be changed to build a permanent FOB there. In the end, my plan half-worked (or half-failed, depending on how you look at it). We were ordered to build two FOBs: one FOB at Ma'sum Ghar for a platoon and one in Pashmul, for a company. This, however, ended up flip-flopping as A Company resided at Ma'sum Ghar and the FOB was built to accommodate them. Since nobody in A Company was physically living in Pashmul, construction of that FOB fell lower on the priority list.

It was mid-to late-September 2006 when 1 Troop, along with some heavy equipment, Rock 47 Route Clearance Package and an Explosive Ordnance Disposal team arrived at Ma'sum Ghar. Due to the fact that we had to return to Patrol Base Wilson to collect some of our engineer resources, we were the last to arrive. Upon arriving, Capt Mike Reekie, LAV Captain for A Company told us that he was impressed by the size of my convoy and the resources I was commanding. Given the four Route Clearance Package vehicles, my Troop's 3 LAVs, 2 RG-31s, 2 ATVs, the 2 EOD Bisons, the "Backwhore" and the D8 dozer, it was a large, unique and slow-moving conglomerate of machines.

A few days prior to moving to Ma'sum Ghar, Maj Wright and I had attended a shura at the Panjwaii District Centre (located just to the south) while MWO Hooyer, Company Sergeant-Major of A Company and WO Rouzes walked the perimeter of our new home. We had planned to construct four Observation Posts atop the highest peaks surrounding the valley that would become our FOB. Observation Post 1 would provide line of sight to the east, Observation Post 2 located on the southern ridge would provide coverage to the south, Observation Post 3 on the northern ridge would face north over the Arghandab River and the entire Zhari District and Observation Post 4 located atop one of the highest points in the FOB, furnishing a view of the southwest. All of these Observation Posts were to be complemented by five LAV run-up positions. Run-up A would support Observation Post 1, run-up B for Observation Post 2 and run-up C, D and E would support Observation Post 3. Due to the elevation of Observation Post 4 we thought that it would be almost impossible to construct a run-up there but as it turned out, run-up F was eventually built at the very end of our tour.

With 31 Echo departing on leave, 1 Troop was down to two field sections. 31 Delta immediately started work on Observation Post 2 while 31 Charlie started work on Observation Post 3, as these were critical in the defensibility of the FOB. In addition to building the Observation Posts, they had designed section-sized bunkers nearby so that troops wouldn't have far to travel to do their surveillance shifts. Meanwhile, Cpl Reid and our D7 dozer began constructing routes within the FOB so that we could have some sort of traffic plan in place. While all of this was progressing, WO Rouzes and I were busy drawing up the stores, equipment and resource list that we would need filled in order to complete the task. We requested the following:

- 15,000m³ ¼-inch gravel
- 10,000 sandbags
- Fifty 10"x10" beams
- Fifty 8"x8" beams
- Fifty 6"x6" beams
- Fifty sheets ¾-inch plywood
- Fifty 2"x4" lumber
- Fifty sheets Corrugated Galvanized Iron (CGI)
- Various sizes and amounts of Hesco Bastions
- Various amounts of nails and bolts
- Power tools
- HP1
- Two Pionjars (gas-powered jackhammers)
- One tracked excavator

- One tracked excavator with hydraulic rock-breaker attachment
- One front-end loader
- Another D8 dozer
- One dump truck
- Two graders
- One pick-up truck
- One donkey

During a Daily Sitrep that I passed back to Capt John Hayward one evening in late September, I also sent this stores request. After a few moments of silence he told me that he'd need some time and that many of these items would not be possible to acquire. I understood, but reiterated that all of these items were necessary. He assured me that he would do what he could in order to get the requisite contracts in place for the majority of my needs, starting with gravel and lumber. Maj Gasparotto and Squadron Sergeant-Major Montgomery, who heard my Daily Sitrep, said that they could bring the HP1 and some pionjars to our position during their next trip to FOB Ma'sum Ghar. Also, the engineer resources that we had brought from Patrol Base Wilson gave us enough for 31 Charlie and 31 Delta to work on Observation Post 3 and 2, respectively.

For the next two weeks Sgt Grignon and Sgt Proulx worked tirelessly to get their Observation Posts constructed. Observation Post 2 posed some unique challenges in that it was sited, intentionally, atop a mountain peak. Therefore, a significant amount of blasting was required to create a level surface for construction. MCpl Foulds was in charge of that task while Sgt Grignon, through sheer talent, managed to manoeuvre the backhoe all the way up the steep southern ridge in order to begin work on run-up B and a road leading up to it. I must say that Sgt Grignon could very well be the most talented heavy equipment operator in the Engineer corps. His skills and knowledge were, by far, one of the greatest combat multipliers in the 1 RCR Battle Group with FOB Ma'sum Ghar, Route Summit, Route Brown and Route Dwyer among his many accomplishments. He made quick work of run-up B and it became the first completed run-up position although Cpl Pleasance and the Headquarters section finished the actual construction of it. Given that 1 Troop was tasked to man run-up B, I decided to move the troop up there permanently as Sgt Grignon had created a fairly large pad for us to use. Shortly after this move, MCpl Foulds informed us that Observation Post 2 was ready for blasting. While elements from A Company went around the town of Bazar-E-Panjwaii to evacuate the occupants of nearby homes, a task I'm told was like herding cats, I went up to inspect the charges. WO Rouzes and I were both quite impressed by MCpl Foulds's ingenuity. Using the pionjar he had bored 38 holes, strategically placed, deep into the ridge peak. In each hole, he had placed a quarter-block of C4 and about 300 millilitres of Trigran pelletized explosive.

Once I received word that the civilians were cleared of the area and that all soldiers were under cover, I gave MCpl Foulds the green light to tell his guys to fire the demolition. Three minutes later there was a loud explosion and a lot of flying rock, all caught on film. When the dust settled we went up to have a look and it was immediately clear that the blast had been successful. The peak had been obliterated and all that remained was a nice flat surface upon which Observation Post 2 could be built. Furthermore, the small rock fragments left over from the blast were perfect for filling the Hesco and this in turn prevented us from having to haul sandbags all the way up the ridge for that purpose although we still had to haul up a few of them for the overhead protection. After the blast, it only took a few days for the Observation Post to be constructed. Meanwhile, other elements of 31 Delta spent their time building a bunker about 50 metres below the peak. This bunker, which measured about 25 metres square, by two metres high was built into the southern ridge in order to make maximum use of the natural protection. Given that no heavy equipment could get to that position, 31 Delta was forced to dig the entire area out by shovel and pickaxe. After about a week of this dogged labour, they had managed to carve out a rectangular prism inside the ridge. Once that was finished, the bunker, complete with bunk beds, overhead protection and a one-metre-thick protective Hesco wall, was in place.

While 31 Delta was busy with Observation Post 2, 31 Charlie was hard at work on Observation Post 3. Instead of blasting, Sgt Proulx decided to chip away at his peak using the HP1. Given that the hose was only about 10 metres long, his section had to haul the 100-pound tool up the talus slope to the peak in order to use it. Unfortunately for 31 Charlie, the HP1 was prone to breaking, so it had to be hauled back down to the maintenance section on an almost daily basis. On one occasion, WO Rouzes and the mechanics had the HP1 stripped right down to the nuts and bolts in order to troubleshoot. They eventually got the thing running and 31 Charlie was

The demolition of one of the peaks at Ma'sum Ghar in order to build Observation Point 2.

able to finish their Observation Post. In order to economize his effort, Sgt Proulx delegated the design and construction of the Observation Post 3 bunker to Cpl Hunt and Cpl Locke, skilled carpenters both. After filling fifteen medium Hesco cells by hand and hauling about 6,000 sandbags the job was finished.

While 31 Charlie and 31 Delta continued with their projects, our heavy equipment (D8 dozer and backhoe) operators were fully occupied constructing routes. The FOB itself had two main entrances; one joined FOB Ma'sum Ghar with Route Fosters while the other was a combat road that had been dozed by 2 Troop for Op Medusa. This road was later named *Stachnik Crossing*. The latter route joined FOB Ma'sum Ghar with the Arghandab River. Both required significant upgrades as the first was extremely narrow and it was thus difficult for convoys to re-supply our position, while *Stachnik Crossing* was quickly turning into a sandbox. Fortunately, WO Rouzes and the Headquarters elements were able use the HP1 to slightly widen the Route Fosters entrance. It was around this time that Capt Hayward told me that we were going to have to give up the D8 dozer as the contract had expired. He assured me, however, that another D8 had been sourced and was en route. Just as we got prepared to load up the D8 and send it on its way, a civilian low-bed showed up at FOB Ma'sum Ghar to do the dozer swap. Had I known what was on this low-bed I probably would not have agreed to let the old D8 dozer go. Much to my disappointment, we had just received a D5, which closely resembled a Tonka Toy. Beggars can't be choosers, so we made the swap and made do.

It was the first week of October when the gravel contract was finally awarded. Nawabi, the contractor's son, came to visit FOB Ma'sum Ghar in order to recce where he would dump the 15,000 cubic metres of gravel. He was a great businessman and told me that his company could provide every piece of heavy equipment that I needed. That night I passed the information to Capt Hayward and within two days a whole fleet of heavy equipment, with operators, arrived at FOB Ma'sum Ghar.

About 600 cubic metres of gravel were arriving daily in loads of about 6 cubic metres. If you do the math, you can see that we had to coordinate the dumping of about 100 trucks every day. It is worth noting that these truck drivers get paid by the load, so, their plan was to simply come into the FOB, dump their load at the earliest possible time and leave. Obviously, we couldn't let this happen as we would have had small piles of gravel everywhere. Spr Lafreniere, who was dump truck qualified and knew how to properly stockpile, was placed in charge of coordinating this. I'm sure he would tell you that it was an extremely frustrating task.

Now that we had gravel and an ample supply of heavy equipment we were able to start shaping the actual FOB. A large Helicopter Landing Site was flattened and gravelled on the south-eastern side of the FOB and all roads were also covered, greatly reducing the dust. In addition, Cpl Reid was able to doze a road all the way up to the sites for run-ups D and E. Once that was done, 31 Charlie had no problem getting in there to build the run-up positions. Run-up C, which was sited on some pretty tough mountain rock, required extensive work. Sgt Proulx, MCpl King and the rest of 31 Charlie had attempted to blast the rock away but there was just too much. Our rock breaker operator, Mohammed Ali, said that he would have no problem creating a route leading up to that position. Unfortunately, this project had to wait, as we needed him to break the rock surrounding the Route Fosters entrance.

It was now the second week of October and solid plans were well under way for the construction of a high speed, well-protected route joining Highway 1 and Route Fosters. This route would generally follow/encompass the Vancouver / Comox / Desperado / Summit (VCDS) routes as well as the combat roads already in place. To be named Route Summit, this thoroughfare was to be as straight as possible, have 50 metres of standoff on both the east and west sides of the road, and be strong-pointed at key areas so as to prevent the Taliban from inserting mines and IEDs. Essentially this road would become the main line of communication between Patrol Base Wilson and FOB Ma'sum Ghar or, more importantly, Zhari and Panjwaii. For ease of command and control, Maj Gasparotto had divided this six-kilometre route into six sectors; sector 1 began at Highway 1 and went south to the old Medusa control line Winged Sword. Sector 2 made a 45-degree turn and headed southwest to the old objective Templar. Sector 3 led due south all the way to Objective Rugby. Sector 4 made a sharp eastern turn and proceeded in the direction of the Old Grizzly Leaguer. Sector 5 would be the eventual bridge crossing the Arghandab River and Sector 6 made another eastern turn, in front of FOB Ma'sum Ghar and linked up with route Fosters. Because of their proximity to FOB Ma'sum Ghar, Maj Gasparotto informed me that 1 Troop would likely be responsible for sectors 4 and 6 with sector 5 being built by an American NGO at some point down the road. The actual construction of the route was going to be contracted out to a civilian company, however due to the urgent need to open this line of communication, the squadron started work on it immediately. This mainly involved 2 Troop working from Patrol Base Wilson and moving south, dozing the 100-metre swath that would eventually become route Summit. This was no easy task as they were attacked by small insurgent detachments on a regular basis.

We were now approaching the second week in October, which was about the time that 31 Echo was expected to return from their leave, while 31 Delta and 31 Alpha were due to start theirs. We were supposed to be transported back to Kandahar Airfield via a Chinook; however, because the pilots were not satisfied with the condition of our landing site, we were told that the helicopter had refused to land at FOB Ma'sum Ghar.

In a desperate attempt to change the pilot's mind Sgt Grignon jumped into the backhoe and did some speedy maintenance. This unfortunately wasn't enough. Instead, A Company formed a leaguer in the middle of the dry Arghandab River bed and the bird touched down in the centre. As 31

Echo was taking over 31 Delta's vehicle, those elements conducted a 30 second handover at the landing site.

WO Rouzes, who was intimately familiar with the plan for FOB Ma'-sum Ghar, as he had conceived it in large measure, as well as the design for Route Summit Sector 6, had no problems commanding the troop during my absence. He was given an updated priority of work and told that he needed to begin construction on the FOB that would be located across the river in Pashmul. The FOB was to be built about 200 metres east of what was once objective Rugby. A Company's 2 Platoon had been living in this location for some time in order to keep an ISAF footprint on the ground in Pashmul. Because the centre of the FOB coincided with the remains of the destroyed Zettelmeyer from Op Medusa, we aptly named it "FOB Zettelmeyer" or "FOB ZL." WO Rouzes and I had discussed the design of the FOB prior to my departure. Due to the fact that the ground was relatively flat and open, the concept was much simpler than that of FOB Ma'-sum Ghar. Its basic shape was a quadrilateral with perimeter dimensions of 100 metres (south side) by 100 metres (west side) by 200 metres (north side) by 150 metres (east side). The walls would be constructed using 10B Hesco cells (the largest kind) and in each corner there would be an elevated run- up position and an Observation Post. The entrance/exit would be an eight-metre wide lane linking up with what would soon be Route Summit Sector 4. WO Rouzes immediately put 31 Charlie and 31 Echo to work constructing the walls, starting with the north and west, as these were the most critical. The Taliban, who obviously didn't like the idea of another FOB being built in their birthplace, launched intermittent nuisance rocket attacks on 31 Charlie and 31 Echo while they were constructing the outer walls. Despite this, they spent the next days finishing the perimeter.

While building the fortifications, WO Rouzes was visited by the local Afghan National Army Kandak Commander as well as his American Embedded Training Team mentor. Since they were the ones rumoured to be moving into the FOB, they wanted to know the status of the progress. When he saw the lack of stores, the embedded mentor told WO Rouzes, "Tell me what you need and I'll get it for you." This issue was also being driven by Maj Gasparotto as he had told the American Embedded Training Team, "If you want your FOB built you need to cough up some stores." Within two days, several truckloads of 7B Hesco were dumped at the FOB.

Eager to settle in, the Kandak Commander stated that as soon as the north wall was finished, his battalion would move in. Upon completion of the north wall, he stated that when the west wall was built, they'd occupy the FOB. Upon completion of the west wall, he stated that when the east and south walls were built he'd take up residence. Again, he didn't. He then stated that when the Observation Posts were built, he'd be there. Nope. In fact, we never saw one Afghan National Army soldier live in that FOB for any length of time.

Meanwhile, work at FOB Ma'sum Ghar had not ceased. Since this base was located in a valley between two ridges, the ground was anything but flat. Thus, WO Rouzes had directed our two dozers to begin moving the dirt so we had flat surfaces to work with. Once the area had been terraced, we could build permanent structures. In some areas (particularly along the northern ridge), he had brought the ground level down about two metres. Conscious of the fact that rain could be a factor he had our excavator dig a one metre by one metre French drainage system throughout the FOB, using the ¼ inch gravel as fill. His foresight definitely paid off as one month later it did rain and there was absolutely no pooling of water within the FOB. He had also directed our hydraulic rock breaker to begin work on run-up C - a task that would take the better part of a month to complete.

In addition, WO Rouzes began work on the grubbing and clearing of what would eventually become Route Summit Sector 6. He tasked both dozers to completely flatten all of the grape fields that bordered the north side of FOB Ma'sum Ghar, as this would become Sector 6. It is worth noting that the landowner received a healthy monetary sum for his land prior to its destruction.

As a bonus, Maj Gasparotto had managed to convince the local Civil-Military Cooperation detachment to give us 500 afghanis so that we could buy ourselves a donkey, which was the last item on our stores list. The hope was that this donkey could be used as a pack mule for carrying sandbags up to what would soon become Observation Post 4. As we were to soon find out this donkey, which had been named Tina, despised all work of any nature and did nothing but eat hay and apple-cinnamon Pop-Tarts.

When I, along with 31 Delta, arrived back in theatre in mid-November, I immediately saw the incredible amount of work that had been accomplished in my absence. The perimeter wall around FOB ZL had been finished, FOB Ma'sum Ghar had become a flat surface and properly drained and the area that would become route Summit Sector 6 had been completely cleared and levelled. With that, WO Rouzes handed control of the troop back to me and he departed that evening on leave.

Around this time, the 1 RCR Battle Group was getting ready to start Op Baaz Tsuka (Falcon Summit in Pashto) with a view to eliminating the Taliban that had been disrupting ISAF movement in and around FOB Spervan Ghar, Zangabad 1, Zangabad 2 (there were two Zangabads) and Zangabar Ghar. Given that this was more or less outside of the A Company's Area of Operations, 1 Troop did not play a major part in the operation. Instead, we maintained an Emergency Response Section and EOD team on standby so they could augment a Quick Reaction Force based on the A Company Combat Team.

Meanwhile, the troop continued working on the two FOBs. 31 Charlie was tasked to continue building the perimeter fence surrounding FOB Ma'-sum Ghar, 31 Delta to progress with FOB Zettelmeyer, and 31 Echo to construct the bunker for Observation Post 1 (31 Charlie had already built the Observation Post). Over at FOB Zettelmeyer, the remains of Hooper's Front End Loader were still sitting squarely in the middle of the site, which was making it difficult for Sgt Grignon to finish the grading. Since it was completely unsalvageable I asked Maj Gasparotto if we could have it buried in place. He agreed that that was the best thing to do; however, he insisted that the bucket, which was still in decent shape, be salvaged and sent back to Kandahar Airfield. So, I snagged the local Material Technician (jack of all trades - from sewing to welding). This we transported back to FOB Ma'-sum Ghar and subsequently sent on a logistics convoy back to Kandahar Airfield. Nine months later, this symbol of the Squadron's involvement in Op Medusa would find its way to the 2 Combat Engineer Regiment lines at CFB Petawawa. With the Zettelmeyer buried in its final resting place one metre below the centre of the FOB, Sgt Grignon was able to finish grading the surface making it ready to be graveled.

Back at FOB Ma'sum Ghar I could see that constructing Observation Post 4 was going to be a tough challenge. Located at the highest point of the mountain and with no quick or easy access up to it, the location was more or less cut off from the rest of the FOB. Following the advice of my staff, I tasked my most talented civilian operator, Mohammed Ali, along with his rock breaker, to start chipping a road up to the top. This road, which would take three months to complete, looked a lot like the Sea-to-Sky Highway in Vancouver, B.C. It required five switchbacks, and that the surface elevation of Observation Post 4 be brought down about two metres. In the end the road was not completely finished until the very end of our tour, and Observation Post 4 was never actually built. Instead, we gave them a run-position (run-up F) that towered over the entire area.

Everything was going well and the FOBs were being built without any major setbacks. However, Mother Nature decided to throw a giant wrench into our plans. For the first time in seven years, Kandahar received rain. And in Kandahar, when it rains, it pours. For about three days straight it did just that. As we were about to find out, this rain was going to cause some significant problems for us. The Arghandab River became so swollen that we could no longer cross with our vehicles. This effectively severed the main line of communication between the A Company Combat Team at FOB Ma'sum Ghar and the Charles Company Combat Team strong-pointing Route Summit. Once the rain ceased I immediately tasked 31 Echo to build a gravel causeway across the main artery of the river and 31 Charlie to repair the Arghandab River entrance into FOB Ma'sum Ghar. Luckily, we had several concrete and metal culverts on hand that could be used for these purposes. After three days of work, Sgt White and MCpl Pittman had effectively bridged the Arghandab and the line of communication was restored. Following this, 31 Delta was able to finish gravelling the inside of FOB ZL and 31 Echo proceeded to construct the vehicle run-up positions. Once complete, all that remained was the construction of the four elevated Observation Posts.

It was now mid-November 2006 and the population of FOB Ma'sum Ghar was about to significantly increase. The tanks of B Squadron had been held in Kandahar Airfield and were finally going to deploy forward into the fight. We had quickly prepared a firing line for them to occupy and had made signs denoting which roads were for tanks and which were for wheeled vehicles. These signs, however, did not influence the tanks' choice of routes.

Everyone in 1 Troop was working extremely hard, that is except Tina the donkey. In fact, she had quickly become nothing more than an amusement park attraction for soldiers passing through. Despite the fact that we were building FOBs and roads in a combat zone, the National Post saw it fit to do a story on Tina instead of the soldiers. She had developed a pretty mean attitude and it appeared that nobody could tame her. Fortunately, Sgt Grignon, who seemed to have some sort of animal sixth sense, was able to calm her down and ultimately ride her. Given his unique ability to communicate with Tina, Sgt Grignon was henceforth nicknamed the "Ass Whisperer." When I passed this information during Daily Sitrep, I'm told that the Battle Group Command Post erupted with laughter. Moments like these helped keep morale high, despite the gunfights, mortar and rocket attacks.

While 1 Troop was busy with FOB Ma'sum Ghar and FOB Zettelmeyer, Capt Dan Clarke and 2 Troop, along with two recently acquired Badgers, were frantically attempting to save Route Summit. The wadis that we had dozed during the construction of Summit Sector 1 had overflowed during the rainstorm because we failed to unclog them. Route Summit was becoming the Summit River. Luckily, Dan was able to use the Badgers to create a berm along the eastern edge of Summit, which contained the water. Given that route Summit Sector 4 was at the lowest elevation of the entire route north of the river, I was concerned that this flooding was eventually going to reach it. In order to get a better feel for how the water would eventually flow into sector 4, Sgt Proulx and I went on a wadi recce. We traveled to the area, dismounted, and began walking north, up into the village of Pashmul in order to inspect the wadis. Engrossed in our quest we soon found ourselves about 200 metres from our vehicles, deep within the village. Realizing that we were in a dubious position, when we saw and heard a Rocket Propelled Grenade launched and land about 50 metres west of our feet, we began sprinting for our vehicle. Not that it was any help, I did however send the following contact report "1 this is Echo 31 Alpha, someone just fired a Rocket Propelled Grenade at us from somewhere, more to follow, out."

We eventually made it back to our vehicle having qualified for the Olympic 200-metre sprint with no time to spare. As soon as the ramp came down Sgt Proulx threw me inside and then followed suit. Fortunately, we were able to get all the information that we needed regarding the wadis and we quickly returned to FOB Ma'sum Ghar. Based on our findings I tasked Sgt Grignon and 31 Delta to begin work on route Summit Sector 4.

In order to build Route Summit Sector 4 properly I ordered some additional heavy equipment, based on Sgt Grignon's recommendations. Two more graders, another front end loader, a water truck, two vibrating compactors and another dozer were acquired. As well an additional 10,000 cubic metres of gravel were ordered for the top layer of the road. Because the road was sited directly through grape fields, marijuana patches and other vegetation, we had to spend the first week of the project grubbing, clearing and levelling the area. Fortunately, two Badgers and a dozer were able to make quick work of this task. There was, however, one problem. This road was running pretty close to Route Vancouver, which had been closed for most of the tour due to the high mine/IED threat. This was where the D7 had been blown up, and the threat still remained. I was, therefore, reluctant to have the AEVs drive within twenty metres of the route. To resolve the problem, Sgt Grignon ordered MCpl Foulds and Cpl Sugrim to physically cut down all of the marijuana using the section machetes. This task completed, resulting in a 150-metre by 650-metre swath of land that was clear, level, free of obstructing vegetation and ready for a road.

Depending on the operational tempo, we either had zero, one or two Badgers at any given time. Their availability played a big factor in the speed at which we were able to build the road. Over the following week (mid-late November) Sgt Grignon started building up the base layer. Because we did not have a soils contract, we were forced to use the soil that was in-situ. Once the base layer was in place, it required about a week of levelling, compacting and watering. The Taliban did not take too kindly to Sgt Grignon's new road project. Consequently, 31 Delta was subjected to a few small arms attacks during the build. These proved to be most inconvenient, as we had to corral all of the civilian operators and move to FOB Zettelmeyer until the firefights subsided.

Once the base layer was complete Sgt Grignon was able to place the top layer of gravel on the road. From there, it was a matter of compacting, watering and grading over and over again. He also ensured that the shoulders were nicely compacted so to allow vehicles to pull off the route with relative ease, should they feel the need.

The project was more or less finished by mid-December. We were struggling to get the work done prior to Eid so that the road would be complete before all the workers went on a vacation of indeterminate length. Route Summit sector 4 was 650 metres long with about 75 metres of stand-off on either side. The route was elevated to a height of 1.5m and there was a gentle slope on each side allowing for easy on/off access. Because all of the vegetation had been removed, FOB Zettelmeyer and Observation Post 3 at FOB Ma'sum Ghar easily observed the route. On the last day of the project and after receiving permission from the village elders, we removed some compounds in Pashmul so that there was a seamless joining of Route Summit Sectors 4 and 3. With the road in place, we finally had the means to bring a low-bed to the north side of the Arghandab River.

This was important because the D7 dozer that had been destroyed in September was still rusting over on Route Vancouver. So, with a low-bed and two 20-tonne cranes, I set out to finally recover the dozer and send it back to Kandahar Airfield, thus clearing the $400,000 debt was on Johnny Hayward's loan card. John was the one who had ultimately convinced the Afghan National Army to lend us their dozer and had signed the paperwork. Prior to hooking up the dozer, I had to get two tanks to drag it 50 metres to the north so that it was close to the new road. Despite doing a detailed search, I was still concerned that there may have been some legacy mines or IEDs underneath the dozer. The giant metal dozer rendered our mine detectors useless, so with everyone under cover, we dragged the dozer without any problems. Once out, the cranes easily loaded the dozer onto the low-bed.

Route Summit was a tremendous accomplishment for Sgt Grignon and 31 Delta. In fact, they did such a fine job that they were tasked to spend the rest of the tour building a route that would connect Route Fosters and FOB Spervan Ghar. Prior to that, however, force protection works at FOB Zettelmeyer still had to be completed. 31 Delta and 31 Echo were tasked to each build two elevated Observation Posts using sea cans as the foundation. Each one was constructed in four days. With that done, the FOB was considered fully defensible, even by a dismounted platoon.

It was now late-December and the rumour was that the "Army of the West Combat Team[29]" (A Company, B Squadron and 1 Troop) was going to spend New Year's Eve in Helmand Province supporting the beleaguered British Task Force. In the end, we deployed close to Maywand District, just bordering Helmand. We spent a few days leaguering in and around the area and conducting presence patrols. The entire combat team, which consisted of about twenty tanks and twenty-five LAVs, was probably the most robust and intimidating force that had ever assembled outside the wire. Unfortunately, 1 Troop was abruptly forced to leave the Army of the West Combat Team because Bravo Company, who was manning the strong points along route Summit, came under a major attack. An after-action review conducted by the CO of our response to the large-scale Taliban attack on the strong points revealed that those strong points did not have the run-up positions required for the Quick Reaction Force to simply pull into a strong point and join the battle. Therefore, 1 Troop's task, along with my two Badgers, was to recce each strong point and create additional run-up positions.

With the FOBs and route Summit Sector 4 almost complete, Maj Gasparotto made the decision to give 1 Troop a change of scenery. He subsequently detached us from the A Company Combat Team and attached us to the ISTAR Squadron, who was set to deploy to Ghundy Ghar.

FROM GHUNDY GHAR TO TRENTON

For the first time since Ex Maple Guardian in Wainright, 1 Troop was attached to Maj Andy Lussier and his ISTAR Squadron. Our task was to support their movement from FOB Ma'sum Ghar up to the peak of Ghundy Ghar and then assist with survivability and further mobility. Armed with two field sections, an Explosive Ordnance Disposal team, a Badger and a Route Clearance Package, we departed for Ghundy Ghar, located about 30 kilometres west of FOB Ma'sum Ghar. In addition to supporting friendly force mobility we were also tasked to build some hasty police checkpoints that would later be manned by the Afghan National Police. We ended up building one such checkpoint in the vicinity of Ghundy Ghar; however, the Police never manned the post and the Hesco that we had used was emptied and stolen by locals.

Upon arriving at the base of Ghundy Ghar we realized that we had our work cut out for us. The only passage was a narrow goat trail that led part way up the mountain. Concerned about the IED and mine threat, I dispatched the Route Clearance Package Husky to get as far up the road as possible. Once completed, I dispatched MCpl Schroder and his Badger to doze a route leading to the peak.

WO Rouzes and I decided to recce the proposed route to be dozed by MCpl Schroder. When we arrived at the top we were surprised to see that the entire peak was covered with old trenches, most likely dug by the Mujihadeen during the Soviet invasion of Afghanistan. We also saw ration packs and water, indicating that other Coalition forces had already occupied this position before. It was later learned that Canadian soldiers from the previous rotation had been engaged in some fierce firefights at Ghundy Ghar.

Once the road was about 75% complete, MCpl Schroder advised me that the Badger was not fully functional and needed some downtime. It was, however, made clear to me from higher that the road had to be finished as soon as possible and that the risk to the equipment was something we'd have to accept. As if God was trying to prove a point regarding the work-to-rest ratio, the engine died twenty minutes later and we were left with no Badgers and a road that was 76% completed. The good news was that enough work had been done to allow the Coyote Armoured Reconnaissance Vehicles to get positions atop Ghundy Ghar. A few days later, the Badger was fixed and returned to service.

With the ISTAR Squadron and a tank troop set up along the high ridges and peaks of Ghundy Ghar, the only place left for 1 Troop was at the very bottom of the mountain in a sort of 100-metre by 100-metre bowl. This was an interesting spot as it carried with it several implied tasks including site security, "gate" security (although there was no gate, *per se*) and liaison with visitors who were mostly Police.

The only task we ever really received at Ghundy Ghar was to construct another checkpoint about one kilometre east of the mountain. The Civil-Military Cooperation crew supplied us with about 50 metal barrels and six shovels. With these great stores in hand we went to the location, offered employment to anyone who passed by, and began setting up. After some initial reluctance, about 30 Afghans were hired to shovel dirt into these barrels, thus creating chicanes along the road. From the outset, the checkpoint was a dilapidated collection of structures and the Police abandoned it not five minutes after it was completed. They were later ordered to return to this location and it turned out to be a major hotspot for the subsequent rotations.

During our three weeks at Ghundy Ghar we responded to about one IED/mine strike per day, some of which were post-blast, some of which were pre-detonation and some of which were non-existent. On one occasion, while MCpl Barrette's Badger was doing some route maintenance, they dozed right over top of an Italian TC-6 anti-tank mine, shearing the top half right off. A clearance would later indicate that this was a solitary mine. A closer look showed that the mine was indeed fused and the only reason it didn't go off was because MCpl Barrette had sheared it right along the seam, thus separating the primer from the charge. Had it gone off there certainly would have been shrapnel injuries within the position. I guess it was our lucky day.

Our days were pretty quiet aside from the IED calls, conducting improvements to the position with limited means and a few patrols. One day

WO Rouzes and I were able to watch all ten one-hour episodes of HBO's Band of Brothers. There were some entertaining moments, however. Some of the intelligence hits that were sent to us were absolutely priceless. On one occasion, the following message was heard on the radio, "The Taliban are planning something, somewhere."

OP DESTRUCTOR

Ghundy Ghar was the last big show for 1 Troop. It was the end of January, 2007 and the tour was coming to a close. We did support two more small-scale operations, one with a tank troop about 50 kilometres west along the Arghandab River and one with the "Army of the West," the latter being the more interesting. Op Destructor, as it was informally nicknamed, was intended to be a demonstration of our capabilities for the incoming Battle Group. At the end of the day, it involved dozing a ring around an objective village, thus providing an outer cordon. Once established, a dismounted force went into the village and did some patrolling. As turned out, the dozed ring was responsible for destroying several parcels of farmland. Judging by the angry look on villagers' faces, I don't think we won their hearts or minds that day.

With the Troop back at Kandahar Airfield, all that was left to do was the relief in place. I met up with the incoming troop commander, and we arranged to head out to FOB Ma'sum Ghar the following day in order to do a handover tour of our Area of Operations. As we were leaving Kandahar Airfield, we found out that Highway 1 was closed due to a collision involving ISTAR Squadron. I recall Maj Lussier asking for a sitrep regarding recovery assets and adding that up to that point, his squadron had already had 16 Rules of Engagement escalations. The situation necessitated a change of the route so I decided to go north around Kandahar City. Never having travelled these roads before, I was unaware of how narrow they were. The difficulty of navigation was compounded by the fact that this was a night move. At one point, inadvertently I hit a utility pole (or more like stick) and ended up tearing down many power lines.

HANDOVER / HOME

After a day touring FOBs Ma'sum Ghar, Spervan Ghar, Patrol Base Wilson and Route Summit, the handover was more or less complete. During the visit to Patrol Base Wilson, I overheard an interesting conversation with the incoming company from 2 RCR Battle Group. Basically, they were unsatisfied with the response times for engineer EOD teams and figured that their Assault Pioneers should be given the explosives necessary to destroy unexploded ordnance. I thought about inserting myself into the conversation and explaining exactly how many ways that plan could end in disaster or death, but decided to let my counterpart know and deal with it. I also attended a Commanding Officer's Orders Group on behalf of Maj Gasparotto and had a noteworthy conversation with one of the incoming OCs. He had asked when Route Summit would be completed and paved, to which I replied about six weeks. He then told me that that wasn't fast enough. I then asked if he had any spare paving machines. The answer was no. We then parted ways.

I travelled back to Kandahar Airfield the next day in the back of the OC's LAV as he had come out with his replacement that morning. The ride back was uneventful, which was fine with me. I met up with the Troop and started packing my bags and getting ready to get the hell out of Dodge. Since 1 Troop had been the first in, we had the luxury of being the first one out. The only issue that we faced was that our flight out of Kandahar Airfield was delayed by one day. Before long, 1 Troop was sipping Mai Tais in sunny Cyprus after a quick layover at Camp Mirage.

Aside from the incident involving Pte Aucoin, (Spr Quesnelle's self-designated alias) found swimming naked in the hotel pool, 1 Troop survived Cyprus with no significant issues. The trip home was long and uneventful; that is, until we hit Canadian airspace. Just off the Atlantic coast we were greeted in style and duly escorted home by a pair of CF-18 Hornet fighters. They patched their radio into that of the Airbus and were the first to welcome us back to Canada. After touchdown in Trenton and a 4-hour bus ride to Petawawa, we had finally arrived.

2 TROOP

Various Authors

DEPLOYMENT

(WO Clucas)

2 Troop had been together for approximately one year before we deployed. During that time most of the troop had bonded and knew what to expect from one another. Even though we recognized that this was achieved in a training environment, we did not expect anything to change once in Kandahar. As we were soon to discover, we were very naïve in our expectations. As had been proven on many battlefields before our own, people change or grow up in unimaginable ways as they become hardened to the environment, to other people and to certain situations.

During training at the Canadian Manoeuvre Training Centre, the Troop performed all of its tasks with the utmost professionalism and resolve. Attached to Charles Company for the better part of this training, 2 Troop formed a certain bond with the members of that company, a relationship which would come into play once in Kandahar.

Throughout the training and eventually the mission, the Troop went through some changes in leadership. The Troop Warrant Officer, WO Perrault, had bone chips in his foot and unfortunately was sent back to Petawawa to heal so he would be able to deploy in August. So, with that, I stepped up to be the Troop Warrant Officer. Unfortunately this occurrence foreshadowed WO Perrault's eventual permanent replacement in theatre when he would become a casualty during an IED strike.

As with every changeover of leadership there were growing pains. Eventually, they were all addressed by the various levels of command concerned, and despite all of that, the Troop continued to provide the engineer support that was demanded of it. Once the training was completed, we returned to Petawawa in order to take some well-deserved pre-deployment leave.

The Troop Commander and Warrant Officer were the first to deploy. They went in early to ensure everything was in order, or in as much order as possible, before the remainder of the Troop arrived. My section, 32 Bravo, was next to deploy, followed by Sgt Carruba's 32 Charlie, Sgt Stachnik's 32 Delta, and Sgt Coates's 32 Echo. Everyone was in theatre by mid-August 2006.

Once in theatre, all the arrival briefs, ranges and in-clearances were performed. As well, in a solemn marking of our arrival, we attended several ramp ceremonies before we headed outside the wire. Then it was time to conduct the handover with members of 11 Field Squadron, 1 Combat Engineer Regiment from the outgoing 1 PPCLI Battle Group. Their vehicles as well as their soldiers were in bad shape. They had been through a lot during their time in theatre with little time for vehicle or personal maintenance. The whole of 2 Troop was saying, "Are we going to look like that at the end of our tour?" We hoped not but only time would tell.

Now the Troop had most of the vehicles and the preparations well underway to get ready for upcoming operations. 2 Troop was pretty much good to go for whatever would be thrown at us, or so we thought.

Op Medusa

The first major operation that would test 2 Troop would be Op Medusa. Dubbed as Canada's largest combat operation since the Korean War and the largest in the history of NATO, the operation would see the following dispositions: the Troop Headquarters along with 32 Charlie and 32 Delta attached to Charles Company. 32 Echo would be split in two, with Sgt Coates taking half of the section to FOB Martello in the north and MCpl Thomas taking the other half to FOB Costall near the Pakistan border. Sgt Clucas' 32 Bravo would be part of Maj Gasparotto's Engineer Squadron Reserve along with EOD 2, 31 Delta and Rock 26, an American Route Clearance Package.

Everyone departed Kandahar Airfield on September 1st. While different routes were taken by the Battle Group's various elements, we all met up in Waiting Area 3, on the north side of Route Fosters. The area was supposed to be free of mines and Unexploded Ordnance but when Charles Company was preparing to leave for the next waiting area, one of their LAVs hit an anti-tank mine. Everyone in the waiting area immediately piled into their vehicles, thinking we were under mortar attack. After things calmed down, and the situation was assessed, the Route Clearance Package cleared a safe route out of the waiting area, enabling the remainder of the vehicles to extricate themselves safely.

Once the vehicles had moved on, there was just the OC's Squadron Reserve. We had to stay to provide security for the damaged LAV until recovery assets arrived to haul it back to Kandahar Airfield. Not exactly a great way to start an operation. Recovery arrived at dawn so it turned out to be a long night. Once the damaged LAV was gone we made our way to Waiting Area 2 and then finally to Battle Position 303.

At Battle Position 303, we had a chance to get caught up on some sleep. Initially, Capt Trevor Norton, the Charles Company LAV Captain had col-located his firebase[30] there with us with. Throughout the day the firebase was firing at the "White School" in Pashmul on the other side of the Arghandab River. By the end of the day, the LAV Captain and his firebase relocated to Battle Position 302 (to be later known as FOB Ma'sum Ghar) in order to assist in the assault on the "White School" on September 3rd, 2006. Once the firebase left, it was just the Engineer Squadron Reserve left on the front part of Battle Position 303 with Charles Company's echelon occupying the back.

ASSAULT ON PASHMUL AND THE WHITE SCHOOL.

(Sgt Justin O'Neill)

On the morning of September 3rd 2006, the assault on the White School (AKA Objective Rugby) stepped off from Battle Position 302 at approximately 7:00 am. The majority of 2 Troop, augmented with two pieces of heavy equipment, was attached to Charles Company for the operation. The crossing of the Arghandab River was uneventful, with the attack force reaching the north side of the river without any enemy contact. With a combined bombardment of 155mm artillery and Close Air Support from Coalition jets hitting the north side of the river, we where not shocked how quiet it had been. All the intelligence stated the night before was that there were "No signs of local activity."

The Charles Company Combat Team was sitting in the open just 100 metres north of the river and about 400 metres south of the dreaded White School where exactly one month earlier the soldiers of the 1 PPCLI Battle Group on the previous rotation suffered three killed in action and numerous non-fatal casualties. 32 Delta conducted searches of vulnerable points while 32 Charlie marked the safe lane across the river. During the searches, 32 Delta found a suspected IED of some sort. Sgt Stachnik made the call on the ground and blew the device in place. At this point all was going according to plan. By mid-morning, with still no enemy in sight, the Combat Team was in a relaxed state of readiness - soldiers walking around 'smoking and joking'.

Heavy Equipment call signs were told to start breaching towards the White School. Cpl Clinton Orr was in the armoured D6 Dozer, borrowed from the UK, on the North Breach with 32 Charlie. MCpl Lance Hooper was in the "Mad Maxed" up-armoured Zettelmeyer on the South Breach. Away we went, heavy equipment clearing the way, with Engineer and Infantry LAVs close behind. The breaches were about 30 to 40 metres apart and were pushing northwest. From my air sentry hatch location all was going to plan and then not 100 metres into our travels, the gates of hell opened and enveloped the entire Combat Team with small arms, machine-gun and Rocket Propelled Grenade fire. It was absolute mayhem on the battlefield.

Breach or no breach, we signalled for the Heavy Equipment call signs to pull back. I then saw a LAV drive into a large ditch and another LAV get hit with what we thought to be a Rocket Propelled Grenade. We would find out later that it was an 82mm recoilless rifle round and it was Sgt Shane Stachnik's vehicle that had been hit.

It seemed to be hours out there but in reality only minutes had passed. MCpl Hooper was out of the breach and the Charles Company Sergeant-Major had set up the Casualty Collection Point in close proximity to his Zettelmeyer. Then, a Rocket Propelled Grenade slammed into the fuel tank on the Zettelmeyer. Hooper, along with several others, was injured. WO Mellish was killed. 32 Charlie provided cover fire for the infantry that had ditched their LAV so that its dismounts could get to safety. Cpl Potzkai, 'T Triple C' qualified, dismounted at the Casualty Collection Point to assist with treating the injured.

32 Charlie returned into the kill zone to provide covering fire for Cpl Orr, who, having failed to extricate the ditched LAV, was now exiting the area at the dozer's best speed of 3 KPH. 32 Charlie and one other infantry LAV were the only vehicles left in the fight - all other call signs had pulled out. Then the word came over the net that there was a 500-pound bomb inbound. That was the signal to get out of Dodge. 32 Charlie then moved to the leaguer in the Arghandab River in order to evacuate the wounded and 're-bomb' with ammunition.

Throughout the attack, the Engineer Reserve was listening very intensely to the radio to try and follow the battle. Other call signs had also moved up to the high ground at Battle Position 303 to get a better view and to provide fire support if required. When the news came about Shane and the status of 32 Delta, nothing was said. The ZAP list had been pulled out and the members of 32 Bravo came into the RG-31 one by one and were shown the list of casualties associated with the ZAP number. Throughout the whole battle communications were intermittent at best with the Engineer Support Coordination Centre back at the Kandahar Airfield. As such, 32 Bravo would act as the relay station, as their comms were working consistently well, passing the info back on a regular basis.

MCpl Justin O'Neill acting as a LAV air sentry.

A-10 FRIENDLY FIRE

(WO Clucas)

On the morning of September 4th, we woke to the sounds of an A-10 attacking the White School. From Battle Position 303, we could see the pilot clearly alter his course towards Battle Position 302 and let loose. Fortunately, if that can be said, he only fired a fraction of what he could have.

Next, we saw Charles Company's echelon move through our location to go to Battle Position 302 to see what assistance they could provide to the mass casualty situation. We couldn't believe it. Then we heard the ZAP numbers starting to come across the radio. We were saying to ourselves, "What is going on here? Yesterday, 2 Troop had one KIA and numerous casualties and today we sustained five more!"

REMAINDER OF THE OPERATION

After sustaining casualties for two days in a row, newly-in-charge MCpl Orvis' 32 Delta was combat ineffective. As such they were sent to Battle Position 303 to recuperate. When 32 Delta showed up at Battle Position 303, they were obviously still in a state of shock as to what had taken place and almost immediately after they dismounted from their damaged vehicle, the emotions poured out. All the members of 32 Bravo, 32 Delta, and EOD 2, sat and talked about the memories and the events that happened a day earlier.

After things calmed down once again, we gathered ourselves and then got the word that the remnants of 32 Delta would be returning to Kandahar Airfield as part of a re-supply convoy. They ended up driving their disabled LAV with only man-portable radios for communication and the pintle-mounted machine gun for protection.

Another day started without incident and remained relatively quiet. It was at this point that ISTAR Squadron moved in. In the latter part of that day, 32 Bravo received orders to go link up with Mohawk, an American unit drawn from the US 10th (Mountain) Division, who were located in behind Battle Position 303. After the link-up, 32 Bravo found out that they would be heading back to Kandahar Airfield for a couple of days to start preparations with 1 Troop for the assault from the north.

Upon our return to Panjwaii, we met up in Patrol Base Wilson with 1 Troop, who were receiving orders from the US Commander of Mohawk Company. After receiving orders, we escorted the dozer to the first breach, which was on the east side of Route Comox. The Route Clearance Package remained in Patrol Base Wilson until it was needed. When required, the dozer would be brought back to Patrol Base Wilson and then we would pick up the Route Clearance Package. This process continued until it wasn't feasible to go back to Patrol Base Wilson as we would be too far along in the breach. Once the east breach was completed we then switched to the west side. This went on for almost one week, and then 32 Bravo finally met back up with the remainder of 2 Troop.

2 Troop's next task was to work with A Company. 1 Troop had worked with them extensively in the past, but this would be our first time. 2 Troop, with 31 Echo, would be working just off Route Chilliwack and heading west. Eventually a reconstituted 32 Echo arrived to replace 31 Echo. This section wasn't the original 32 Echo, but included Sgt Coates with two members of his original section and the rest of the uninjured sappers from 32 Delta. 32 Delta's Dragoon crew remained back at Kandahar Airfield recovering from wounds sustained on September 3rd and awaited a replacement LAV. During 2 Troop's time with A Company, we carried out various dismounted patrols to check different routes in order to ascertain if those roads were trafficable by LAV for a further push west.

On September 16th, orders were received for 32 Bravo to head back to Kandahar Airfield the next day with a convoy for 48 hours R&R. Sgt Coates was now the only engineer element supporting A Company.

SUICIDE BOMBING – SEPTEMBER 18TH

(Sgt Neil Coates)

On September 18th, 2006 32 Echo was attached to A Company for dismounted operations in the vicinity of Route Abbotsford. A Company was planning to carry out two patrols a day so it was decided, in conjunction with the OC, that the engineer section would be split so we could provide support to both patrols. On that morning my section second-in-command, MCpl Orvis and I switched so that he could take the morning patrol and I would take the evening one.

We mounted the section into our Bison and departed the harbour, which was also the patrol's start point. On arrival, MCpl Dwayne Orvis, Cpl Johnny Lalonde, Cpl Denver Williams and Spr Mike McTeague kitted up and moved to link up with the patrol commander. Along with my crew, I stayed with the vehicle in preparation for the move to the pick-up point.

Approximately 10-15 minutes later I heard a loud explosion in the area I believed the patrol to be in. Almost immediately a mass casualty situation was broadcast over the net. The person sending the radio report was very excited and the first details were confusing. The A Company Sergeant-Major came on the net and ordered the vehicles to move to the nearest accessible point bringing all available medical supplies and stretchers. We moved to a point about 150m from the scene. I left my soldiers with the vehicle and grabbed the medical jump bag and the two stretchers we were carrying and ran.

I confronted the chaos, after rounding a corner in the road. There were numerous wounded being treated on both sides of the pathway. A ground-sheet covered those who were killed and I could see three pairs of boots. I grabbed the first medic I saw and gave her the jump bag. I then placed the stretchers next to two wounded soldiers who were being treated on the ground. Then it was time to find my soldiers.

I first came across Cpl Lalonde. He was propped up on his bag, which contained prepared C4 charges. He saw me, smiled and said "Hey Sarge, make sure my OT[31] paperwork goes through!" I asked the medic what his injuries were and was informed he had two suspected broken ankles. One was definitely broken judging by the angle of his foot.

I saw Cpl Williams next. He was in serious shape. There were two people working on him. He had several penetration wounds that I could see. When he spotted me had said in his best Jamaican accent, "They done got me Sarge". Denver had complained only a few days before that the Taliban were after him personally because he was black!

Spr McTeague was the third soldier in my section that I saw. He was lying on a stretcher with several people treating him. He looked to be the most seriously injured so far. He had numerous entry wounds and was in a lot of pain. The medics were in the process of administering morphine. Mike didn't say much as I helped dress some of his wounds. His right arm was hanging at a strange angle.

MCpl Dwayne Orvis was across the path from McTeague and I went to see how my friend was doing. He was lying on his right side as a 'T Triple C' qualified soldier worked on his injuries. He had several wounds across his body and more in his right arm. When he saw me he motioned for me to lean down so he could talk. When I asked him how he was doing he asked me for a smoke. I lit one and held it to his lips while he took a long drag. We both laughed when the medic said that was an unhealthy habit and that he would not be allowed to smoke on the helicopter.

While I was finding my section members the casualty evacuation helicopters had been called and now we could hear them approaching. A Black Hawk and a Chinook were in-bound. The Sergeant Major called for Priority 1 and 2 casualties to be loaded last so they would be the first off in Kandahar Airfield. Mike and Dwayne were both Priority 1, Denver and John were Priority 2. When the Chinook touched down I helped load McTeague. When we picked up the stretcher his arm dangled loosely. I yelled at the guy on that side to watch his arm and when we placed him on the ground to wait for the load-master, his arm went under the stretcher. I hit the guy on the helmet and pointed to his arm. We adjusted his position so his arm was secured. Next up was Dwayne. He went straight onto the chopper without delay, and then I grabbed the next up who was Denver. When we placed him on the floor Dwayne said something that I couldn't hear, when I leaned over he said "Don't place him next to me, he will bitch and moan all the way back to Kandahar Airfield!"

When all the wounded had been loaded, and the birds left it was unusually quiet. Then A Company's Sergeant Major took control and soldiers started gathering up gear and weapons. We then received a threat warning that an attack was imminent on our position. As I was getting my gear I ran into Cpl Mike Maidment who took me to his vehicle so I could contact Maj Gasparotto to give him sitrep. He was aware of the situation in regards to the bombing but did not know that we had engineers injured. I passed the ZAP numbers and priorities over the net. It was not until later that I realised that the whole Squadron was listening in and that there were many friends of the wounded hearing the news.

Shortly after, we mounted up and moved back to our harbour area. My section had been reduced to a driver, an air sentry and myself. Once back at the A Company leaguer, the OC convened an Orders Group. Details of the bombing began to surface. The suicide bomber had waved to the members of the patrol, while pushing a bicycle. Once he was within the patrol and soldiers were gathering around he detonated what is now known to be a vest that contained M40 grenades and large ball bearings. OC A Company told me to mount up my guys and join another call sign that was heading back to Patrol Base Wilson. That Platoon Commander and I walked away. He was visibly upset at what had happened to his patrol. He said the guy looked friendly, which is why he allowed him to come into the perimeter. During all my time with A Company, I stressed to the Platoon Commanders to stop anyone from approaching. My comment to him was "A tough lesson to learn, Sir."

We departed the harbour area and headed back to Patrol Base Wilson, where we met up with WO Perreault who was also on his way back to Kandahar Airfield for a break. The final outcome was four dead and 16 wounded, including a civilian male and two small children.

32 Echo Section Commander, Sgt Neil Coates.

BETWEEN OP MEDUSA AND ROUTE SUMMIT

(WO Clucas)

Now, most of the Troop was back at Kandahar Airfield for a break. Everyone had time to relax, get a shower and reflect on the last couple of weeks. We sat around with each other and just basically talked about everything. Once our R&R was done, we were back out. On September 23rd, 2 Troop's Headquarters, Bravo, Charlie and Echo sections headed out to FOB Spervan Ghar to once again meet up with Charles Company. For the next week, the Troop remained there, providing engineer support. Orders for the construction of Route Summit eventually split up the Troop, yet again. On September 29th, my section, 32 Bravo was left to support Charles Company at Spervan Ghar, while the remainder of 2 Troop moved to link up with Maj Gasparotto and started centralized road construction operations.

During 32 Bravo's time with Charles Company, they conducted a recce to see what force protection measures were required yet feasible. At some point, Charles Company moved out and ISTAR moved in, bringing with it the inevitable changes to the defensive plan. Therefore, more stores and equipment had to be ordered, which surely made our Squadron Headquarters' day. Along with 1 Troop starting construction on FOB Mas'um Ghar, they now had to try and scrounge up stores for another FOB.

(Capt Dan Clarke)

Almost two years later, I look back at my time with 23 Field Squadron in Afghanistan with incredulity. My world was turned upside-down in mid-September of 2006 when I was told that I would be immediately deploying to join 23 Field Squadron in Afghanistan. At that time I was commanding 4 Troop in 24 Field Squadron, 2 Combat Engineer Regiment, and was enjoying the garrison life of a young troop commander. Like the rest of the rear-party in the Regiment, I was closely following the heroic actions of 23 as they deployed and became engaged in combat that was unlike anything Canadians had seen for a generation. I was shocked to be told that I would be deploying as a replacement to assume command of 2 Troop. This was an organization that had been badly depleted by casualties and enemy action. As a result of the fighting of September 3rd, the friendly fire incident of September 4th and finally the suicide bombing of September 18th. This was a troop that had suffered greatly.

The preparation to deploy was a whirlwind process. I was given the word on a Thursday and signed for my tan uniforms and other additional kit that afternoon. I received my immunization shots on the Friday, conducted final administration at the unit (and winterized my house) on the weekend and turned in my baggage on the following Monday morning. On the Tuesday I was on a plane; first to Budapest, then to an airbase in the Middle East and then on to Kandahar Airfield. Throughout all of this, I struggled to come to grips with this new challenge. I thought about what I would say when I met the Troop, how I and they might react, and how I could be expected to lead this group of combat-tested veterans who had already been through so much.

More than all of that, I struggled with an overwhelming sense of being unprepared. This Battle Group had readied themselves for over a year in preparation for this deployment. They had undergone countless courses and training exercises. They had been confirmed and re-confirmed, and they had worked hard to prepare themselves for the challenges of combat. I had missed all of this. I was unfamiliar with the majority of their tactics, techniques and procedures. I did not know any of their reports or returns, and I had not worked closely with most of the key personalities in the Squadron. I hadn't even been in a LAV turret for over a year. I felt anxious and intimidated.

I landed at Kandahar Airfield in the last week of September and spent the next four days trying to digest as much information as possible. I hung out in the Battle Group Command Post, and endeavoured to bring myself up to speed on the rhythm of the ongoing operations. I eventual secured a ride to Ma'sum Ghar with an American EOD team, along with Cpl Chris Ashton, who was on his way to the newly established outpost at Spervan Ghar. Cpl Ashton was to be the only Heavy Equipment operator at that FOB for most of the next month, and literally built it from the ground up. I spent a night at Ma'sum Ghar before catching another lift north to Patrol Base Wilson and finally married up with my new troop.

My first days in the Troop were a blur. I arrived in the afternoon and met up with WO Perrault. At this point, the Warrant had been leading the Troop for a couple of weeks and by all accounts had risen to the challenge doing an outstanding job. I had no intention of making immediate changes, and was very comfortable with observing and learning from the Warrant as I found my feet and became more at ease with my new role. After some brief introductions I had to work quickly to come up to speed on the tasks at hand. The Troop was acting as the Quick Reaction Force supporting the ISTAR Squadron operating out of Patrol Base Wilson. Quick Reaction Force tasks are often assigned to units in an effort to give them some time off of the front line. It is a waiting game, and can be a chance to rest and conduct some necessary personal maintenance and administration. At the same time, the Quick Reaction Force must be ready to mount up and head out the door on a moment's notice. As previously stated, 2 Troop's complement had been badly depleted and as it awaited replacements for casualties, this Quick Reaction Force task was clearly intended to give it a moment's respite. The intent, however wasn't always realized. Within a few hours of my arrival we received a Quick Reaction Force call and 15 minutes later we were rolling out the gates of the camp. It seemed we had barely returned from that call when we were called out again, early the next morning, to respond to an IED strike. This strike had unfortunately claimed the life of yet another Canadian soldier, Trooper Mark Wilson. My novel adventure had suddenly become starkly real for me as I found myself coming face to face with the tragedy of war. The pace of operations seemed to only increase from then on. On that same day we were forced to shift gears and set our sights on the construction of Route Summit.

Route Summit was conceived as a tactical solution to the mobility challenges presented by the canalized roads and high mud walls that dominate the Zhari and Panjwaii districts of Kandahar Province. Before Route Summit, the Coalition Forces had to rely on a series of winding roads that could not be adequately observed. This left us highly susceptible to ambushes and IED strikes. Summit was to be a new direct route that would join Highway 1 and Patrol Base Wilson to Route Fosters and the then- fledgling Canadian camp at Ma'sum Ghar. The Troop had already been working on Route Summit for the previous week, clearing and grubbing[32] in some of the sectors further south. During this time the Battle Group elements providing security to the route had taken serious casualties, including five killed in action (Pte Josh Klukie, Sgt Craig Gillam, Cpl Robert Mitchell, Sgt Darcy Tedford and Pte Blake Williamson).

Our task, on my second day with the Troop, was to commence clearing and grubbing from the north and link up with those southern portions that had been previously started. Working with only two small dozers, we were attempting to quickly open up at least a narrow combat road and allow some improved movement for our own forces. This day's work was especially time-sensitive, as it was occurring in concert with a clearance operation being conducted by 3 and 7 Platoons, under the leadership of OC 23, Major Gasparotto. We were pushing through extremely difficult terrain, dominated by mud-walled grape fields. These vineyards were comprised of a series of mud walls, each approximately four to six feet high by 1.5 feet wide. These walls were spaced at approximately six-foot centres. Running throughout the grape fields were a series of large irrigation canals (large enough to hide a LAV or a Humvee) spaced every 100 feet or so. Pushing a road through this terrain would be difficult under ideal conditions, and was extremely demanding when under constant threat of enemy attack.

At this point our two dozers were probably the two most valuable pieces of equipment in the entire Task Force, and we did our best to protect them. We would clear forward with dismounted troops, and then the dozers would push ahead to make a cleared space large enough for a LAV to at least turn around. One LAV would then move up and provide observation to our front as the dozers worked to improve the short segment of road directly behind. This obviously left the lead LAV in the compromising position of being unable to manoeuvre, but I felt it provided the best possible security, given the resources at our disposal. There were four deep irrigation canals that crossed this northern portion of what would be Route Summit. Each of these canals had already been destroyed in four places where the original breaches had gone through during Op Medusa. Ideally we would have preferred to have had temporary culverts to put in these wadis as we filled them in, but that wasn't practical given the circumstances, nor did we have them. We advanced with as much speed as we could effect, eager to complete a lane before last light. I was providing constant updates to the OC on our progress, and it was clear that we were not progressing fast enough to suit the overall plan.

While the new combat road inched forward, we simultaneously worked to create a troop defensive position. It was important that this new road not be left unattended during construction, and we prepared ourselves to spend the night sitting on and guarding our newly made combat road. We were accompanied by 4 Platoon, led by Capt Piers Pappin. With Piers's help, we established a defendable position that our two platoon/troops could occupy for the coming nights.

With about an hour of daylight remaining, we punched through the fourth canal, and finally married up with the OC and 7 Platoon. An existing road of unknown status was now all that separated us from the southern portions of Route Summit that had been previously cleared. The Warrant and I met for a quick conference at the OC's LAV, and it was decided that we would doze a hasty lane that would connect the entirety of the route. Cpl Parker advanced in a D6 while WO Perrault and I turned to make our way back to my LAV. I broke into a jog as the OC mounted up and prepared to head south.

As I neared my LAV, I was rocked by a large explosion. The OC had hit an explosive device as he rolled off of the road into the marijuana field to our south. In shock, I climbed into the turret to give a situation report to the Squadron Headquarters, before trying to get a grip on the state of casualties. The Warrant had been thrown off his feet and was clearly disoriented. It wasn't until later just how serious was the trauma he had suffered in the blast. The OC's crew was obviously quite shaken up, his gunner having received flash burns to his forearm and face. I've always felt that I handled this post-blast situation poorly, and with the OC being a virtual casualty from the blast, I failed to step up and provide adequate leadership. Despite the confusion, we eventually managed to extract the casualties and the damaged vehicle back to Patrol Base Wilson, before occupying our Troop defensive position for the night.

During the four days that I had spent in Kandahar Airfield on my arrival in Theatre, I had asked countless questions in an effort to get myself current. The answer had often been the same. "The Warrant has a handle on that…" or "You'll need to confirm that with the Warrant when you get on the ground…" Now, just a few days later, the Warrant had been evacuated and suddenly I felt alone. I am grateful for the help and guidance of my crew during this period. My driver, Cpl Brian Scott, and my gunner Cpl Matt King both showed outstanding leadership after WO Perreault was wounded. Sgt Neil Coates also did an excellent job of filling in as the Acting Troop Warrant during the weeks after WO Perrault's evacuation.

During the weeks that followed we continued with clearing and grubbing along the new route, as control of the Route Summit area of operations passed to Charles Company, under the leadership of Major Steve Brown. Steve had been promoted and assumed command of Charles Company in the aftermath of the friendly fire incident on September 4th, after Major Matt Sprague was wounded. As work on the route advanced, we provided assistance with the establishment and improvement of Platoon Strong Points[33] along the route. Named Strong Points North, Centre and West, these platoon positions were in a constant state of evolution as they rotated between rifle platoons (and in the case of Strong Point West, an Afghan National Army Company).

Progress was a challenge, as our borrowed British dozer became unserviceable following the failure of its starter, in addition to the regular troubles endured with our one Canadian D6 Dozer. Most notably, while creating a lane to connect Strong Point West to Route Summit, MCpl Lance Hooper struck another IED. We were lucky that it did little more than damage the hydraulics and smash the windshield of the dozer, but I'll always remember Hooper leaning out, looking back with his head shaking and holding up three fingers. This was the third time that Hooper had been "blown up" in a little over a month.

Construction was also slowed greatly by the constant insurgent threat. We repeatedly had to drop tools and respond to various enemy actions. While not altogether accurate, mortar fire was a regular occurrence at both Patrol Base Wilson and along the Route and the Strong Points. The insurgents also employed occasional "shoot-and-scoot" tactics, where they would fire off a Rocket Propelled Grenade or a few bursts of small arms fire before disappearing. This exchange would inevitably cost us an afternoon's work, as we would be forced to adopt a more secure posture.

There was only one larger-scale attack mounted by the enemy during this period. On the afternoon of October 14th we were simultaneously attacked at several locations along Route Summit. At the time we were finally widening the portion of the route where the OC had hit his IED two weeks earlier. Cpl Parsons was operating our one working dozer, and my LAV as well as Sgt Neil Coates's LAV was providing local security. We were without Sgt Carruba's LAV at this time, as we had damaged the transmission trying to pull out a tree that was blocking the route. The lesson learned was to pull in reverse with the LAV in order to avoid damage, as the automatic transmission does not do well pulling heavy loads forward. This knowledge came in handy several times later when loosening stuck vehicles during the rainy season. I was also without my regular LAV crew due to mid-tour leave, so I was being crewed by Tpr Wittman in the driver's hatch and Cpl McCafferty (on loan from 1 Troop) in the gunner's seat. Just moments before we were attacked we received a threat warning over the Squadron net that an imminent attack was possible in our area. These threat warnings had proved accurate in the past, so I knew to take them seriously. We immediately increased our posture, and I am confident that this moment's warning saved lives. I laud the diligent work of our higher headquarters to ensure that that sort of information was pushed down to the lowest level as quickly as possible. There would be many times that we would receive those warnings and nothing materialized, but I had certainly learned not to dismiss them.

Moments after hearing the threat warning we received a barrage of incoming small arms and Rocket Propelled Grenade fire. At the same time, the radio crackled to life as a platoon came under attack to our south at Strong Point Centre. We quickly moved up to the dozer and Parsons jumped into the back of my LAV. I later learned that Cpl Nason had at the same time been forced to dismount under fire to get out of the back of his LAV and into the driver's hatch. We tried to identify the enemy positions as we jockeyed to the north and took more effective firing positions in vicinity of Strong Point North. We continued to engage the sources of enemy fire, as we heard the tragic news over the Charles Company net that two soldiers were "Vital Signs Absent." Medics and soldiers in the field are not qualified to make the ruling that a person is dead; therefore the acronym "VSA" is used. In this case, Sgt Darcy Tedford and Pte Blake Williamson had been killed by enemy fire. Shortly after, our LAV identified and engaged two dismounts carrying a large weapon that may have been a recoilless rifle.

As the battle carried on, a Bison Ambulance was dispatched from Patrol Base Wilson to recover casualties from Strong Point Centre. As the Bison moved through our position, it hit a deep rut causing one of its front wheels to break free. This created a great deal of confusion, as it appeared at first to us as though it had been hit by enemy fire. That Bison was now immobile, and as the sun set, it waited for recovery as a stationary target.

This Bison mishap was only the first of what quickly became a series of errors. The forces at Strong Point Centre had used a great deal of ammunition in the firefight, and wouldn't be able to wait for morning to be re-supplied. A pair of LAVs from the Battle Group Headquarters was dispatched from Patrol Base Wilson loaded to the brim with ammunition and escorting a wrecker (military tow-truck) to recover the broken ambulance. As these vehicles moved through our now-darkened position, the wrecker misjudged the location of the route and found itself stuck in a deep rut. At the same time, one of the two LAVs began to overheat. We were then forced to move down and assist, first with towing the ambulance to safety, then with the re-supply operation, and finally with the recovery of the wrecker. We moved alongside the struggling LAV and transferred the ammo from vehicle to vehicle before moving down to "bomb-up" another Platoon. After that re-supply run, we moved back up and used the dozer to free the stuck wrecker. After coming to the rescue, and well after last light, we escorted the dozer to Patrol Base Wilson, before reoccupying our Troop leaguer for the night.

Things took a welcome turn for the better in late October when Armoured Engineer Vehicles suddenly bolstered our ranks. These beasts, known as Badgers in the Canadian Army, are like a combat engineer's Swiss army knife on a tank chassis. Along with a squadron of Leopard C2 tanks from the Lord Strathcona's Horse (Royal Canadians) in Edmonton, an armoured engineer troop from 1 CER, including four Badgers, was added to the 1 RCR Battle Group on short notice. This reinforcement was in part in response to the list of deficiencies made evident during Op Medusa. The first Badger that rolled out of Kandahar Airfield was attached to 2 Troop as we continued our work on Route Summit, and improving the platoon strong points along the route. We were mortared at Strong Point Centre on the first day that Badger was employed, which I believe marked the first time that Canadian Armour had been engaged in combat operations since the Korean War.

ROUTE SUMMIT PHASE 2 AND THE STRONG POINTS

Late October also ushered in Sgt Sam Ross and the rest of the replacements that had been sent to fill the voids left by the tragic events of September 2006. The Troop was somewhat reorganized, and a new Section was formed which we chose to call 32 Foxtrot. A three-section field troop would normally label its sections Charlie, Delta and Echo, but it was decided that Sgt Stachnik's call sign, 32 Delta, should be retired and this new section should take on a new moniker. Cpl Scott Thompson from 32 Echo was promoted to MCpl (while so employed) and added some combat experience to this new section by stepping in as the Second-in-Command.

Southern Afghanistan had been suffering from a drought that stretched back years. While we knew that our new road would eventually require appropriate drainage, it seemed a secondary concern as we laboured under the heat and cloudless skies of October. In fact, Strong Point North had been constructed inside a large irrigation canal or wadi. That had clearly made tactical sense when it was first sited but in the case of heavy rain it would seem questionable. On November 15th we were working at Strong Point Centre when it began to rain lightly. I immediately became concerned about Strong Point North, then occupied by 5 Platoon. I checked with him several times throughout the day to confirm that water was not accumulating in the wadi upstream from their position. They continually confirmed that it was dry. At day's end we returned to Patrol Base Wilson and were beginning to wind down for the night when we received an urgent call over the Charles Company net. The upstream (eastern) portion of the wadi in which 5 Platoon was living had filled with water and had started to pour out over top of Route Summit. If this continued the water would no doubt make its way overtop of the route and spill down into the Strongpoint. We raced down from Patrol Base Wilson with a Badger and worked quickly to redirect the water. The Badger in this case was being operated by Cpl Clint Orr and was actually being temporarily crew commanded by Cpl Carl Desjardins. With no time to spare, we managed to build a hasty berm of soil and redirect the water away from the Strong Point.

Over the following week it continued to rain and we struggled to maintain mobility over an increasingly soggy Route Summit. All four of the irrigation canals that crossed the northern portion of the route filled with water and began to spill out. Had I planned properly for the eventual rainy season we might have dug a ditch in advance that could have redirected all of this water south towards the Arghandab River, but this hadn't been done. The only alternative I could see after the flooding had started was to form a long berm to contain the flooding to the east side of the Route. This is what we attempted to do, and I can say that it was at least somewhat successful, given the circumstances.

It rained on and off for most of November, and water continued to spill out on to parts of the Route in many locations as it tried to make its way from east to west. At one point Lt Hiltz's Platoon at Strong Point Centre was virtually cut off, as only tracked vehicles could traverse the slop that surrounded their position. On a few occasions we used our lone Badger to cross through the mud, but this risk was not taken lightly. Not only did this make a mess of and further deteriorate the Route, but we would obviously have found ourselves in a difficult circumstance had our one Badger become stuck. Where at all possible, we tried to stick to a standard operating procedure of always having a minimum of two pieces of armour acting together in a particular Area of Operations. For example, our three Badgers would usually be split up with two of them in one area and the third co-located with one of the Armoured Recovery Vehicles in the Task Force.

There was also an alternate way to reach the cut-off Platoon at Strong Point Centre, except that involved using restricted routes that had been largely unobserved and that we felt posed a high IED threat. On three occasions during this period we opened this route for the course of a day to enable the re-supply of Strong Point Centre. This entailed a deliberate and methodical route clearance using mine detectors and prodders. On one occasion this route clearance was interrupted by enemy fire. Sgt Ross' 32 Foxtrot was approximately 50 metres short of completing their clearance when a small group of insurgents directly to their east began engaging Strong Point Centre. Sgt Ross quickly weighed the risk of traversing the remaining un-cleared portion of the route. As the same section had previously opened that route only a few days earlier, they decided the risk was justified. Quickly mounting up, they rolled forward and took a position where they could effectively engage enemy forces. Simultaneously, Strong Point North began taking fire from two grape-drying huts to its southeast. At the time, I was dismounted, supervising a Badger. The Badger was helping some elements of A Company dig themselves in, as they had been tasked to keep observation on this newly-cleared portion of route for that coming night. We were only about 400 metres outside of Strong Point North, but when the firefight started I felt very exposed and quite far from my vehicle and turret. As the enemy small-arms fire continued, I ended up hopping on top of the Badger and crouching on the exposed deck of the vehicle for a ride back to the Strong Point and the rest of the Troop.

As we continued to improve the defensibility of our Strong Points, it was often necessary to remove or level some nearby structures or tree lines. These obstructions often hampered line of sight and fields of fire, while at the same time providing covered avenues of approach for the enemy. While it was preferred to accomplish this using heavy equipment, the nature of the ground would often make access extremely difficult. In these cases it was necessary to deploy a patrol to move to the obstruction and remove it through explosive means. This usually involved a field section being paired with a rifle section from the infantry to form a demolition patrol. The patrol would move out loaded down with up to 30 ten-block satchels of C4. The standard demolition charge consists of a 1.25 pound block of C4 explosive. These blocks can be easily cut, moulded or bundled to create the appropriate charges for the given situation. The rifle section would provide a secure perimeter while the field section would prepare and place the charges. For the average mid-sized grape-drying hut or small tree line this was usually about a one-hour operation.

During the course of the firefight on November 20th, Strong Point North had received direct fire from two large grape-drying huts to its southeast. In order to improve its defensibility, it was decided that these huts should be removed to improve fields of fire. On the morning of November 21st, 32 Foxtrot was paired with a rifle section from 5 Platoon. They proceeded with the demolition of the two huts, achieving the first one without difficulty. The infantry section moved forward to secure the second hut, while 32 Foxtrot regrouped at their vehicle and reloaded themselves with demolitions. On the return trip they had to cross a small creek, which was difficult considering they were each carrying over 50 pounds of explosives above and beyond their normal fighting order. MCpl Thompson was looking for another place to cross when Cpl Mike Barnewall from the rifle section came back to assist the Engineers in crossing the creek. As he approached the Section, Cpl Barnewall stepped on an anti-personnel landmine in the soft earth. The loud blast that followed filled me, and most others that heard it, with dread. With the amount of explosive they were carrying, our first reaction was that we might have just lost two sections of soldiers. Fortunately, that wasn't the case, although the circumstances were still tragic. After recovering from the shock of the blast, 32 Foxtrot quickly dropped their packs and scrambled to assist. Cpl Barnewall had suffered injuries to his leg and arm, while the rifle section commander had suffered head injuries. MCpl Thompson, along with other 'T Triple C' providers in the rifle section began treating the casualties. The OC's gunner, was also rushed to the scene to assist. Medics were quickly dispatched from Strong Point North and the casualties were loaded onto stretchers and into waiting LAVs. Cpl Barnewall was loaded into my borrowed LAV, and with the OC providing care in the back, we rushed him north to Patrol Base Wilson. Cpl Barnewall ended up loosing his right leg just below the knee. After the casualties had been evacuated, 32 Foxtrot conducted a quick post-blast investigation of the scene. They then destroyed a Canadian M72 rocket that had been damaged in the initial blast, before walking back to Strong Point North.

From the time that WO Perrault was evacuated as a casualty, through until the end of October, the Troop was without a dedicated Troop Warrant Officer. While Sgt Neil Coates, as well as the other Senior NCOs in the Troop did an excellent job of filling this void, it was relief to all involved when a more permanent solution was finally found. 2 Troop's recce section, 32 Bravo, was re-roled into 37 Bravo, a recce section from the newly arrived 7 Troop. That Troop had deployed with only a LAV crew for its recce detachment, but no dismounts. Sgt Peacock and his crew therefore, inherited what was left from 32 Bravo; while Sgt Scott Clucas was elevated to the role of the 2 Troop Warrant Officer. The positive impact on the Troop was instantly noticeable. Sgt Clucas had been a leader within the Troop since the very beginning, and his presence helped to quickly solve many of the small administrative issues that can have a huge impact on the overall effectiveness of the Troop.

When Sgt Clucas and the rest of the original 32 Bravo crew went on mid-tour leave in December, Sgt Ted Peacock came over from 7 Troop as the acting Troop Warrant Officer. We continued to support Charles Company on Route Summit during the first half of December. We began repairing one of the key irrigation canals that crossed Route Summit in an effort to promote the drying of the soggy route. At the same time we were providing guidance and supervision to the civilian contractor who was finally preparing the route for paving.

OP BAAZ TSUKA

In the middle of December, we were finally able to hand over responsibility for the Route Summit corridor to Bravo Company and their supporting engineers from 31 Bravo. This was a long awaited and welcome moment, as we had been working in and patrolling the same 5 square kilometres of the "Route Summit Range and Training Area" for almost three months. The Combat Team rested in a leaguer in the desert for a few days before heading back down to Ma'sum Ghar to receive orders for Op Baaz Tsuka.

2 Troop's principal task during the first phase of Op Baaz Tsuka was to support the Charles Company Combat Team operating in the town of Howz-e-Madad. Here, the construction of a police checkpoint in support of the Afghan National Police was deemed a priority. However, the actual task of constructing the checkpoint fell to an attached troop of British engineers, so we were more concerned with specific support to the needs of the Combat Team. As we were to be the first ones on the ground in Howz-e-Madad, we had a Recce Sergeant from the UK Troop attached to us. He spent several days riding along as we completed our battle procedure for the operation. Also there were two explosive detection dogs with their contracted handlers. It took a certain amount of creativity to figure out how to put these two dogs, with their kennels, in the back of a LAV.

Prior to the start of the operation, I had the opportunity to go on a helicopter flyover of the area, as well as drive through the town on a reconnaissance. On December 20th the town was secured. We supported the Afghan National Police in conducting searches, while also helping the UK Recce Sergeant conduct a more detailed recce for the Vehicle Check Point. Near the end of that first day, based on a map grid reference and a timing, 2 Troop moved to the border with Helmand Province to marry up with the UK Forces. On our way, I very nearly backed my LAV into a potential minefield that was not identified on our maps. We saw the painted rocks in the nick of time and stopped quickly. We generally have very good data on the locations of legacy minefields left over from the conflict with the Soviets, but you can certainly never be too careful. We eventually joined with the Scimitar-mounted UK Light Dragoons and the Royal Engineers.

We returned to Howz-e-Madad and I was impressed with how quickly and efficiently the Brits got to work. Working with white light throughout the night, they didn't stop until the project was done. Our two Badgers also got involved and lent a hand to keep the task on schedule. My favourite memory from Howz-e-Madad came the next morning, after the checkpoint was complete. A short line of British Sappers formed, digital cameras in hand, wanting their picture taken with the big bad Badgers.

The morning of December 21st also represented the Regimental birthdays for both the Royal Canadian Regiment and the Royal Canadian Dragoons. To commemorate the occasion, the entire Battle Group celebrated with the Ortona Toast, enjoying a delicious hot toddy made of dark rum, water and brown sugar. This tradition dates back to December 21st, 1943, when the same mixture was imbibed at the Ortona Crossroads in Italy. I broke out a box of Cuban cigars that had been sent from friends at home, and we felt like kings as we savoured the sunrise, drink and cigar in hand.

After spending a few days camped at the outskirts of Howz-e-Madad, we returned to FOB Zettelmeyer just in time for Christmas. I don't remember the day especially clearly, except that it was rainy and we shared a traditional dinner, served by Gen Rick Hillier. Shortly afterward, Sgt Clucas returned from leave and received a well deserved promotion to Warrant Officer. We conducted a quick handover and I headed in to Kandahar Airfield and off on a leave of my own.

When I returned, the Troop was operating out of Ma'sum Ghar. They were helping with the constant improvements to the FOB and supporting B Squadron and Charles Company, who were also using that locale as a base of operations. We continued in this manner through our last few weeks before heading back into Kandahar Airfield to meet our replacements and begin our relief-in-place.

HANDOVER

As part of the relief-in-place with the 2 RCR Battle Group, we conducted a handover with 2 Troop from 42 Field Squadron out of Gagetown. This new troop was commanded by Capt Billy Dixon, whom I knew well from our phase training. The incoming troop was well prepared, and had no difficulty in getting a quick handle on the state of operations. We conducted as much of a handover as was possible in the secure confines of Kandahar Airfield. All that was left was to give them an actual tour of the ground. In conjunction with Matt Arndt's troop, a "guided tour" was planned to visit some of the key tactical infrastructure throughout the Area of Operations. We rolled out of Kandahar Airfield in the wee hours of the morning, with Matt leading. I rode along in one of the air sentry hatches of my LAV. Billy and his gunner were up in the turret, but I was in the back giving the play-by-play over the intercom. Things went well until we made a wrong turn driving through Kandahar City.

The lead vehicle stopped quickly, and due to what was likely a factor of inexperience, all of the LAVs in the convoy who were moving too fast and too close together, one after the other piling into each other. I was rocked hard back and forth in my hatch. I remember taking a moment to catch my balance before losing consciousness. When I came-to, I was lying on my back on the floor of the LAV. Billy came over the intercom and said that the lead vehicle was looking for some help with navigation. I stood up and poked my head through the hatch as our damaged convoy rolled through the darkened streets of Kandahar City. We were disoriented, but trying to limp our way to Camp Nathan Smith. In my state I was no help with the navigation, but we eventually found the front gate to the camp and rolled inside. The medical staff met us and performed a quick triage. Fortunately, the most seriously injured was a LAV gunner who had lost his front teeth. There were numerous other scrapes and bruises, and my suspected concussion. There was also serious damage to some of the vehicles.

That was unfortunately the end of our show-and-tell tour of the area. The injured personnel were airlifted back to Kandahar Airfield via Chinook. I was held for observation for most of the day and given a CAT scan. I was eventually released with little more than a headache, a stiff neck, and a bruised ego. The incoming 2 Troop returned to Kandahar Airfield by road in order to enable repairs to their damaged vehicles. In the end there was not enough time remaining to give them a proper tour, although I'm not sure if it would have been of great benefit.

GOING HOME

We spent our last few days in Kandahar Airfield conducting much-needed administration and performance reviews. When it finally came time to leave, our flight was actually delayed by a day because of a snowstorm in Ontario. We eventually made our way out and flew on to Cyprus, where we took part in three days of mandated "reintegration." This involved a series of briefings from different counsellors and mental health professionals, aimed at lessening the shock of the return from war. While most of the troops were just eager to get back and see their families, I believe this sojourn to have been a valuable and necessary process. After our fun in the sun, we flew through Germany and on to CFB Trenton on March 3rd, 2007. It was a proud moment when a CF-18 Fighter came alongside and gave us a salute as we crossed into Canadian airspace. In Trenton we were met squarely with a full dose of winter weather and a slow drive back up to Petawawa and to everyone's waiting families.

Most of the Troop had about a month-and-a-half of well-deserved leave before coming back to work full-time. When we did come back, we had the luxury of staying together as a formed troop for a few weeks as we became re-accustomed to life in garrison. Some obviously struggled more than others with this adjustment, and I'm thankful for the support structure of the Squadron and Regiment and for their patience in this slow process. I eventually handed over the Troop over to Lt Dave Walcott, as I was moved to the Regimental Headquarters as the Adjutant. At the same time, many other returning Squadron members had to be moved due to postings and other career progression.

I am very grateful to have been given the incredible opportunity to command 2 Troop on operations. 2 Troop and 23 Field Squadron had already earned some of the most celebrated history in the Canadian Military Engineers and what was accomplished on our rotation only added to those accounts. I particularly want to recognize the foundation of the Troop as I knew it - WO Roger Perrault and WO Scott Clucas, for their outstanding leadership. Further acknowledgements are owed to the strong Senior NCOs of the Troop: Sgts Neil Coates, Oli Carruba, Rob Kennedy, Ted Peacock and Sam Ross. I'd like to restate my appreciation to the crew in my troop headquarters for helping me along and keeping the Troop going through hard times: MCpl Steve Matte, MCpl Justin O'Neill, Cpl Brian Scott, and Spr Matt King. I'd like to thank the OC for giving me a mission and allowing me the freedom to command within my arcs. Finally, I offer my most sincere condolences to the family of Sgt Shane Stachnik. While I didn't know your son well, I had the honour of serving in his troop and with his comrades. The respect held for him as a soldier, a leader, a son, a brother and a fiancé is obvious and overwhelming. We will remember him.

Chimo!

EXPLOSIVE ORDINANCE DISPOSAL

Sgt John Valois

HANDOVER

Everyone in the Team had finally shown up. We had conducted our handover, and had completed our validation with the outgoing EOD teams. This transition period had given me an opportunity to talk to some buddies I had not seen in a very long time. On August 21ˢᵗ we said our good-byes to the rest of the EOD teams at the Kandahar Airfield and left in the convoy for the PRT. When we arrived Mike Scoretz greeted us. Mike and I have a continued history together; our careers seemed to parallel each other. I relieved him in Bosnia, I attended the Advanced EOD course after him, I relieved him in Kabul and now I was relieving him in Kandahar.

We also shared some stories, conducted a quick handover, did a tour of the PRT and then we got ready to go for supper. The next day, Mike and his crew left early in the morning, and then it was officially us. I tore apart the EOD Bison and started rearranging kit in the way I was more familiar with. Just after finishing, I ramped up the Bison and plugged everything in.

As I was walking back to the tent, a huge explosive went off. I remember thinking, "Holy Shit that was close," and it was - just outside the front gate of the PRT. Over the loudspeaker we heard "EOD to the Command Post." PO2 Jimmy Leith took off running to the Command Post and I gathered the guys to start getting ready, found the Quick Reaction Force Second-in-Command and got the order-of-march. Jimmy came back and said, "It was our guys, just outside the gate." We rolled out the front gate, turned the corner, and right there in front of us was a LAV and G-wagon completely engulfed in flames. I told the driver to move in front of the packet as I informed the Quick Reaction Force Commander over the radio what I needed for a cordon and what I was going to do. Over the net, I heard that all personnel had been evacuated, one was Vital Signs Absent (Cpl Braun was killed) and three others were Priority One casualties.

We moved forward to start conducting a search of the area. Leith and

Lightle dismounted and moved to the left side of the Bison. All of a sudden we started getting shot at from the west. The incoming rounds hit all around the buildings, I turned the C-6 machine gun to the west and yelled at both of them to get back behind the Bison. I told the Quick Reaction Force Second-in-Command what had happened, and that I couldn't see where the rounds had come from. As it was a populated area, I wasn't just going to open fire. A LAV was sent around to try to flush out the shooter.

Back at the post-blast site, the fire still raged. An Afghan fire truck showed up and started pumping water on the vehicles. As soon as the water hit the LAV, rounds inside started cooking off. A man, carrying his young child, who was injured in the blast, walked by our position. As a father, I couldn't even begin to imagine what that was like. Over the radio, I asked if our medics could check out the child, but they were already busy with the casualties on the other side of the site. The flames were intense and various shops in the area were also burning. In about 15 minutes, the Afghan fire fighters completely contained and extinguished the blaze. It was an impressive demonstration of their skills.

In order to verify that the area was clear of secondary devices, we reverted to conducting our search. Once the area was confirmed to have no secondary devices, we started conducting our post-blast investigation. The heat still coming off the vehicles was intense. A molten slag was beginning to drip off the LAV, indicating how fierce the fire had been.

Once all our information was complete, the Counter-IED Team showed up and I handed over to them. They were a group of people that investigated each explosive incident, collecting biometrics (DNA, hair, soft tissue), device fragmentation and component parts in order to determine the likely perpetrators – a CSI Kandahar type of outfit. It was weird how the crater wasn't that big, but the engine block was almost 75 metres away. Pieces of the bomber were nearly 200 metres away.

Suddenly to the north of us, there were gunshots. The Quick Reaction Force Second-in-Command grabbed his headsets, "What the fuck just happened? Who is shooting?" he inquired. Down on a side road where a section had dismounted and were holding a cordon, two people on a motorcycle were approaching. The soldier ordered them to stop. The motorcycle didn't even slow down. Again he commanded them to halt, this time raising his weapon to his shoulder. It was as if the driver didn't see them. Two other soldiers raised their hands and yelled, "Fucking STOP." As the motorcycle got closer, the first soldier fired his weapon. The bullet went through the driver and into the child riding behind him. The bike went off the road, as the soldiers quickly moved in to check them out. They were unarmed and did not have any explosive devices. The soldiers started treatment for the gunshot wounds.

Once the Post-Blast Investigation was complete, the difficult task of getting the burnt-out vehicles back to the PRT commenced. I offered my Bison to drag the LAV back, but was turned down by the Quick Reaction Force Commander, stating the PRT had a trailer that could handle the task. We waited nearly 3 hours for the trailer and other recovery assets to show up. I have no idea why the wait was so long, as it was only 100 metres to the front gate. So we sat in the Bison on site until everything was picked up and all vehicles headed back into PRT. The Quick Reaction Force Commander called for an After Action Review right after we got back. At this point we received the rest of the details about the shooting. We also worked out that recovery assets would deploy with Quick Reaction Force. I made a plea that diesel jerry cans should not be strapped to the exterior of any vehicle. I had noted that once the flames reached the jerry cans strapped to the outside of the LAV it was then that the fire got out of control. This had been the second post-blast incident that I had witnessed in which a vehicle with jerry cans had been targeted. However, at the time, the recommendation fell on deaf ears.

AUGUST 28TH, 2006

A radio-controlled IED connected to a landmine; some young platoon commander telling me "I'm in charge;" me replying, "OK, I'll go home then, you deal with it."

AUGUST 29TH, 2006

Just after lunch, a suicide bomber hit a logistics convoy that was moving from Kandahar Airfield to Patrol Base Wilson, through the PRT. They were about 2 kilometres east of the Arches (a concrete *McDonald's* "M" looking structure that straddled the highway). As it was a natural choke point, suicide bombers often targeted convoys travelling through that location. When we got on scene, camera crews and media were all over the place. I counted at least 6 television cameras. The site was crawling with people, civilian and military. My first thought was, "Well there goes my threat of secondary devices and all my forensics evidence." The main vehicle that was targeted was a large military truck that was towing a trailer. According to witnesses, the suicide bomber was initially unable to accelerate enough to get his vehicle up the ditch. He then proceeded to floor it on the second attempt. This extra second or two helped the driver get the cab out of harm's way.

As it happened, there was also a civilian dump truck driver in the area. It was his vehicle that sustained damage from the blast. He was coming from Kandahar and travelling eastbound toward Kandahar Airfield and had just stopped to pick up a hitchhiker who was on his way to a village down the road. The hitchhiker sitting on the left side of the vehicle sustained wounds from the bomb's shrapnel and died instantly. It was reported that the driver got out and started kicking the dead but fairly intact suicide bomber.

AUGUST 30TH, 2006

It was sometime in the morning when we got called out to support British Forces in what was being called a possible IED, on Route Black Ice. Upon arriving on site we deployed our "TEO" robot, directing it towards the obvious freshly-dug hole in the road. There were a few exposed wires. I started using TEO to pull each and every wire I saw and soon had quite a collection. After about an hour and a few dozen pieces of scrap wire later, I told Jimmy Leith, "I'm not finding anything." He decided that he would go forward on a manual approach using a prodder and mine detector. After 20 minutes I leaned on the horn, a signal for him to come back, but Jimmy looked up at the robot and signalled he was OK. Thirty minutes, under the Afghan sun in a bomb suit, sifting through the dirt must have felt like a lifetime. As the ditches on either side of the road dropped about 2 metres, we had to rearrange the vehicles to maximize coverage and not roll off the road.

When Jimmy came back he said, "I didn't find anything. Prep me two blocks, I'm going to explosively investigate." Out of curiosity, I raised my eyebrow, as I wasn't familiar with this tactic. "What is the purpose for this?" I asked. He replied, "If anything is in there, then the two blocks will set it off. Or I can stay here all day digging." It worked for me. I prepared the 2 blocks and a 1-minute initiation set and handed it to him. As he moved from the Bison back the incident site, I drove TEO back to the vehicle.

Jimmy set the charge, pulled the M60 igniter and made his way back to the first Bison. Once inside the vehicle, the driver started driving backwards. It appeared as though he just put it in reverse and floored it, consequently the Bison got really close to the ditch on the right side. All I could think was, "Great, we just get here, and lose 3 guys to a vehicle rollover." Luckily the Bison stayed upright and the 2 blocks detonated safely without a larger explosion. We must have looked like a gong show to the Brits.

We then packed up, and moved back to the PRT. I asked to see Jimmy privately to discuss the incident with the Bison. I also spoke to Ivan Peters, who was the driver, to ascertain what happened. He stated he was just following orders. His crew commander apparently didn't realise that you could safely be as close as he was to an explosion if you were in an armoured vehicle – yet another lessoned learned. When we got back we were issued the first set of orders for Op Medusa. If I had known this operation would last as long as it did, resulting in us not seeing the PRT until the end of November, I would have eaten more yoghurt.

NOVEMBER 27TH, 2006

It was probably just after breakfast and I remember clearing garbage out of the Bison. My team, EOD 4, had just returned from Ma'sum Ghar where we had been stationed for roughly a month. We got pushed forward to the PRT, as it would be easier to pick the guys up for mid-tour leave. Kevin Chiasson and Paul O'Brien were next in line for leave and were very excited. I remember talking to them about their plans while we did vehicle maintenance. We had to change one of the tires, which had a piece of shrapnel cut into it. We put the tools away, Kevin went to go play his PSP and I went to the mess for a coffee with some Irish Creamer in it - it had become my drink of choice. I was walking back when I heard the non-secure phone ringing in our tent. I ran over and picked it up.

"EOD. MCpl Valois."

"Johnny, it's Jimmy, get the boys ready. You're getting launched on a big post- blast." It was Jimmy Leith; he was acting EOD Chief, as Knobby was on his mid-tour leave.

"Is it one of ours?" I asked.

"Yep, I got two words for you." He paused then added succinctly: "Fuck you." Why was he telling me 'fuck you?' What had I done? "Okay thanks Jimmy, talk to you later."

"Stay frosty out there." That was Jimmy's saying, every time we deployed he said something like that.

"OK Boys, we got a post-blast, start getting ready." One by one Scotty Elson and Kevin came out of their bunks. Jon Leclerc had headphones on, so he didn't hear me right away.

I took off to the Command Post, and knocked on the door. The duty officer opened the door very surprised.

"I was just about to call you and the Quick Reaction Force."

I answered. "I know, Kandahar Airfield called, it's a post-blast." The remainder of the Quick Reaction Force call signs showed up. The attack was on Highway 1, just a few kilometres south of the Arches. It was a rapid set of orders from the Quick Reaction Force Commander and we were ready to leave. I headed to our Bison and Scott was already in the Crew Commander's hole. We developed this procedure, so that I could get dressed in my Personal Protective Equipment and not delay the convoy. We left via the front gate and headed toward the site. It only took a few minutes to arrive and when we did it really did look like a bomb had gone off.

I still remember that the day was completely overcast - very dark and gloomy, threatening rain. As we pulled up, a crowd of people had already started to gather. To the right side of the road, there were at least a dozen dead or wounded camels. There were also wounded people walking around. *How big was this blast*, I thought to myself.

Scotty came on the intercom. "Monty's out front." We pulled off to the left side of the road about 100 metres away from the blast. I got out and met Monty, our Sergeant- Major. I walked up and as my eyes focused, I noticed that he had blood on him but it didn't look like he was bleeding. A Black Hawk helicopter took off in the distance.

"Park your vehicles over here and start moving forward." MWO Montgomery said. "People have already been all over the scene, so your search for secondary devices should be good," he told me. I just nodded. I left him, turned and motioned to the Bisons, indicating where I wanted them to park. Once set, everyone dismounted. This was when I discovered an extra person. MCpl O'Brien had taken it upon himself to bring along an air sentry as there were only two personnel in his vehicle and in Kandahar City you needed eyes in the back of your head.

"Who are you?" I asked

"I'm Master Corporal such and such," she replied. I wasn't really listening as the chaos in the background reminded me that I had a job to do.

"Everyone knows their job?" Everyone nodded their heads. "You stick with Paul," I told the newest member. I then looked at Scotty and said, "Let's go." Scotty and I pushed forward and completed a full search for secondary hazards. It turned into a cattle-herding event trying to get people out of the blast scene in an attempt to save some forensic evidence. After our search, we found a grenade that was in very poor repair, so we moved that off to the side to destroy later. When the scene was safe, we gave the thumbs up to the boys and got on with our post-blast investigation. Just as we started it, the convoy that got hit turned the scene over to us, and returned back to Kandahar Airfield. I waved at Capt Busbridge and MWO Montgomery as they drove by.

The way I had my team set up was that Scotty and I first checked the area for secondary devices, then we would investigate various points of interest. Kevin took the pictures, Jon did a site sketch with grids, and Paul questioned any witnesses. We pushed forward and completed our investigation as best we could. I called all the team back at the Bison and asked if everyone was done. As each person said yes, I asked if they had completed certain tasks and asked if they had seen anything we needed to pay attention to. I walked over to the Quick Reaction Force Commander and told him that I was finished. This was when he told me that the Counter-IED Team was on the way.

We were waiting for about five minutes when they showed up. Two of them were good friends of mine – CPO2 Darrell Colwell and WO Brian Waters. I went over to Darrell right away and gave him the info I had, then he started his investigation. Next, I spoke with Brian. He was getting biometrics off the suicide bomber's body and was trying to get a good picture of the face but it was in several pieces. I still had my gloves on so I slide my hands underneath and reassembled the face as best I could so Brian could get a good picture. Remember that crowd that I said was there? Well they left after they saw me do that.

Counter-IED completed their investigation, mounted in their convoy and left. After receiving permission, we blew up the grenade. The disabled Bison was loaded on the flatbed, the convoy rearranged, and we got ready to go.

As we were heading back to the PRT, Kevin was the first one to talk.

"Everyone at the unit is going to have to get ready for another ramp ceremony."

Confused I said, "Which unit?"

He replied "Ours - 2 Combat Engineer Regiment."

Still uncertain, I asked, "What are you talking about?"

"Well that was Louis Proulx's Bison," he said. Apparently, while I was doing other tasks, the team had gathered at the disabled Bison and had convinced themselves that it was an Engineer call sign that got hit.

I told him "That wasn't Louis' Bison, that was the Niner Tac Convoy - he isn't part of that." But there was no changing his mind and the rumour spread like wildfire. The entire team thought for sure it was Louis Proulx's Bison. Kevin's friends Joe Lafreniere and Jason Legros were Louis' drivers and now they feared that they were all dead.

As soon as we got back, I took off for the Command Post. I told them we were back, and that we needed about an hour to sort out all the evidence and be ready to leave again. I also confirmed that is was Niner Tac that got hit and not Louis.

I went back to the tent, and gathered the team together, to disseminate the information. I listened to everyone tell me what information they had, and made notes. I then told them it was a Niner Tac call sign that was targeted, not an engineer field section. Kevin argued the fact, maintaining that it was our friends.

I looked at Kevin, "Kevin how often have you seen an Engineer Bison with such a small amount of equipment in it? Had it been an Engineer vehicle it would have been fully loaded with everything!" He still didn't believe me. I wasn't going to continue the conversation as I had a report to complete. It wasn't until I was typing the report that it clicked - the two words that Jimmy had said to me when he first called. They were the two words that RSM Girouard had said to the entire 1 RCR Battle Group back in Petawawa, when it first stood up. They were *"Fuck you!"* It was in reference to anyone who was bad-mouthing the unit or complaining about things that were beyond everyone's control.

It was the RSM and his driver that got killed. It was his blood on Monty. I started going through the *rolodex* in my head. Stormy was his driver. Cpl Albert Storm, an infantry soldier and a former assault pioneer. He was a great guy. A give-you-the-shirt-off-his-back sort of guy. He was like an honorary sapper and had done lots of live-mine training with us. As

I was typing the report, I heard Kevin talking, still going on about it being Legros and Proulx.

I stopped and walking out said "Kevin, it was the Niner-Charlie call sign - the RSM. The RSM and his driver are the ones that were killed."

Grasping, he continued his protests "No, they had to have gotten the call sign wrong, they must have meant 31 Charlie."

Exasperated, I said, "How do you get 31 Charlie out of Niner Charlie? Kevin, it's not - it's the RSM!" I walked back into my tent and continued my report. Suddenly the phone rang, it was Jimmy. Scotty asked him, right away, "Jimmy, who got hit?" Jimmy must have given him the same two words he gave me earlier. I got on the phone and, just as I thought, they wanted that report ASAP - as in yesterday. By the book I had eight hours to get the report in but with it being a high priority, it needed to be in right away. I hung up the phone.

Scotty was confused and asked, "What was Jimmy talking about"?

I said "Scotty, who used to use that expression? The RSM."

DECEMBER 1ST, 2006

A private security contractor turned in a Radio Controlled IED on the same day as the CANCON[34] Show.

DECEMBER 3RD, 2006

We had just finished lunch and I was walking back to the tent with a coffee in hand. Over the loud speakers I heard "EOD to the Command Post." I thought, *oh great...what now?* All the other Quick Reaction Force personnel were already there. You would figure being such an important part of the Quick Reaction Force they would at least give me a radio.

There had been an IED strike on Highway 1 in Kandahar City. No details as to who got hit, but I knew Jimmy would be on the radio to give me that info as soon as I got on the Engineer net. Sgt Mike Davidson of the Close Support Military Police Platoon was the Quick Reaction Force Commander. He gave me the Readers Digest version of what was going on and the order-of-march. I went back to the vehicle and told the guys. We got mounted up and took off. The incident site wasn't too far from the PRT. I gave a quick sitrep on the Engineer net and heard Jimmy's familiar voice. Prior to the radios cutting out, I heard him say it was a British callsign.

We arrived on scene. The first thing I noticed was that the civilians were already cleaning up the area. It must have been some time from the strike to us arriving on scene. The remains of the car were already loaded up on a flat bed ready to be taken away. Once again, Scotty and I took off doing our search for secondary devices. I told the interpreter to talk to the tow-truck guys and have everyone stop what they were doing inside the scene. Once the search was done Scotty jumped into the back of the flat bed and started looking for evidence. Everyone else broke off and started their usual jobs. I sifted the blast seat[35], and then began looking for fragmentation further out. I noticed two Afghan Police walking away, one of them had a cord in his hand. It looked like a piece from the blast. I ran after him and when he stopped he showed me he a plastic coated bike lock. He indicated that he used it as a crowd control tool.

Once the blast part of the investigation was finished, I realized that something was amiss. I asked Kevin and Jon, "You guys see any body parts?" They both replied, no. So the search started, then we found a piece. Not sure which piece, but it had hair on it. I wasn't ready to get a hair sample that possibly came from a suicide bomber's groin, so the search continued for a more suitable piece. After a while, villagers came out with shovels full of the bomber's body parts and just tossed them into the street. I looked over a wall and found a piece of the hand. I hopped the wall and there was a hand, with two fingers. I asked Jon to get me something I could take a fingerprint with.

There is now a picture in the Squadron Video of me taking a fingerprint using a black marker and paper and Jon Leclerc standing over me. I had no idea someone was taking the picture.

The Counter-IED Team showed up and I gave them the info that I had. They took a few pictures, then took the hand and left. After telling Sgt Davidson that I was done, we mounted up and returned to the PRT. When we got back, we had a quick debrief and the guys told me what they found. The convoy that had been struck had carried on through to their objective. They also had an Apache helicopter providing overwatch on their patrol. I went to the Command Post and jumped on the secure radio to talk to Jimmy, telling him we had no information about the convoy.

DECEMBER 5TH, 2006

Kevin Chiasson and Paul O'Brien were getting ready to go on leave. Everything was all set. A convoy was going to come through and pick them up and another convoy was going to drop off their replacements. Everything was going to be great. An hour later, the convoy was cancelled; 30 minutes after that, the convoy was back on. 10 minutes before the time, we found out that the convoy was not stopping at the PRT at all - so many changes in such a short period of time. The phone started ringing. "EOD to the Command Post." When I got there, the Operations Officer told me "I know you guys have people going on leave, so do we, there's a Chinook coming in an hour, have them ready."

"Where is it coming from, I need to get their replacements out here" I asked.

"I dunno." was the reply. So I went back to the tent to tell the guys the good news, and made a call to Jimmy on the satellite phone to let him know about the Chinook, inquiring if he could get the replacements on the bird.

The Chinook landed and Kevin and Paul left. We returned to the tent, with no replacements. Then what I feared might happen, happened. I heard "EOD to the Command Post." As I was running to the Command Post, I passed MBdr Croft and asked him, "Kent, I need a crew commander, you available?"

"Yeah…when?" he said.

"Right now," I said.

"Shit, well let me get my stuff." was his answer. When I arrived at the Command Post, sure enough, it was another post-blast incident. A suicide bomber had struck a convoy coming back from Patrol Base Wilson just at the turn-off to go to Ma'sum Ghar. I ran back to the Bisons. Jon was working like a madman to get both of them ready. I told the guys what was going on. My plan was to have Jon and Scott in the EOD Bison, and I would drive the Bison and have MBdr Croft crew-commanding. That way I could tell him what to do in regards to the Electronic Counter Measures. I gave a quick sitrep to Jimmy on the Engineer net. Jimmy and I had a laugh about the fact I knew this was going to happen, then the radios stopped working. When we got on scene, someone must have had mercy on me. Jerry Henwood was there (he was another one of our Electronic Counter Measures operators) and had worked with me before. He knew how I ran my team for post- blast; he had questioned all the witnesses before I got there. I parked the vehicle and did a quick search.

Jerry ran up to me and said "Johnny, let's get out of here."

"Well you're on your way, follow me. Tell me a story" I said. As Scotty and I conducted our search, Jerry told me what happened. Once the area was clear, I gathered the team together and told them "Kent, I need you to take pictures. Take them of everything. Take at least 100 to 150 pictures, close up, far away, all directions. Scotty and Jon you guys know what to do."

We broke off and started our post-blast investigation. Once everything was close to being done, I went over to the Quick Reaction Force Commander and told him that we would be done in about 5-10 minutes. He told me that we might have to wait longer than that, as a flat bed was en route to move the disabled RG-31. Not wanting to wait, I instructed Jon to get an A-Frame and hook up the RG-31 to our Bison.

Suddenly one of the interpreters came over with a guy from the Afghan National Police. We were informed that when the Police were moving the suicide bomber's body they found something in his pocket. Scotty and I walked over to the body and sure enough it was a grenade. It was wrapped in so much fabric that it was easy to miss with a quick search of the body. I went to the Bison to get a hook and line kit and a metal detector. I told the Quick Reaction Force Commander to put everyone under cover so we could investigate further to see if anything else was up. We did a quick sweep with the metal detector, tied a line around the dead man's arm, hid behind a wall and conducted our pull[36] - no boom. We did another search and found nothing. Once everything was sorted out and the convoy was ready to move, I noticed that Jon had already hooked the RG-31 up to my Bison. "That was excellent," I thought, because towing the RG-31 made us a huge target. After confirming with MBdr Croft that he had taken several pictures, we moved in the order-of-march, and headed back to the PRT.

When we got there, they had a flatbed ready for me. I backed that RG-31 up on that ramp like I had been doing it all my life. Finally, towing guns back from my artillery days came in handy. The next day, Cpl Wilson and Cpl Hulan showed up as the Team's replacements.

DECEMBER 6TH, 2006

It was a cold but sunny Wednesday morning. The boys were already outside having a smoke. As usual, I was the last up. I came out, had a huge stretch and yawn and said, "Well boys what do you say about breakfast, I'm buying." All of a sudden we heard a huge explosion, just outside the gates of the PRT. "Oh for fuck's sake, can't you guys wait until after breakfast!" I cried out to anyone that would listen, then adding "Well time to go to work boys." I then took off for the Command Post.

I was the first one there. The Operations Officer didn't know about it. He got on the phone to the front gate. It turned out the front gate wasn't even aware. Impossible I thought - it was a huge explosion. He got the Quick Reaction Force to the Command Post and quickly dispatched them. We were held back until Quick Reaction Force could establish what had happened. So I went back to the vehicle and waited and waited. Gator ATVs started coming back with bodies and hurried them into the Unit Medical Station. I got tired of prompting the Command Post to launch us so I told Scotty to just go. We got right outside the front gate. A suicide bomber had targeted the private security company that was located directly across from the PRT. The man at the head of the company was named Jack. I had only met him once when he turned in the Radio Controlled IED earlier that week. Most people knew him and he was well liked at the PRT. Jack, his bodyguard (a Gurkha soldier) and their interpreter were leaving their compound to go into their waiting vehicles on the other side of the road. The bomber approached them, detonating himself as Jack's bodyguard raised his weapon ordering him to stop.

I gave a quick sitrep to Knobby. He had already discussed the issue with Capt Busbridge. Since this was a private company, a full post-blast was not required. We were to conduct the investigation, give basic details, and that was it. So that's what we did. I did a very quick post-blast investigation; we mounted up and headed back. Two gators drove by with body bags in them. It was Jack and his bodyguard. They were being put in the freezer. The interpreter had already been placed there. Later that day some direction came down as to what was going to happen. The private company was coming to get the bodies, and they wanted the post-blast report and all evidence to be handed over to them. At around suppertime they showed up. I handed over all the evidence and told them I was keeping a copy of the investigation solely for the reporting purposes. They agreed. We got ready to leave that night for Ma'sum Ghar.

DECEMBER 7TH, 2006

What a great day. We were heading to Ma'sum Ghar - finally getting out of the PRT, possibly to have a break. We left with the convoy, did a quick handover with the team in Ma'sum Ghar. They took our spots in the convoy and we took their beds. It was great to be forward again, as it had a completely different feel to it. When you are deployed you feel like you are actually doing your job, that you have a sense of purpose. We got up and adopted the usual morning routine with someone manning the radio at all times. It was around lunchtime that an Operational Mentor Liaison Team call sign (OMLT or "Omelette" for short) had discovered something in the road. We mounted up and drove around the mountain to link up with them. As the OMLT operated mainly on foot, I dismounted and moved forward. Scotty followed us in the Bison. I told their team leader that I needed some people to give me a cordon and to make sure nobody is watching or can come in. He pushed a group of soldiers away from the device and moved them to the other side of the road. I used my binoculars and determined that it looked like a landmine that had been knocked out of place. So I walked up to it. When I got there, I noticed it was a pressure plate linked to a landmine, which had low-ordered (not fully exploded). By rights I should have turned around and let Scotty deal with this, since I was not officially IED-disposal qualified; however, I had enough experience to handle it, and besides, I was already there. I pulled out my big anti-tank knife, and started prodding all around, uncovered all the parts and pieces and cut some wires. I then walked back to the vehicle to get the hook and line kit, and made my pull. Then I went back to pick everything up. Darren Wilson just shook his head at me, in disbelief. It wasn't the first time I had to dismantle a device however the other times I had already taken it apart with the robot. I honestly thought this was a simple landmine. Furthermore, I had convinced myself that I was already there, and not to act would have drawn the whole situation out way too long. However, I wasn't going to make it a habit.

FEBRUARY 9TH, 2007

Elements of the 2 RCR Battle Group had started coming in. They began to conduct the handover patrols and one had departed a few hours earlier to the west towards Ghundy Ghar. I was part of EOD Team 4 and we were based out of Ma'sum Ghar. As per standard operating procedure we always had someone in a Bison listening to "The Game," as I called it, on the radio. The new company from the 2 RCR Battle Group was asking for EOD assistance in the area of Patrol Base Wilson. As Route Summit was extremely well protected, we often moved in a two-vehicle convoy and I told the guys to start getting ready. While the boys were doing this, I contacted the Squadron Headquarters, told them the situation and asked for permission to support. We were dispatched from Ma'sum Ghar at roughly 5:00 pm and were on scene in about 20 minutes. I linked up with the Company Sergeant-Major and asked him what was going on.

By way of background, in order for us to continue building Route Summit we needed to get more material, namely dirt, from another source, which was just west of Patrol Base Wilson. It was a good spot because the security there could also have constant observation of that location. The mine clearance of the road into that area was contracted to a Japanese de-mining company. The status of the area was open to debate. According to our database this location was a known minefield. The locals and the Afghan National Security Forces, however, believed it to be clear. This discrepancy was not unusual as nothing was ever straightforward on this mission. As a grader was expanding the road, it uncovered parts of a landmine. Thus the grader operator contacted our forces at Patrol Base Wilson, who in turn contacted us.

I established the cordon and got a LAV to move down the graded road just to have eyes and cover for protection. The Quick Reaction Force positioned to the east and west on the highway and blocked traffic. As this was a main thoroughfare, in fact the only one, the traffic soon started to quickly build up.

I moved forward to do my recce and found that the grader had completely sheared off the pressure plate of an Italian-made TC-6, anti-tank mine and also the fusing mechanism of a PP-MI-SR anti-personnel bounding fragmentation landmine. I had to laugh at the complete dumb luck of it all.

So I walked back to my vehicle, got a camera, a shovel and a hook and line. I told the guys what I was going to do and returned to the landmines. By this time the traffic had begun to really build up. I rigged up my equipment, made my way behind the LAV, confirmed that everyone was under hard cover, ensured that an air space Restricted Operating Zone had been established and conducted my pull. Everything popped out of the ground without any problems. The Company Sergeant-Major came up to me and asked what to do about the traffic jam.

I told him, "They can divert the traffic around to the south, as long as they don't come anywhere near me."

Top: EOD 2 group shot.
Bottom: MCpl Mike Maidment.

Top: LS Bruce.
Bottom: An EOD Operator dismantling an IED by hand.

An IED Operator with his TEO Robot.

I returned to the scene, confirmed my pull, moved everything off to the side, then got down on my belly and started clearing the hole by hand. All of a sudden, there was a sound like a starter's pistol being fired. I looked up and the traffic all took off. Instead of being diverted to the other side of the road, they proceeded everywhere. It looked like a Baja Race. There had to be at least 50 cars passing on either side of me in a known minefield. My teammate, Scotty Elson moved forward to offer me some type of cover. I looked up at him and asked, "What's going to happen if one of those cars hit a landmine?"

Scott replied, "Well hurry up so we don't have to find out!"

So I completed my clearance, searched for the fusing and pressure plate, cleared the surrounding area. I then packed up my gear, got back into the Bison and got out of there. I gave a sitrep to the Squadron Headquarters, jokingly telling them to start contracting grader operators for de-mining, as they were far better at defusing landmines then any of our tools. What a hell of a way to finish a tour.

Squadron Sergeant-Major

MWO Brad Montgomery

September 1st, 2006: Engineer Reserve Moves to Panjwaii District

It was 55 degrees Celsius and we were all marshalled and sitting in the compound 100 metres west of our Squadron office complex. This was the day that we were to start our move to Ma'sum Ghar for Phase One of Operation Medusa. I walked the vehicle line a couple of times while waiting to move out and talked with the US Route Clearance Package troops. They seemed very confident and had a certain calm about them, like it was business as usual. We would see this demeanour many more times in weeks to come when, even under fire, their professionalism would stand firm. Cpl Poulin and a few of the troops had started up a poker game in the shade under the front of their Bison, and by the smile on his face I figured he was taking everyone for their money. Others were just trying to stay comfortable by finding whatever shade they could to sit in.

The Squadron OC had given orders a day or two prior and we were all ready. Everyone knew what to do including loading water, ammo, stores, expendables and whatever luxuries you might have room for. This time it all seemed a little more deliberate though, as it wasn't training, it was for real. I'm sure a lot of the troops' minds were thinking hard about what was in store for them. There would be no slipping back into base to grab whatever kit might have been forgotten.

I had only been in theatre for a couple of weeks myself as I pushed the last large group of the Squadron out of Canada. It was planned this way to allow me to take care of any personnel issues and it would be the same at the end of the tour as I would bring the last of the Squadron out. You always hope there's not going to be any disciplinary issues but something always crops up at the 11th hour. For example when during the end tour decompression leave I found out that PO1 'Knobby' Walsh was the first Warrant Officer on Gatorade Platoon[37]. Once again 23 Field Squadron led the way in firsts.

I was not yet acclimatised to the heat, which was still overwhelming, so the water consumption was right up there for me. I remember the whole trip sweating profusely and doing things that I would never do in normal situations, like standing in the shade of a vehicle. Not that I don't like shade, but standing close to vehicles that could move unannounced out in the Area of Operations was also not good for your health. IEDs were often initiated by the weight of a vehicle and anyone standing close wouldn't have much of a chance. As the tour went on I distanced myself further and further from moving vehicles. Self-preservation, I guess.

The trip to Waiting Area 3 was done in the midday heat with numerous stops, lots of 5- and 20-metre searches around the stopped vehicles, and a whole lot of wrong turns. The maps just didn't show the routes south of Kandahar City clearly. Once arrived, we rolled into the waiting area and linked up with the infantry company that was present. You think you have planned for everything, but every time there is something that takes you by surprise, such as female washrooms in this case. I didn't even think of it until Cpl Fretter, our medic, came up and asked. I said "No problem, give me 10 minutes and I'll have something sorted for you and Cpl Hicks." I hung up a SKOP kit (green tarp) and everyone was happy, except the infantry sections between whose LAVs I had hung it up.

Everyone's mind was focused on the battle ahead, so when an infantry LAV backed over a landmine, we all immediately thought 'mortars' and bailed into our vehicles. I guess the chunks of LAV tire flying over our heads should have given us a hint that it was a ground-initiated charge. As I turned my head to check the mine data on the map in the back of the LAV, Maj G simultaneously asked where the closest minefield was. The closest one on our mine map was 400 to 500 metres to the west. The OC used his attached US Route Clearance Package to clear tracks out of the danger area. Who knew what was there after all. It could be a single mine or, worst case, we were sitting in an unmarked minefield. It was all night before recovery got the LAV onto a flat bed. We ended up having to tow it out to Route Fosters where the LAV was loaded onto a waiting low-bed.

Most times a plan will not go 100% as planned and this was one of those times. Everyone in the world had to know that Waiting Area 3 was now compromised, possibly one mine, possibly a minefield. I'm not sure who the call sign was but they took painful measures to navigate around our vehicles to get into Waiting Area 3 as that was their plan and no one was going to stop them from getting there.

The OC came across the intercom, "Sergeant-Major, stop those vehicles!" I shoved my head up out of the hatch to see a whole convoy entering Waiting Area 3. PO2 Walsh later complimented me, "I've never seen a man sprint that fast with body armour, tactical vest and weapon before." I stopped the lead vehicle and informed him to not move, I let him know he was in a suspected minefield and I would have the Route Clearance Package come over and clear him a route out. "Do you understand?" I asked. "Do not move."

I thought it was clear but as I walked away they all turned left and drove back out to Route Fosters. I remember thinking, "I'm sure I told them in English. Oh well, less work for the Route Clearance Package tonight."

As we sat for the evening watching the mass exodus from Panjwaii it was almost mesmerizing. You didn't know what was coming down the road next. A van stuffed and 10 people on top, a horse at full gallop with a cart full of people, speeding vehicles loaded all the way up and donkeys hauling carts - all getting out of Dodge before the show started. It was quite obvious that they knew we were coming and that there was going to be a gunfight.

By afternoon we were at Ma'sum Ghar and linked up with Niner Tac on the north forward slope of the hill facing across the Arghandab River. It was a desolate area and I couldn't have dreamed at that time that 1 Troop would turn that hill into an impenetrable FOB by the end of the tour.

SEPTEMBER 2ND - 3RD: MA'SUM GHAR

We spent a couple of days at Battle Position 302 on the northern forward slope of Ma'sum Ghar. As a Sergeant-Major, what stuck out in my mind was once the stress of the big show is on, how quickly you forget about all the basics that are second nature during training – latrines for example. I know I mentioned this back in Waiting Area 3 but here we were again, 200 soldiers on Battle Position 302 and not one shitter was set up, no ablutions, no refuelling point, etc. Even though it wasn't my position to be worried about it, I'm to blame more than anyone, because that's what I'm responsible for as a senior non-commissioned officer - ensuring that camp routine is smooth. After two days, there was used toilet paper all over the side of the mountain. If we had known that we were going to turn this barren mountain into a permanent FOB, we wouldn't have left it in the state we did. It didn't happen again though. Whenever we pulled in somewhere

I would ask whoever owned the place about the facilities and if they weren't up to code I'd make them into what was expected.

The OC had been in constant conversation with the CO about the conduct of the battle to come. I remember hearing the CO on the Battle Group net on numerous occasions bringing up the question of where the Company of Afghan National Army was, as they were supposed to be in support of Op Medusa. The whole time I can only remember seeing the solitary Afghan Army tan Toyota Tacoma pickup truck with a .50- calibre machine gun mounted in the rear and four occupants. I remember this well because they never seemed to be parked more than 20 metres from our LAV. In fact, at one point when engaging the enemy on the far bank they were parked behind us, firing their .50-calibre while we had our ramp down. The only traversing and elevating mechanism on the gun was a set of toothpick-size Afghan arms and that was all that was deciding if the rounds went over our LAV or filled the back of it with lead. That was enough.

I signalled to the gunner to cease fire, guided the driver 20 metres to the right side of our LAV, gave them the thumbs up to continue their fire and just about took their keys away from them. As I made my way back to the LAV, I regretted not ensuring that they had their emergency brake on so as not to uncontrollably free wheel down the side of the mountain if the driver fell asleep.

When the order came down early on the 2nd of September that we were crossing the Arghandab several days early, I remember the CO on the radio persistently objecting and trying to buy us precious time. One day of bombing instead of three days of bombing sure didn't sit well with anyone. Maybe the people giving the order knew something we didn't. We were the ones looking at the far bank from a kilometre away, so the rationale behind the decision escaped me. The OC wasn't happy with it and for good reason; our boys would be in the lead with the breaching tasks, and in "Mad-Maxed" heavy equipment at that.

The last conversation I had with Sgt Shane Stachnik wasn't about anything important but I will remember it forever because it was 12 hours before he made the crossing. He was walking by the back of the OC's LAV and I called him over. Knowing the boys were going across the next morning I called over anyone that came into view and had a chat with them. The conversation was light and more just to see what the mood was with the troops.

"How you doing Shane, ready for tomorrow?" I asked.

"Good to go, Sergeant-Major," he answered. We had some idle chat about motorcycles and that he had his back at his home all winterized. He was just up the hill taking care of some last-minute administration and was heading back to his section.

"Take care of the boys tomorrow buddy." I gave him a slap on the upper right arm.

"Yup, good to go Sergeant-Major, talk to ya later." If a guy knew how the next day was to unfold there would have been a hell of a lot more said.

The next day, sitting on our position listening to things unfold was tough. It is safe to say we were glued to every word on the radio. When the message came across about 32 Delta, the OC looked back over the turret and I nodded in confirmation that I'd heard. After the battle an infantry section commander specifically sought me out back at Ma'sum Ghar to tell me of the events. His section was behind the 32 Delta LAV when the round struck its side. It was as if a giant shock wave had encircled the vehicle. He said they couldn't see the Taliban as they lay waiting in the three- to four-metre-high marijuana plants.

The RSM and I spoke later about this green belt and how we could have been wrong about pushing so hard for the tan Tactical Vests back in Canada. A green vest with the tan uniform broke up your colour providing better camouflage, just like you do in winter by adjusting and wearing just the white bottoms and staying green on the upper to blend into tree lines.

I later inspected the LAV and saw where the round had entered the right side turret ring and penetrated the crew commander's and gunner's seat supports. An infantry section commander commented on MCpl Dwayne Orvis and he explained how Dwayne had taken control of the section after the devastating loss of Shane and refocused them to get the section and crippled the LAV out of the kill zone. Realizing the importance of this info, I immediately asked him for a statement. Something that had not even been thought of was the writing of honours and awards. It's been so long since our army has been in a war that this didn't even come into focus until September 3rd for me, and by end day September 4th we had four decorations on the table to write up. The Charles Company Quartermaster also came and sought me out, knowing I was on the opposite bank of the Arghandab. He wanted to inform and assure me that four fellow senior non-commissioned officers had placed Sgt Shane Stachnik on a chopper.

It was early and we were all conducting our morning routine. Maj G and his gunner were manning the turret putting fire across the river at targets of opportunity. Cpl Hicks was in the back with a headset on and Cpls Fretter and Kravjar and I were out back sorting kit. The morning calm was broken by a spray of sparks coming from just down the hill out in front of the LAV. I told everyone to mount up because we were under attack. We did so and raised the ramp. The OC was monitoring the radio while in the turret and he knew the situation as fast as it came across the net. An A-10 had mistakenly identified the burning garbage behind Charles Company as his target. I didn't yet have my headset on and heard the OC yell over the LAV engine noise.

"Sergeant-Major, go and help the RSM!" It all really sank in at that point, bright sparks, three second delay, followed by a dull burping sound: we had taken A-10 fire in our lines. Kravjar dropped ramp and I looked for Fretter, she was already gone. She had realized it before any of us and grabbed her medical bag and was already on site. When I was running down over the hill I can remember thinking, *good God this is going to be carnage*. Thankfully, my mind was playing it out worse than it was, although tragically we lost one soldier. If the A-10 pilot hadn't instantly realised his mistake, and he had gone with a full three to four second burst rather than one-second burst things would have been catastrophically worse. There were approximately 35 troops lying everywhere, wounded. I sought out Cpl Fretter and started feeding her shell dressings as she was going through them fast. The RSM was organising the injured into groups by priority, the Blackhawks would be here soon to take out the Priority One casualties.

At one point, I made my way around the front of the vehicle line to make sure there were no other injured soldiers who had been missed. I found a couple of troops treating a soldier under the front of a LAV. They looked like they needed a hand so I made my way over. I went to work on his leg wound and once it was all dressed we rolled him over on his back. It was my neighbour from back in Petawawa!

"Ian, how you doing buddy?"

"Good Sergeant-Major. Guess I'm going home eh?"

"Yeah buddy, looks like it." I didn't talk long with him, as there was more work to be done.

After all the casualties were treated, we waited for the helicopters and I moved through the rows of wounded checking on them. Many were lying and taking comfort with photos in hand of loved ones back home. I had come across Maj Sprague, OC Charles Company, lying on his back with his head bandaged. His sergeant-major had been wounded the day prior and now he was to be taken out of the battle. Although he would return later in the tour it was going to be a hard blow to his company. I told him the chopper would be here soon and he nodded his head in acknowledgement. Our Squadron also had five wounded in the attack and I got the chance to see them all off onto the chopper. Sgt Kennedy, our senior Dragoon crew commander, had to be the happiest wounded soldier I've ever seen. With a hunk of shrapnel through the leg, his morale didn't drop for a minute and he continued to keep up the spirits of the wounded soldiers around him.

The Black Hawks had come and gone now and the Chinook was inbound. It flew right over our heads and across the Arghandab River. I made a dead sprint for the RSM yelling that they were going to land on the enemy side of the river. I'm not sure who, but somebody called them off over the radio. I've logged many hours in Chinooks and never seen a pilot make a side bank like this guy did. It was obvious he had realized the situation he was in.

Back in Canada, the RSM had insisted on practicing a Mass Casualty Collection Point during the Maple Guardian Exercise. It paid tremendous dividends on that day. It was all very organized and panic-free, with all the wounded evacuated in an orderly manner. Cpl Fretter gets a lot of the credit for the treatment of the wounded. I witnessed first-hand her unceasing efforts to provide care. As more medics showed up on site it was her they saw leading the triage and they sought their initial direction from her. She was awarded a Chief of the Defence Staff Commendation for her actions. Cpl Potzkai, who is 'T Triple C' qualified, is another that needs to be recognized for his efforts as he worked on the wounded from the minute of the attack until the last soldier was loaded onto a helicopter.

The RSM and I boarded a helicopter on September 7th to travel back to Kandahar Airfield for the Ramp Ceremony and meet up with the CO and Maj G who were back sorting out the new orders for the second assault on Pashmul.

SEPTEMBER 27TH, 2006: EOD 2 – IED STRIKE

The ISTAR Squadron Sergeant-Major, MWO Steve Lehman, struck an IED when traveling south on Route Vancouver while conducting a re-supply mission. His vehicle suffered minor damage; however, when EOD 2 responded from Patrol Base Wilson the next day to investigate, their Bison struck an IED that resulted in a large hole being ripped in the bottom rear of the vehicle. PO2 Leith was the crew commander, Cpl Maidment was the driver and Cpl Lightle was in the back as the air sentry. Lightle sustained a broken leg when the blast broke the robot loose from its tie downs and it crushed him against the inside wall of the LAV. He was brought to Patrol Base Wilson and I was waiting at the Medical Station for him after listening to it all on the radio. He was in pretty good spirits - in fact damn good spirits because of whatever they gave him for the pain - probably morphine but I am not sure.

Lightle was laughing. "Hey Sergeant-Major, how's it going? I think I got a homer here"

"Yeah, I think you do buddy." We talked while the medics prepped him for the ride back to Kandahar Airfield. He was feeling absolutely no pain.

OCTOBER 3RD, 2006: GUNFIGHT

During Route Summit construction we had set up a leaguer with elements from ISTAR Squadron who were located at the meeting point of Sectors 2 and 3 of Route Summit. The Route Clearance Package and our dozer were part of our grouping. Maj G and I were in the rear of the LAV when an imminent attack warning came across the radio and was to happen in our vicinity. We had heard many of these before but the OC looked over and gave direction to have everyone suit up because we were moving in five minutes.

The first group I went to was the Route Clearance Package. "Suit up boys. We've received an early warning of an attack planned against our position." Back at the LAV, I mounted up and we circled around the north side of Rock 26. It couldn't have been three seconds later when explosions hit the leaguer. The OC came across the intercom indicating mortar attack and ordered hatches down. As Cpl Kravjar and I pulled our hatches over, a round (what I now know to be a Rocket Propelled Grenade) struck just behind the LAV and showered dirt in on us. It was close because the concussion knocked the two months of dust off the interior sides of the LAV and

Kravjar and I sat there squinting to see if the other was OK.

Rock 26's explosive storage trailer and a Humvee had been hit in the attack and they had taken casualties. The OC was on the radio telling Lt Webb to gather his casualties and make his way out to the road and that we would provide escort to Patrol Base Wilson. Lt Webb initially had problems locating which LAV was ours, but once he did, he and his two Humvees were on us like glue until we dropped them at Patrol Base Wilson.

Once night came, we were sitting on Route Comox with a broken-down Husky and damaged Humvee. We were all manning our fire positions in our LAVs and the infantry platoon with us had dispatched a section to put out trip flares to the south for early warning of infiltration. I could see their helmet infrared strobes blinking about 400 metres to our south. The OC dispatched me to assess if we could move the crippled vehicles to Patrol Base Wilson or not. He was weighing his options and had to make the decision whether to stay in place and adopt a defensive posture or get everyone back to Patrol Base Wilson. I could tell he wasn't favouring the idea of staying in position.

Before dismounting, I had Kravjar switch sides and cover to the west because it had the higher vegetation and was harder for me to see into that area with my night vision goggles while dismounted. I walked towards the Husky and remember thinking, if it still has four wheels then it can be towed and I'll do my best to give the OC the option to go to Patrol Base Wilson if he so decides.

I met up with the Rock 26's Sgt Krantz. I knew the operator wasn't there as he was one of the wounded we took to Patrol Base Wilson. I looked at the Husky. Good, no flats. This meant slip it in neutral and tow it home. I was quickly informed that the only one who knew how to operate it was the driver.

"Well Sergeant, hop on in there, I've got all the faith in the world that you can find me neutral on that baby." It took him a couple of minutes and I gave direction to have it hooked to a LAV. "Do the wheels turn on that thing or are we just dragging it?"

"I think they're good to go, Sergeant-Major," he answered. I looked around and we actually had a substantial quantity of firepower in location, including, from what I can remember, 2 Troop's LAVs, a platoon of infantry and the OC's LAV with Rock 26 assets.

I gave the OC a sitrep that all vehicles could move, but that it would be a slow trip. We then made our way to Patrol Base Wilson. As I looked behind us through my night vision goggles it looked like a slow-motion snake winding its way north on Route Comox. The three-kilometre trip took about 45 minutes to complete but we made it there safe and sound.

OCTOBER 21ST, 2006: BADGERS ARE DEPLOYED

From day one, I couldn't understand why the Army deployed its Engineers without their Badgers. I've never gone anywhere without them, save to Africa, but we were only a troop-sized entity at that time. Higher-ups think there must be tanks for Badgers to be needed but that isn't so. Engineers will always need these armoured engineer vehicles to both provide and deny mobility, whether we are using a wheeled or tracked fleet in theatre. The Badger has proven itself over and over again by destroying grape huts, building roads, digging in positions or simply executing recovery operations.

At one point, during the flooding of Route Summit it was the only vehicle that could move in the area. The dozers had completed daunting tasks for their capability and lack of armour. A big 'well done' for the troops that operated them but I breathed a big sigh of relief when I met MCpl Schroder at midnight and guided him and his Badger into Patrol Base Wilson. One drawback was the temperature inside. He tossed me out a bottle of drinking water that was probably even too hot to shave with and this was October. Imagine what the temperature was going to be inside during the summer.

When I guided MCpl Schroder into Patrol Base Wilson the front dozer blade cleared the walls on either side with about 4 inches to spare. It was supposed to be flat bedded out to keep the operating time down to minimum but he had driven the whole 60 km route to Patrol Base Wilson. The Armoured Recovery Vehicle was to follow the flatbed but it had mechanical problems so they had swapped positions.

Badgers will not do as pretty a job as a dozer as it doesn't have an articulating blade. The trade-off is armour, guns, an excavating arm, 60 KPH maximum speed and can dig itself a defensive position in minutes. They are maintenance-intensive, but after what we had seen with the dozers, I think it took less to keep the Badgers running and we got more results. Also, I don't think my small pack could have handled hauling another 25 kilogram D6 dozer starter from Kandahar Airfield to Patrol Base Wilson.

Later in the tour the Tank OC, Maj Cadieu, commented on the skill of our Badger operators. Different from a tank, the driver is given much more latitude for manoeuvring and this is mainly because he operates everything from the excavating arm to the dozer blade as well as driving. He has to be a master at manoeuvring and manipulating the vehicle implements at the same time. Cpl Orr, a heavy equipment operator, was thrown into the job of Badger operator when we went short one. He had already proven his capabilities in a dozer on September 3rd, receiving a Medal of Military Valour, and now was to take the Badger and show he could master it also. Throughout the remainder of the tour the Badger crews worked tirelessly, operating and maintaining their vehicles to achieve the desired end state of each mission.

NOVEMBER 27TH, 2006 – NINER TAC IED

It was 7:30 am and we marshalled our vehicles in the usual place at Kandahar Airfield waiting for the CO to come from the Command Post. Once he arrived, his crew commander gave us the routine packet brief and we all took note of what vehicle was in front and behind as usual. We'd been through this 30 or 40 times now so it was routine but the only difference was that the RSM had replaced his RG-31 with a Bison. The order-of-march was the CO's LAV, the RSM's Bison, the Engineer OC's LAV and finally the Artillery Battery Commander's LAV. I can remember after the briefing spending a few minutes at the back of the RSM's vehicle and being a bit jealous of the space he had to transport goods to his troops at the front lines. I had a G-Wagon assigned to me that couldn't leave Kandahar Airfield so if I was to get out seeing the troops at all it was with the OC's LAV. Every trip out, I would monopolize all the extra space in the back with what the troops needed. Things like tentage, HP1 hydraulic units, mail, replacement clothing, vehicle parts, etc. The RSM didn't have much in his Bison this time as he hadn't the time to stock it.

Niner Tac departed Kandahar Airfield at approximately 8:20 am and made its way towards Kandahar City on Highway 4, ultimately destined for Ma'sum Ghar. It was all routine. We passed through the various checkpoints where everyone would put on their game faces, drop down to chinstrap defilade in their hatches and start watching their arcs. We then made the turn north towards Kandahar City. 20 minutes later, about 500 metres short of the Golden Arches Niner Tac came under contact from a suicide vehicle IED. I remember hearing later that it was one of the largest ones seen to date. At the time it didn't sound that loud, possibly because I was behind the turret and shielded from the sound and the shock wave. There was no doubt what had just happened due to the debris passing over our heads. The suicide bomber had 'sharked' the convoy. He pulled out from the opposite side of the road and positioned himself in front of our lead vehicle. When the lead vehicle sounded its horn for the vehicle to clear the road it pulled over to the right side and waited to detonate as we passed.

Capt Busbridge was covering off for the OC because he was heading out on mid-tour leave the next day. He came across the intercom stating that he thought everything was all right because the RSM's Bison kept moving through the blast as if unaffected. Unfortunately, it was just the momentum of the vehicle that took it through because it then veered to the left coming to stop in a depression alongside the road.

It was only seconds later that the CO came across the convoy net and directed us to investigate, as he didn't see any movement from the RSM's Bison. Adrenaline kicked in at that moment, and not knowing what frequency Capt Busbridge was monitoring, I answered, "Echo 39 Charlie, dismounting now." while simultaneously discarding my headset and dropping the ramp. The CO had already sent the Contact Report in to the Command Post.

Once out the back of the LAV, I signaled Cpl Vomastic to grab all the medical gear and to come with me. While approaching the Bison from the rear right I could tell it had nosed into a shallow depression on the left side of the highway. I made my way around the front. I was on the driver / crew commander side of the vehicle and I could see no one in either of the hatches and no answer when I called out to them. I considered climbing the side to check on the crew then stopped, realizing I was on the opposite side of the vehicle to where the other LAVs could provide any cover fire from secondary attacks. I called myself an idiot out loud and changed my approach to the rear of the vehicle. This would also make it easier to extract the wounded. I recalled that when talking with the RSM prior to departure, noticing that the back of his Bison was pretty empty. There would be lots of room to treat the injured in the back under cover.

From the south side of the road a lone individual broke into a run towards our vehicles and I brought my rifle up and put the sights square on his chest. He was about 30 metres out when he stopped abruptly and grabbed a sack from the roadside, then turned and ran off in the direction he came from. He probably had no idea how close he came to being shot. He was undoubtedly an unfortunate bystander who dropped his belongings when the IED went off and had returned for them. There were also about seven camels on the side of the road that had been injured, they all laid there, contorted in different positions, moaning, bleeding and slowly dying.

Once in the back of the Bison I realized that there would be no treatment of the wounded. The injuries sustained by the RSM, CWO Robert Girouard, and his driver, Cpl Albert Storm were lethal and instantaneous. The shrapnel from the blast had come up across the bow of the Bison where both driver and crew commander were positioned with their heads out. Good God, we've just lost the Battle Group RSM and his driver, I thought. The soldiers respected and admired their RSM and it was going to be devastating to hear he was a casualty. The CO had also lost his most trusted confidant and I could only try to imagine how it would affect him.

A Black Hawk helicopter was on site within 15 minutes and extracted the RSM and Cpl Storm back to Kandahar Airfield. EOD out of Camp Nathan Smith was on site by now and I handed over to them. I identified an un-detonated grenade, likely from the suicide bomber and the suicide bomber himself, whose lower torso was hanging from some power lines and whose upper torso was lying in the north side ditch. I gave them whatever else they needed. Frankly, I don't remember much of the handover, as my mind was still on the incident realizing the enormity of it. The Battle Group net was completely quiet and I can remember thinking everyone out there must be waiting to hear who had been killed.

I don't even recall what our destination was, probably Ma'sum Ghar, but at that point we turned back the way we came and returned to Kandahar Airfield.

DECEMBER 2006: – SECOND NINER TAC IED STRIKE

Niner Tac was making a trip to FOB Spervan Ghar with the usual composition of vehicles and a platoon of infantry who happened to be travelling to the FOB. On this particular occasion WO Gombert was accompanying us to get him some face time within the Area of Operations when he would cover off for me, once I departed on leave. Capt Busbridge remained as the acting OC since Maj G was still on leave. This move was also being used as an opportunity to relocate additional personnel around to different tasks. MCpl Waugh and Sgt Dix were being moved to FOB Spervan Ghar to link up and work with 2 Troop.

The third vehicle, an infantry callsign, was hit by a pressure-plate IED on Route Fosters. It was about 800m short of Route Brown leading into FOB Spervan Ghar. The rear left wheel, hub and axle where completely blown off and the occupants in the back of the LAV received minor injuries. Niner was the vehicle directly behind the stricken LAV, and ours was the next vehicle behind Niner.

Upon hearing the report by Niner on the radio, I had MCpl Waugh prepare the mine detector and, once ready, we dropped the ramp just short of touching the road and dismounted to check out the area for any secondary devices. We immediately cleared our way off the road where we knew there was little chance of IEDs. I looked at Waugh and said, "We're safe now, we can't do shit to rectify what has happened but it gives everyone else confidence to see people with the balls to actually get out and deal with things."

It was Waugh's first time in a strike so I took a second to brief him on past experiences. If we weren't taking fire immediately after an IED strike then there was little chance it was an ambush and in the multiple times I had dismounted to do vulnerable point searches, I had the utmost confidence in the turrets and the people who had their fingers on the triggers covering me. He acknowledged and I sensed his confidence grow. He had a purposeful look in his eyes and a confident grasp on the mine detector.

Once safely off the road we made our way up the verge past the CO's vehicle, stopping briefly to give a sitrep on our intentions. Once we confirmed that all the occupants of the stricken LAV were all right we started checking spots of likely interest on the road such as depressions, freshly moved dirt and any odd objects. I knew teams were coming from FOB Spervan Ghar but as I mentioned before, it gives people confidence to see others actually conducting decisive actions and dealing with the situation at hand rather than sitting waiting. I took a quick visual in the direction of the FOB and could see that our location was in their direct sight about one kilometre away. Not really talking to Waugh or anyone in particular, I said under my breath, "What the fuck? I can see the Coyote mast from here, how the hell did a pressure plate IED get installed under our noses?" The Coyote is an armoured reconnaissance vehicle with a tremendous surveillance suite. First impressions: I guess the Taliban are just masters at crawling around on their guts and digging in IEDs.

A Coalition Force EOD team stationed out of the FOB at the time was the first group to arrive on site with their Quick Reaction Force. The speed of their route clearance and lack of detail was quite apparent, not only to me but to the CO as he called me over to comment on it.

"Sergeant-Major, I'm no engineer but it doesn't look like very thorough clearance drills to me." They took approximately four minutes to cover a 300-metre distance. I informed the CO we should wait until Sgt Coates's section arrived until we ventured any farther on the route. Coates's section arrived within the next 10 minutes. I remember seeing them starting their clearance 300 metres to our west and felt no small comfort knowing they were the ones checking the route. They completed the clearance up to the stricken LAV and, along with Quick Reaction Force, took over the site allowing us to continue on to the FOB. An hour and a half had elapsed by the time Waugh and I mounted back up into the LAV. I sat and took a relaxing breath and looked over at Gombert and said, "Wait for it buddy, you've got four weeks of this when I'm on leave and that's only two weeks away!"

WO Gombert gave his usual confident chuckle and the LAV started to roll forward to Spervan Ghar.

DECEMBER 20TH, 2006 - OP BAAZ TSUKA

The Operation was to be executed in conjunction with the Brits. After we went in to Howz-e-Madad (a town 10 kilometres west of Patrol Base Wilson) and secured the area, the Brits would launch from one of their bases in Helmand Province and arrive to set up one of their expedient checkpoint packages. It was another one of those plans in which we didn't know what to expect from each other or just didn't know each other's capabilities. In the end the Operation was a success but wasn't without its hiccups.

We received our British Liaison Officer a couple of days early and he met us at Patrol Base Wilson. He was to travel with us in our LAV. The Liaison Officer was accompanied by his radio operator.

The move to Howz-e-Madad was a rather impressive show of force. Tanks, LAVs and echelon vehicles all moved as a combat team. We leaguered up just north of the town and monitored Taliban movements for the next 24 hours. At one point, the Intelligence cell had stated that Taliban were dressing in burkas so as to freely roam the area and pick up their dead.

I remember thinking, "Great, now we have Taliban insurgents dressing in drag. They have to know this isn't going to work."

The next day we broke leaguer and moved the whole element cross-country east towards Patrol Base Wilson. As I recall it, two tank troops, our 2 Troop, Charles Company and Niner Tac made up the combat team. It was quite a grouping of vehicles moving across the countryside. I'm pretty sure the CO's intent was to see what he could stir up for enemy movement. We swung back south to the highway and came back west to Howz-e-Madad and leaguered up again about one kilometre north of the previous leaguer.

The Badgers had cleared the foundations for the checkpoint and it was now time for the Brits to perform their part. Capt Busbridge gave the Liaison Officer permission to contact his organization and launch their assets.

I can remember his conversation, over cell phone, back to his headquarters, quite well. First, he couldn't get in contact with anyone. Once he did they informed him they would need about 12 hours to prep everything to go. I'm was not in the picture as to what kind of orders the Brits received but I couldn't help but think that if there was an operation of this magnitude on the go, they should really have been ready to launch at a moment's notice - passage of information possibly, or poor interpretation, I'm not sure. Once they did arrive it was impressive to watch the speed with which the checkpoint went up.

SQUADRON HEADQUARTERS

The unsung heroes of the tour resided back in Kandahar Airfield both in the Command Post / Engineer Support Coordination Centre and the Squadron Quartermaster lines. The process of contracts, getting goods forward to the troops and managing administrative issues was a 24/7 endeavour and our people handling it all back in Kandahar Airfield put the best foot forward that I have ever seen. WOs Marcoux and Mazerolle were our resident Badger experts who accepted and prepared the Badgers for deployment forward, doing so above and beyond their gruelling shifts in the Command Post. WO Gombert, qualified on heavy equipment and with a couple of years experience in the job, could troubleshoot just about any supply and equipment problem that came his way. He was expertly assisted by our resident Technical Quartermaster, Sgt Bernie French. Capts Busbridge and Hayward were constantly on the go, working everything from administration to smoothing over the conflicts between organizations and fighting the ever-evolving future-planning monster. We had the foresight to push for a Geomatics Cell within our structure. Having built the capability from scratch, Sgt Isabelle Couture and MCpl Chuck Caissie worked around the clock performing terrain analysis and producing maps.

We cut ourselves short on staff when we created our 6th field section, which meant all the troops back in Kandahar Airfield pretty well worked two jobs rather than one. Cpl Hicks did her expected signals job but also pulled 8-hour shifts in the Command Post as well as Cpl Power as the Motor Transport Representative. They all pulled miracles to keep us going, for which I will be forever thankful.

I can remember pulling the Command Post staff out behind the building one day after Op Medusa to thank them for being the voice of calm on the radio. Things can be going to shit out in the field but their job was to address things on the radio with poise and invoke a sense of calm into the situation, which they did very well. The OC was a master at this. I can remember his IED strike. I was back in Kandahar Airfield helping out in the Command Post, and he came across the radio coolly and methodically so not to instil panic in anyone else. The only one who panicked was me when he said the blast blew his boot bands off. Before that he had passed probably the worst nine-liner I'd ever heard.

I was at the Hospital to see the OC's gunner when he arrived. The medical staff had already completed all their treatments before I was allowed to see him. The burns on his arm were already bandaged up along with his eyes but I was informed there was no problem and his sight would be just fine. I had a few minutes to chew the fat with him and provide some comfort before the Padre came in to do his required visit and provide the opportunity for him to contact his family. I bade him farewell but then had second thoughts and felt that I should remain on the sidelines until the Padre was done. It was a good thing in hindsight. The Padre gave him the usual spiel and told him that as a wounded soldier he was required to inform his parents prior to his name being released to the press. Having his eyes bandaged, he accepted the Padre's offer to dial the number and initiate the call.

The words are still fresh in my mind. "Hello, this is the Battle Group Padre calling from Afghanistan about your son ...oh my gosh, she hung up.... guess I could have handled that better." If I could have forecasted the conversation I would have grabbed the phone and handled it myself.

He responded, "You'd better call my Aunt. She lives down the road and can go check on my mother and see if she's all right." In the end, the message was passed to his mother and all was good. During the second call I made my way back to the Squadron Headquarters knowing that he had made contact with a family member.

THE HANDOVER

The Squadron prepared for the relief-in-place starting on the day we took over. A few weeks prior to the new Squadron arriving we stepped up our preparations. Vehicles were maintained and handed over in serviceable condition. Section Commanders and up would have face time with all their counterparts. We would also vacate our accommodations to make room for the incoming as they had a job to do and it wasn't proper to do it from transient quarters.

I think we moved three times before permanently settling in our quarters for the tour. Many on the previous tour could not see past their own departure date and nothing else mattered. We had sappers deployed forward with their kit still in temporary quarters only to return and move again. We moved to the "Big-Ass Tents" or "BATs" for short, so the incoming engineers could move straight into their permanent quarters and get on with their mission. The quarters were cleaned, and every effort was made to have the heater and air conditioning units operational.

As groups left for decompression leave in Cyprus and we received numerous updates about their escapades, it looked more and more like the last group (i.e. mine) would only be allowed coffee or tea once there. The first crew out had apparently utterly dismantled the resort on their first night. More news came back steadily about each subsequent group. Gatorade Platoon was established for those who were cut off of alcohol and no booze was allowed in the rooms of the resort.

By the time Capt Busbridge, the rest of our group and I arrived, the rules were set out quite firm and there wasn't much room for interpretation, although I did manage to get liquored up enough one night to end up in the resort pool naked. The statute of limitations has run out on this one and there aren't any pictures. I blame Capt Busbridge because he had a bottle of rum in his room contrary to the rules.

There were a lot of mixed feelings about Decompression Leave. Some thought it was a waste of time and just wanted to get home to their families while others felt that it was a necessary activity for our troops prior to returning back to Canada. I personally think that the opportunity to unwind and decompress was absolutely essential as evidenced by the events that unfolded at the resort. People argue that those events wouldn't have taken place in Canada and it was simply a group of soldiers feeding off each other that was the cause of any unruliness. I believe that many of those same soldiers would have got together back at home to let off steam in much the same way. The difference being that it would have occurred at home rather than in the third location. Decompression Leave, from my perspective, successfully allowed the soldiers to unwind and return to their families in a healthier state of mind.

On March 6th, the last 31 soldiers of 23 Field Squadron loaded up on buses and made their way to the airport. As when I deployed into theatre, in order to settle any administrative and/or disciplinary matters I, along with Capt Busbridge, accompanied the last group out. Once the wheels folded up into the plane and we were airborne I remember thinking this is it, next stop home. Everyone was very relaxed and we were going to be arriving in Trenton Ontario sometime in the evening and subsequently getting into Petawawa by bus after midnight, thus ending our time with Task Force 3-06.

SQUADRON HEADQUARTERS

WO Derek Marcoux

It is May, 2008 and I am back at Kandahar Airfield with the Joint Task Force Afghanistan Headquarters, Roto 5. It is just over a year-and-a-half since I left Kandahar Airfield the first time around, after having participated in Roto 2 with the 1 RCR Battle Group, and specifically as the Operations Warrant Officer with 23 Field Squadron. My overriding personal thought on that deployment is one of pride in the accomplishments of that sub-unit. I remain eternally grateful to Maj Gasparotto for selecting me to be his Operations Warrant Officer. If I understand the story of how that took place correctly, there was no hesitation on his part to pick me and it came about rather quickly one evening in November of 2005. I am incredibly proud of the soldiers I served with. They are the best this nation has to offer and they proved their fortitude and integrity on many occasions. As I look back I can see the things that happened, but it is as if some other guy was there, and it is very much like watching a movie.

I have read the draft copies of the war diary, and the events described therein, and they have prompted some memories of events, so I thought I might put a few words to paper from the Headquarters side of the Squadron. The lead-in to our Roto was very hectic and the training was intense. In retrospect I think that it was good, and that it did prepare the troops for what they were about to face. I remember I spent long hours in the office with Captain John Hayward, the Squadron Operations Officer, going through the extensive direction that was given to us by Maj G for the Squadron training.

Maj G was an outstanding OC. He was all about mission command: state the intent and desired end-state, give him a quick back brief, sometimes there would be a few modifications, and then we would execute. He respected his Non-Commissioned Officers and Warrant Officers and he always took the time to listen and understand where we were coming from. Because of that, we would follow him anywhere. I don't know if he knew that, but I think he sensed the loyalty and commitment. There was no greater punishment that could have befallen us than to hear him say that he was disappointed in the outcome of some venture and fortunately I only heard him say that on two occasions, once in training and once in theatre. And so the training came and went.

DEPLOYMENT

I came into the picture somewhat late in the development of the Squadron and throughout the whole time I was in the organization I felt like I was sinking. It wasn't because the tasks were too difficult, or anything else like that, it was because the pace was so incredibly fast. Time was something that I never had enough of because there was always something extra I could do to increase the value or quality of training by enhancing the basic plan.

This tempo carried on throughout the deployment as well. In any case the deployment date came and our group got on a bus at 1 RCR's lines on a hot day (high 30s Celsius) at the end of July 2006 and we went left for CFB Trenton. We then got on an Airbus and flew to our staging base in the Middle East, with a stop in the UK along the way. When we got off the plane at the staging base it was 52 degrees Celsius with about 80% humidity. It was at that moment that I knew this mission was different. Things moved along there quickly and then we were aboard a Hercules. One motor started, two motors, three motors... and then we were back off the aircraft until they fixed the problem. Oh by the way, it's hot, full kit and no air-conditioning. OK, let's try again. We all got back on the plane and this time it took off. I remember thinking that it would cool off when we got up around twelve thousand feet... wrong! It was just as hot and miserable all the way to another hot and miserable environment to further do incredibly demanding things in even more hot and miserable conditions. That is why I am so proud of them.

Anyway, we got off the plane in 40 degrees Celsius heat at three in the morning at Kandahar Airfield, and were welcomed by a crusty Sergeant-Major from the in-place force. He told us what we could and could not do, where, when, and with whom. I was paying attention at the time, but most of what he said escapes my consciousness now. The next outstanding memory I have is meeting WO Ted Gombert at our shacks. It was a good meeting.

The next day we started our theatre indoctrination training. Of note, I volunteered to be an Assistant Range Safety Officer for our chalk. That was a mistake. I spent the whole morning on the firing line, nowhere near acclimatized to the 55-degree heat and the sun. I drank sixteen 500-milliliter bottles of water and almost passed out at 10:00 am despite that. That afternoon I went back to have a sleep. I set the air-conditioner at 30 degrees Celsius and was found shivering in my bunk under a blanket by Sgt Scott Clucas at about three in the afternoon. The heat was absolutely crazy!

At the time, I don't think anyone realized how lucky we were to have the expertise of WO Ted Gombert, Sgt Rene Grignon, Sgt Ron Dix and myself included in the Squadron. Our knowledge of how to execute heavy equipment and armoured engineering operations would prove invaluable. Between the four of us we had to have close to 80 years of experience. Just as an aside, it is my view that the Army made a poor choice when, among other reductions, they removed the Engineer Heavy Equipment trade. I know all the justifications that were made for it and I also know the promises that were made to ensure that the capability would remain at the standard it was in the mid-nineties. Those promises never came to fruition and because of that, there is now a generation of engineers coming up that don't know what we experienced soldiers know. Also, there are now officers coming up that won't ever know the true potential of the force they may have the privilege to command, at least not for another few years, because that is how long it is going to take for the corrections that were made post-Roto 2 to take effect. Why must we learn every lesson over and over?

And so we began our handover. I took over from the Operations WO from 11 Field Squadron. He showed me around the base, I made contacts with the key players and I politely listened to how he executed his day-to-day tasks. It wasn't the same as ours and I knew what my chain of command expected from me, so I asked the pertinent questions about the things I knew I would have to integrate into our operations. One key point I noted was that they did not man their Engineer Support Coordination Centre 24 hours a day, but that was because they rarely had guys out past dark. That would change.

The first battle that I would have intimate details of occurred on the August 3rd. It was chaotic in the Command Post and it was my belief that once our battle group was in control it seemed to me that the environment in the Command Post was much calmer. In the end, I was wrong on this point, but at the time it was my perception. Two days later I attended my first ramp ceremony. The thing that struck me the most was how bright the red and white maple leaf stood out against the desert sand. I went to many, many more. So many I lost count, so every now and then I would go up to the alcove by the Battle Group Operations Officer's office and look at the faces of all the fallen, so that I would not forget.

August 19th arrived and the Transfer of Command Authority between the 1 PPCLI Battle Group and ours was barely completed when we got into our first major battle in the Panjwaii. A Company went in and shredded the Taliban pretty well. We didn't suffer any casualties and it was a successful night. I remember thinking that, "Hey, we're pretty damn good". We were, but what I think I did at the time was underestimate how good the Taliban were. You see the troops from Edmonton were pretty much out the door and we saw them as an exhausted force. Now we were here and we were going to change the world. I must reiterate that all of this was my opinion of events, and how I saw them at the time. Looking back, I do not hold that same view at all.

The first real violence I witnessed personally was an air strike that Capt Tim Spears, our Joint Terminal Air Controller, called in from the Command Post on a compound that was about 10 kilometres west of Patrol Base Wilson. I watched the attack on a plasma TV screen that was receiving a live feed from an Unmanned Aerial Vehicle. I witnessed countless others in the same fashion and, much like Maj G's experience on Op Medusa where he described being so far away from the target that it didn't seem so personal, I understand, but also with the realization that it's not the same either.

Op Medusa had almost commenced and the Squadron was making its way out the door. I was scrambling along with WO Gombert, Capt Hayward, Capt Busbridge and the rest of Squadron Headquarters to try and get them ready. The state of the equipment and vehicles was absolutely horrendous. It was busy and we all took turns manning the Engineer Support Coordination Centre desk, going to meetings, etc. Ted and I spent quite a bit of time down at Maintenance smoothing the waters with some old friends we knew, attempting to get our stuff to the front of the line. At the time, our biggest problem was finding equipment for mobility support. In fact I remember a heated conversation we had in the Engineer Support Coordination Centre where we (the heavy equipment operators) were accused of saying that we could do breaching operations with the Zettelmeyer. To this statement, I replied that yes, we did say that, but in the absence of being informed that we were going up against Rocket Propelled Grenades and heavy machine guns. This information would have changed our answer. At that point nobody really realized (read: we were in denial) what we were getting into. All of us were still in "Bosnia mode," which was a product of a decade-and-a-half in that theatre. God help me for saying this, but the Canadian Forces School of Military Engineering had the right approach through all those years that I complained about fighting the Soviet 40th Motor Rifle Division. Now they have defeated the friction of the ages and the Cold War is over they are trying to become more mission-centric in their training. I hope they don't, they had it right the first time. The basics kicked in and our outstanding leadership from top to bottom was, in my humble opinion, what got us through the whole ordeal.

OP MEDUSA

Here are some of the Highlights that I remember.

It was the start of the operation and we had no mobility in Zhari-Panjwaii. The terrain was just too tough for the LAVs to negotiate. The roads were narrow, they were laced with IEDs and the cross-country routes were not negotiable at all. The landscape was all mud walls and grape fields that had furrows that were over a metre in height. Main battle tanks could not negotiate these fields without the assistance of some kind of bulldozer blade as we found out after they arrived.

So the solution to all these obstacles was to get bulldozers. I remember the Commanding General of Regional Command (South), coming around the Battle Group Command Post and asking what we wanted or needed. To a man we responded, "Tanks". Two months later they arrived in theatre.

The interim solution was to use the heavy equipment that we had. We didn't have much - a twenty-year-old Zettelmeyer front-end loader and a thirty-year-old D6 bulldozer. Crazy, but that is all we had. So we brainstormed and came up with the idea of welding armour plate on the equipment, well onto the Zettelmeyer anyway. The D6 Dozer already had an armoured cab. Then we went scavenging. We found another armoured D6 Dozer at the end of the runway and found out that it belonged to the Brits. They let us use it because it was due to be repatriated anyway and I think they were hoping that we would blow it up. We also borrowed a D7 dozer from the Afghan National Army and we rented a D8 dozer from a contractor. Both were civilian pattern – yellow, unarmoured and with an open cab. The Material Technicians did an outstanding job of welding the armour plate on the equipment and are responsible for saving MCpl Hooper's life at least once, if not twice. I do not know if they were ever recognized for their efforts, but they made a difference in the lives of many.

I remember going down to their shop to have a look at the D7 dozer while they were working on it. Poor old Cpl Daryl Parsons was the operator and he was circling that thing like a scared rabbit and I don't blame him one damn bit. At this point I must tell you that Capt Rich Busbridge and I had, and still have, an outstanding relationship, but at this point we had a bit of a disagreement. He was being pushed to get that dozer out, not now, but *right fucking now*! I called back and said "No way, it ain't gonna happen." He told me to get it on the low bed and get it going. There was no way; I mean there was zero protection. The boys were working as quickly as they could; there was no way I would have operated it like it was and at least I would have had three meals and a bed in Edmonton at the detention barracks, so I wasn't going to order a Cpl to do it and I told him so.

No one was happy with that answer, well, except Cpl Parsons, the poor bugger. So I pushed the Material Technicians and they said six hours. Everyone up top relented, and so it was. The Heavy Equipment Transport was coming in six hours and it was going whether it was done or not. As it turned out they got the job done. And the quality? Well, good enough, although I understand that a few of the smaller plates fell off when they unloaded it.

The Afghan National Army D7 toughed it out until one day when the "bomb magnet" MCpl Lance Hooper, who is one of the most dedicated leaders I have ever had the privilege to serve with, was scraping the top layer off of Route Vancouver. He hit an IED and there it stayed for the better part of four months. He injured his back in the blast and Cpl Reid who was outside took a piece of shrapnel in the forehead. Just imagine if you will - 85 000 pounds of steel being lifted and turned 90 degrees in a second. If we had of been using any of our lighter equipment his injuries very likely would have been much more severe. Both returned to the field two weeks later. In the end we ended up building a road nearby in order to by-pass the IEDs. Many months later, Sgt Grignon took a couple of cranes we had rented and conducted a tandem lift to get it out of there. Again, here were years and years of heavy equipment experience to the forefront. If it had been others, that piece of equipment very likely would still be sitting there.

CALMING 1 TROOP

I received a call on the radio at about two in the morning, two days after 1 Troop occupied their position on Ma'sum Ghar. "3, this is 31".

"3 send over".

"31, are there any known friendly forces at grid ### ###? Someone is shooting down there and we can't tell who it is." So I gave them a wait and checked with the duty officer. No, there weren't any friendly forces there and the grid given was about two and a half kilometres away. So I checked with the guns. Yes, they were shooting at that spot, so I told 1 Troop's WO Rouzes all this, and I could tell he was not convinced. He said that it seemed a lot closer and that it was coming towards him. So I checked again. No, I had the facts straight. So I repeated all of what I had just told him and he was good with that. Not two minutes later...

"3 this is 31A... can you confirm that it is outgoing artillery?" Well holy shit! But I had to stay calm and patient because I know I would have been the same, if not worse. After two more days they wouldn't report anything unless it actually hit them or came within twenty feet of hitting them, plus they could give vector data and what it was. Amazing.

MY FIRST MONTH WITH NO SLEEP

Working in the operations cell is a tiring and thankless job. I can't believe I'm doing it again. That Squadron Headquarters was stacked, and it still wasn't enough at that time. I would start the day at about nine in the morning. Sgt Mazerolle started at six. I would go in and follow up on the Daily Sitreps from the evening before and try and get my situational awareness up. I would take over the desk at around 2:00 pm or so. It was steady. Meetings, reports, organizing the movement of troops and stores, and if something was going on I couldn't leave the desk. We had guys all over Hell's half-acre. Some had good communications, some had none and it was anybody's guess as to when they would show up, or where. We had guys stuck in Spin Boldak for over two months with only a satellite phone. Then there was all the organizing of convoys and lots of horse-trading with other elements in order to fit vehicles or personnel into convoys. Then the troops needed all sorts of things, like steel I-beams for instance. After six weeks of being asked about it, I finally asked if the guy requesting them had seen any steel mills out there anywhere and that quieted him down for a little while. I must admit, I used to dread the evening reports. While some found "the fire side chats" entertaining it never dawned on them that after this two-and-a-half hour marathon of taking notes I then had to decipher then translate Cpl Chris Coady's scribbling from "Newfanese" to English then to something presentable to our higher headquarters. Not to mention the fact that there were some issues where we just couldn't get the required stores for the troops in anything that seemed like a timely fashion. And then there was so much going on that some things just got lost throughout the day. So I usually finished my day at about 3:00 am exhausted. I did that for the first month and a half then I went home on leave and slept for three days straight. When I came back I tried to pace myself a little more, and in the end when winter came on it did let up a little.

FIRST BADGER INTO A COMBAT ZONE

This particular bit of history is important to me because I spent ten years as an Armoured Engineer. At one point in the mid-nineties the Canadian Armoured Engineers were on the cutting edge. Other nations would call us for information on how best to employ their Armoured Engineer Vehicles and Armoured Vehicle Launching Bridges, ironically, even the Germans (as our vehicles were German made). Then in the latter part of the nineties the Iron Horsemen became neglected and all the skill that Canada had in this field was dispersed and the equipment was left to rot.

As it turns out the Badger was the single most important piece of equipment in the entire Canadian fleet for providing mobility and it still is as I sit and write this in Kandahar now on Roto 5. Let it be known to all, that the first Canadian Leopard chassis that drove into a combat zone under its own power was a Badger crewed by Engineers. The CFR was 81655 and it is the very same Badger that was the first of its kind off the train in the former Yugoslavia in 1992. Having said all that I don't know how Kosovo measures up against this but in any event, *FIRST IN, LAST OUT, UBIQUE and CHIMO!*

KNOWING IT WAS TIME FOR MAJ G TO COME IN

God bless Maj G, he was and is a very pragmatic and reasonable officer. However, after a week or two outside the wire it became very difficult to communicate with him on the radio. Basically he would leave camp with a high level of awareness about what we were dealing with in regards to equipment, stores, etc. After a while, when things went off the rails, he would be expecting things that we just didn't have the horsepower to deliver. So sometimes the order would come but we couldn't execute for whatever reason. Some days we would get a blast with no way to explain "why" because you just cannot argue an OC into a counter-order when the whole Squadron is listening on the net. So the answer always is, "Roger". Then you have to try and find some way to get the messages out to him that explains why things got all fucked up – satellite phones were great for secure and personal communications. Anyway, when we got two barks in a row we tried to give some subtle hints that maybe what we needed was that '9' behind his name to get some stuff done, and usually he was in within the next couple of days to recharge and sort shit out.

The main lesson to take away from this is that yes a commander has to be out front leading the troops but he also has to check the rear every once in a while to ensure that the intent and main effort are being met. A commander always needs to be located where he or she can best influence the battle. Sometimes that is back at camp when dealing with higher headquarters or national rear-links.

One instance of this was when one of the Badgers was down because of a parts issue and, as I stated previously, this particular piece of equipment was and remains vital to success with regards to mobility. We determined that we could swap out the part with the operational reserve Badger that was at Kandahar Airfield. So Maj Gasparotto says, "Go ahead, do it".

"Well, it's not that easy", I said. "We need authorization from someone with a nine behind their handle." This meant either the Battle Group Commander or the Task Force Commander, because ultimately it's their equipment.

"Well I've got a fucking nine," he says. Now I must categorically state that I had no intent of insulting him. It's just that a General had chased me once before for cannibalizing a Badger and I didn't want either of us to go through that because we both should have known better. I got away with it as a sapper but I had a feeling that given the circumstances we would both be in big trouble for screwing with the General's Badger. So anyway, I aggravated the situation by telling him that he didn't have enough nines and that's when Capt Busbridge took over the radio. A day later he came back in, and I explained what I was trying to tell him and we were good. I was just trying to keep him out of trouble.

TURNING DOWN 2 TROOP

This is something I wanted to write about so all can understand the logic behind the decision. I know that the senior leadership in the Squadron was privy to this, but not all the soldiers were. After WO Roger Perrault was injured by the IED strike on Maj G's LAV there came a point when it became clear that he would be going home.

Sgt Mazerolle, Sgt Clucas and I had heard all kinds of rumblings about what might happen in terms of his replacement. I thought to myself, *you had better nip this one in the bud.* So I asked Capt Busbridge out one evening to sit under the Afghan stars and have a little talk with me. He obliged and I explained to him that they (the officers) shouldn't keep this one under wraps and that they weren't going to offend anyone with their decision or cause any friction amongst us.

I told him that I would happily be 2 Troop Warrant Officer if I could keep Sgt Clucas as the Recce Sergeant, because frankly if I was going to be the new Troop Commander's right hand man this was something that had to be.

As it turned out, this was not an option because I would have to be replaced and it was going to be internal, so therefore it would have to be Sgt Clucas. I did not think that this was fair for the soldiers in 2 Troop. They had lost a Section Commander, the Troop Warrant Officer, and the Troop Commander they had deployed with and if the move took effect, their Recce Sergeant. The only continuity in leadership they would have been left with were two Dragoon Crew Commanders and two Engineer Section Commanders. I thought that this was too much, and Sgt Clucas was the only "glue" they had left, not to mention the fact that we would both have to "learn" new jobs in a combat zone.

I told Capt Busbridge that I understood what this meant and that I had no problems with that. I thought and still think that it was the right thing to do. Furthermore, I believed Sgt Clucas was more competent at the job than I could have been given our backgrounds, he being a Field Engineer all of his career and I being primarily a Heavy Equipment and Armoured Engineer. As it turned out, I believe I was right. WO Clucas did an outstanding job.

MY TRIP OUTSIDE THE WIRE

And so it came to pass that I was to take a trip outside the wire to see first hand the ground we had fought over. Oh boy. I was nervous, but once

I got out there doing stuff I forgot about my own mortality. The unfortunate thing about the trip was that it should have been made much earlier, but having said that, I gained an appreciation for the Squadron's accomplishments.

It was absolutely amazing. I learned a great deal while I was out. It was nerve- wracking moving around in that part of the world - the explosive and enemy threat and the incredibly tough environmental conditions. I had three great sleeps (despite being woken up for radio watch) when I was in Afghanistan - they were all outside the wire and they were all due to the fact that at the end of each day I was exhausted.

Another thing I learned was that, during day-to-day ops I think the guys outside the wire had a better quality of life than those who stayed in Kandahar Airfield. I will fully qualify that statement with the caveat "when there was no kinetic or explosive activity," because I was out there when MCpl Jody Mitic (a 1 RCR sniper) was wounded.

I hope that those who were out there on a daily basis understand what I am trying to say. I saw all the key terrain we were operating in and Maj G gave me a history lesson as we travelled. It helped me to visualize much of the radio traffic I received from then on when I got back to the Engineer Support Coordination Centre, and it also aided me in understanding reports and requests much more quickly. If I were to do things over again I would have insisted on going out much earlier in the operation.

I flew out in a Black Hawk to Ma'sum Ghar. When I arrived there was no one there to meet me from the Engineers so I walked up the hill to where the Engineer flag was and waited. Cpl Parsons came along, offered me some Kraft Dinner for lunch and then he took me for a tour of the FOB. I ran into MWO Pynn (I used to be his driver in an Armoured Vehicle-Launched Bridge) and we caught up. He was out managing the paving of Route Summit Sector 6. It was a good meeting because I came away with a few points that I was able to help him out with later. Then Maj G came in and we went for a quick drive up to Patrol Base Wilson. We returned and settled in for the night. The next day we went out to Howz-e-Madad and then on to Ghundy Ghar. The day after that we travelled down the Arghandab on the south side of the river, not quite to Spervan Ghar and observed an operation near Sangsar. The final day I stayed in Ma'sum Ghar and caught a flight back to Purgatory and a bunch of work that had piled up in the Engineer Support Coordination Center, much enlightened, and over my feelings of failing the troops who were out.

Life on Kandahar Airfield

Life on Kandahar Airfield for the "HESCO hobbits" was repetitive. Everyone starts off with the attitude that everyone has a job to do. For me that still applies but there definitely was some friction at various points during the Roto. Everyone gets tunnel vision after a long haul like that. My buddy Sgt Ted Peacock made me a "Kandahar Airfield Medal", it was a picture he drew of a single cell of HESCO. I still have it, and I will keep it.

The camp is huge. I knew a triangle no bigger than a parade square for the first month or so. I only found out where the movie theatre was during the last seven days of the Roto. I actually took the bus for a couple of hours on the last day there, just to see where it went. So basically, what I'm saying is that it wasn't all peaches and cream just to clear up that urban legend.

Talking With Stormie

I remember very clearly the day before Cpl Albert Storm died. It was November 26th, 2006 and he was sitting in the dining facility closest to the Battle Group Command Post. I sat down with him and had lunch. We chatted a bit about the heat and sports. He told me how excited he was to finally have a chance to get out of the camp and go out and do something. I'll never forget what I told him, I said, "Stormie, be careful what you wish for." The next day I woke up to news of his and RSM Girouard's death. It stung.

My Final Thoughts

In hindsight, knowing what I know today, I might have advised differently on some issues, but the readers of this chronicle have to keep in mind that this was, for all intents and purposes, new to us. I have analyzed some of the decisions and actions taken by the collective Canadian leadership over the course of our deployment and I must force myself to not be critical, especially where there was loss of life. What happened, happened, and hopefully those who came after learned, because that is all they could reasonably be expected to do.

Critics of past action have nothing to offer if they choose not to learn and address mistakes constructively. In Afghanistan everything is easier said than done. If you go into the area of operations with nothing, then that is what you will have to get the job done. There is never a yes or no answer.

There is good enough with varying degrees of better or worse. There is always a 'maybe' answer. Hope is not a plan, despite the best efforts of many people to convince us otherwise. Tomorrow means some time in the future, not tomorrow. In Afghanistan the sun rises, then the sun sets, and nothing else matters. The Taliban have more patience than we do. We have rules they do not.

23 Field Squadron is a storied sub-unit indeed. I am grateful to have served in the Squadron, not once but twice. My previous service was in 2003 in Bosnia. Times have changed since that deployment. I believe that the sappers who went before us would have been proud of the things that we accomplished in this desolate and unforgiving land. There are sappers who walk the halls of 2 Combat Engineer Regiment today who have seen as much combat action, if not more, than some of the Sappers who fought in the World Wars and Korea. They overcame a very difficult set of circumstances and provided outstanding support to the 1 RCR Battle Group. We have much to be proud of.

ENDNOTES

1 "Dien Bien Phu was the decisive engagement in the first Indochina War (1946–54). It consisted of a struggle between French and **Viet Minh** (Vietnamese Communist and nationalist) forces for control of a small mountain outpost on the Vietnamese border near Laos. The Viet Minh victory in this battle effectively ended the eight-year-old war." "**Battle of Dien Bien Phu.**" *Encyclopædia Britannica.* 2010. Encyclopædia Britannica Online. 02 Mar. 2010 <**http://www.britannica.com/ EBchecked/topic/162678/Battle-of-Dien-Bien-Phu**>.

2 Ghar is Pashto for Mountain.

3 Grossman, Dave. "The Bullet Proof Mind." Mental Preparation for Combat lecture. CFB Petawawa. 2006 (LCol Grossman is the the author of the books *On Killing* and *On Combat*).

4 The Canadian Military Engineers' greeting or toast is "Chimo. This expression is also often used as a closing on correspondence between Engineers. The word Chimo is derived from the Inuktitut greeting: "saimo" that means "hello," "goodbye," "peace be with you," and similar sentiments. The current spelling and pronunciation is based on a Caucasian adaptation of the native language. *Canadian Military Engineers Association.* 2008. CMEA 2 March 10 <http://www.cmea-agmc.ca/redbook/CME_Customs_Ch03_e.pdf>

5 To Breach - A tactical task where any means available are employed to break through or secure a passage through an enemy defence, obstacle, minefield, or fortification - usually done under fire.

6 Badger is the nickname for the Canadian Armoured Engineer Vehicle. It is based on a Leopard 1 tank chassis; has no turret but has a dozer blade and an excavator arm.

7 *Clearing* is the total elimination or neutralization of an obstacle that is usually performed by follow-on engineers and is not done under fire.

8 In western France (e.g., Bocage Normand, Bocage Vendéen), a well-wooded district in distinction to the *campagne*, which denotes a hedgeless tract of farmland characteristic of old-established areas of open-field agriculture. The fields of bocage country are small, irregular,

and enclosed by hedges and groves of trees. "**bocage**." *Encyclopædia Britannica.* 2010. Encyclopædia Britannica Online. 02 Mar. 2010 <**http://www.britannica.com/EBchecked/topic/ 70827/bocage**>.

9   You'll have to ask him why he is nicknamed "Knobby".

10 A Ramp Ceremony is held at Kandahar Airfield and involves the procession and loading of the deceased in flag-draped caskets onto a Hercules aircraft, which starts them on their final journey home.

11 Zuehlke, Mark. *Ortona.* Vancouver: Douglas & McIntyre, 1999.

12 A Pressure Plate is a method of triggering a device. The circuit is completed, in this case when two metal plates are connected when pressure (i.e. a vehicle driving over or a person stepping on it) is applied.

13 Two IEDs had been struck and many more had been discovered in a highly localized area in Pashmul (centred on the "White School") immediately following the end of major combat operations (September 13th, 2006). These IEDs had been emplaced well prior to the commencement of the BG's attack on Taliban forces in Pashmul on September 3rd, 2006. Non-legacy IEDs refer to the ones emplaced after September 13th, 2006 by the Pashmul IED Cell.

14 (Minus) refers to an organization that has detached one or more of its integral elements.

15 Texas Barriers are large free-standing concrete barriers.

16 Combat exhaustion will start to set in after approximately 30 days of continuous combat. Grossman, David. *On Killing.* Boston: Little, Brown and Company, 1995.

17 A Company, based on its occupation of FOBs Ma'sum Ghar and Zettelmeyer could dominate the southern Sectors (4 – 6) of Route Summit.

18 When the Canadian Forces replaces its aging and eclectic fleet with new heavy equipment, it is requested by those who use this equipment that we purchase said items, all of which need to be armoured, from a single source, reputable, solvent and international company. Caterpillar immediately comes to mind.

19 An M72 is a light-weight, man-portable, shoulder-launched anti-tank weapon.

20 ZAP numbers are used to identify soldiers on the net without using their name.

21 Sledge, E.B. With the Old Breed. New York: Presidio Press, 1981.

22 Adoption of the Hindi term *pukka* – meaning *"genuine, of good quality, reliable"* – into English usage has its origin in the days of British rule in India. To recognize individuals outside the CME who demonstrate these sterling qualities and who have given outstanding service to the Engineers, the highest honour the CME can bestow upon an outsider is induction into the Order of the Pukka Sapper. The sponsoring unit should treat inducted Pukka Sappers as members of the extended CME Family. Canadian Military Engineer Association. 2008. CMEA. 2 March 2010. <http://www.cmea-agmc.ca/redbook/ CME_Customs_ Ch03_e.pdf>

23 Frost, Robert. "The Road not Taken." *Modern Poems*. Ed. Richard Ellmann and Robert O'Clair. New York: WW Norton and Company, 1989.

24 Shakespeare, William. "Henry V." *The First Folio of Shakespeare*. Ed. Charlton Hinman. New York: WW Norton and Company, 1968.

25 Spoil refers to the pile of dirt that lines either side of a lane as a result of a tank ploughing the ground in order to remove buried mines.

26 A typical and manufactured fascine is a collection of open-ended plastic pipes bundled together in a steel chain net. They are placed into ditches, allowing vehicles to drive over them while still enabling water to flow through.

27 This rule stipulates that from receipt of orders to the time that the mission starts, a commander will deliver his/her set of orders no later than one third of the time in, thereby leaving two-thirds of the time remaining for his/her subordinates to conduct their own battle procedure.

28 Dragon's teeth are a collection of sharp tire-puncturing metal triangles fastened to a rod used at a road block to control traffic.

29 A Company, 2 PPCLI and B Squadron, LdSH were the only western based sub-units within the 1 RCR Battlegroup.

30 A Firebase is a grouping of weapons systems (often stationary) on the battle field that allow for the controlled concentration of direct fire onto an objective. It is typically an elevated location that provides superior observation of the surrounding area.

31 OT stands for Occupational Transfer, meaning a change in military trade.

32 Clearing and grubbing refers to the removal of all surface and subsurface (roots) vegetation and rocks.

33 A *Strong Point* is a location that has been hardened or fortified allowing

a force to occupy it and defend the surrounding area.

34 Canadian entertainers deploy to theatre once every tour to perform for the troops.

35 The blast seat refers to the location where the device exploded – typically the crater.

36 Using a hook and line kit or rope as an expedient tool, A pull is conducted to remove material form the ground or to ensure that an object is not booby-trapped.

37 Soldiers who misbehaved during the post-tour decompression leave were assigned to Gatorade Platoon – i.e. they were forbidden from drinking any alcohol for the duration of their punishment.

INDEX

5860358R0

Made in the USA
Charleston, SC
12 August 2010